Media Law in Hungary

Media Law in Hungary

Fourth Edition

Judit Bayer
Ágnes Urbán
Gábor Polyák

This book was originally published as a monograph in the International Encyclopaedia of Laws/Media Law.

Founding Editor: Roger Blanpain
General Editor: Frank Hendrickx
Volume Editors: Peggy Valcke & Eva Lievens

Wolters Kluwer

Published by:
Kluwer Law International B.V.
PO Box 316
2400 AH Alphen aan den Rijn
The Netherlands
E-mail: lrs-sales@wolterskluwer.com
Website: www.wolterskluwer.com/en/solutions/kluwerlawinternational

Sold and distributed by:
Wolters Kluwer Legal & Regulatory U.S.
920 Links Avenue
Landisville, PA 17538
United States of America
E-mail: customer.service@wolterskluwer.com

ISBN 978-94-035-1578-6

e-Book: ISBN 978-94-035-1588-5
web-PDF: ISBN 978-94-035-1598-4

The Authors

Judit Bayer is an associate professor at the Department of Communication at the Budapest Business School and a guest professor at the University of Münster, Institute for Information, Telecommunication and Media Law. She taught and researched at the University of Wellington, New Zealand, in 2006 and at Tama University, Tokyo, in 2009. She previously taught legal subjects at the International Business School's Oxford Brookes BA (Hons) programme in Budapest (1998–2002). Judit acquired her LLM from Eötvös Loránd University (ELTE), Budapest, in 1992 and her PhD on 'Freedom of Expression in the Online Environment' from the Department for Constitutional Law of ELTE in 2005. She pursued constitutional free speech studies at the Central European University in 2000. She also carried out a research project at the Open Society University in 2001–2002 on information policy issues and led a project at the Hungarian Academy of Sciences on the regulation of public service television from a perspective of European competition law. She participated in several other research projects, specializing primarily in media regulation from a freedom of expression perspective and in freedom and regulation of new media. Judit Bayer is frequently asked to speak at conferences and expert workshops or deliver legal or policy analyses. She is the author and co-author of several books and author of numerous articles, both in English and in Hungarian. She is the chief editor of the quarterly *Médiakutató*, a reputed media research journal. Judit Bayer was a member of the executive board of the Society for Communication Research in Hungary between 2010 and 2017. She acquired her habilitation in Hungary in 2015 in the field of media law and data protection.

The Authors

Dr Ágnes Urbán is an Associate Professor and Head of the Department of Infocommunication at Corvinus University of Budapest (CUB). She received her PhD degree at Corvinus in 2006. Her areas of study include digital media, media consumption, and media policy. Dr Urbán is head of the media policy think tank Mérték Media Monitor, which aims to monitor the changes in the Hungarian media landscape and evaluate the impact of media policy decisions. She is the author of some 60+ Hungarian and English-language international publications in the fields of media and infocommunications. Her publications include books, book chapters, journal articles and conference presentations.

Gábor Polyák is a lawyer and an associate professor at the University of Pécs and at CUB. He is the leader of the Standards Media Monitor (*Mérték Médiaelemző Műhely*), a non-governmental organization (NGO) financed by the Open Society Institute, dealing with the effect analysis of the Hungarian media law. He graduated in Law and Media Sciences from the University of Pécs. After completing his LLM in ICT Law at the University of Vienna, he received his PhD from the University of Pécs with the title 'Forming the Media System'. He is currently the chief editor of the Hungarian professional journal, '*Infokommunikáció és Jog*' (Infocommunications and Law). He is the author of numerous publications and expert papers in media law, information technology law, and telecommunications law. He worked as an advisor at the National Radio and Television Authority during the presidency of László Majtényi. He is a fellow of the Bolyai Scholarship of the Hungarian Academy of Sciences.

Table of Contents

Table of Contents

List of Abbreviations

AH	*Antenna Hungária*
API	Application Programming Interface
Ásztv.	Act LXVI of 2011 on the State Audit Office *(2011. évi LXVI. Törvény az Állami Számvevőszékről)*
AVMS Directive	Directive 2010/13/EU of the European Parliament and of the Council, OJ L95/15
Basic Law	Basic Law of Hungary (*Magyarország Alaptörvénye)*
Bszitv.	Act CLXI of 2011 on the organization and administration of courts, effective from 3 December 2011. *(2011. évi CLXI. Törvény a bíróság szervezetéről és igazgatásáról)*
CAS	Conditional Access System
Civil Code	Act V of 2013 on the Civil Code *(2013. évi V. törvény a Polgári Törvénykönyvről)*
Criminal Code	Act C of 2012 on the Criminal Code *(2012. évi C. törvény a Büntető Törvénykönyvről)*
DTT	Digital Terrestrial Television
Dtv.	Act LXXIV of 2007 on programme distribution and digital transition *(2007. éévi LXXIV. Törvény a műsorterjesztés és a digitális átállás szabályairól)*
DVB	Digital Video Broadcasting
ECJ	European Court of Justice (please note that since the Lisbon Treaty entered into force on 1 December 2009, the official name of the European Court of Justice is now the 'Court of Justice of the European Union' comprising the Court of Justice, the General Court (formerly the Court of First Instance) and the Civil Service Tribunal)
ECHR	European Convention on Human Rights
EctHR	European Court of Human Rights
Eht.	Act C of 2003 on electronic telecommunications (*2003. éévi C. törvény az elektronikus hírközlésről)*
EPG	Electronic Programme Guide

List of Abbreviations

EU	European Union
FOI	Freedom of Information
GDPR	General Data Protection Regulation
Infotv.	Act CXII of 2011 on informational self-determination and freedom of information (effective from 27 July 2011) (*2011. évi CXII. Törvény az információs önrendelkezésről és az információszabadságról*)
IPTV	Internet Protocol Television
ISP	Internet Service Provider
Ket.	Act CXL of 2004 on the general rules of administrative procedure and services (*2004. évi CXL. Törvény a közigazgatási hatósági eljárás és szolgáltatás általános szabályairól*)
MEME	The Association of the Hungarian Electronic Media Service Providers
MHP	Multimedia Home
MP	Member of Parliament
MLE	Association of the Hungarian Journal Publishers (*Magyar Lapkiadók Egyesülete)*
MTE	Association of Hungarian Content Providers (*Magyar Tartalomszolgáltatók Egyesülete)*
MTI	*Magyar Távirati Iroda*
Mttv.	Act CLXXXV of 2010 on media services and mass communication (*2010. évi CLXXXV. Törvény a médiaszolgáltatásokról és a tömegkommunikációról*)
MTVA	Media Service Support and Asset Management Fund (*Médiaszolgáltatás Támogató és Vagyonkezelő Alap)*
NGO	Non-governmental Organization
NHH	National Telecommunications Authority *(Nemzeti Hírközlési Hatóság)*
NMHH	National Media and Telecommunications Authority *(Nemzeti Média és Hírközlési Hatóság)*
NVB	The National Election Commission *(Nemzeti Választási Bizottság)*
OBH	National Office of the Judiciary (*Országos Bírói Hivatal)*
OBT	*National Judicial Council (Országos Bírói Tanács)*
OIT	National Judicial Council (before 2012) (*Országos Igazságszolgáltatási Tanács*)
ORTT	National Radio and Television Body (*Országos Rádió és Televízió Testület*)
OSCE	Organization for Security and Co-operation in Europe

Ötv.	Act CLXXXIX of 2011 on the local governments of Hungary *(2011. évi CLXXXIX. törvény Magyarország helyi önkormányzatairól)*
Pp.	Act III of 1952 on Civil Procedures *(1952. évi III. törvény a Polgári Perrendtartásról)*
SAO	State Audit Office
SIP	Media Service Providers with Significant Influencing Power
Smtv.	Act CIV of 2010 on press freedom and the fundamental rules on media content *(2010. évi CIV. törvény a sajtószabadságról és a médiatartalmak alapvető szabályairól)*

Acknowledgement

We would like to thank the editors of the IEL series for their work and Dr Ildiko Vincze for her invaluable insight and selfless help on legislative changes.

Acknowledgement

Foreword to the Fourth Edition

This book cannot ambition to describe the full story of the Hungarian backslide in media freedom and pluralism. From its beginning, it has restricted its scope only to introduction of the written law and case law of media and of freedom of expression. Its authors have consciously refrained from forming opinions and providing their own interpretations. They have ample publications where they publish their scholarly analysis of the media system in Hungary, including their assessments and policy proposals.

However, by 2023, the Hungarian media law has grown to be the most prominent known example of creeping governmental occupation of independent media. Rather than using classic tools of censorship, the Hungarian government captured the official bodies and occupied media outlets through hostile takeovers; it leveraged imbalanced distribution of state advertising, accompanied by advertising of state-owned companies and government-friendly businesses in the government-friendly media; proxy ownership and the following 'donation' of the owned media companies to a holding; and also internal censorship within the public service television. These well-documented actions at last raised concern with the European Union (EU) after several years of benevolent tolerance.

In 2018, the European Parliament triggered the Article 7 procedure against Poland and Hungary. Ever since then, the Council has avoided voting about the next step, which would be to determine whether there is 'a clear risk of a serious breach' of the EU's common values.

On 15 July 2021, the Commission started an infringement procedure against Hungary for violations of fundamental rights of LGBTQ people based upon the anti-LGBT legislative package that is also described in this book below.[1]

Media freedom and pluralism have been highlighted among the main problem areas in the 2021 Rule of Law Report on Hungary. The main concerns expressed related to the independence of the Media Council and the Media Authority, the imbalanced placement of state advertising that permitted the government to exert indirect political influence over the media, and the restrictions on access to public information during the pandemic, among others.[2]

On 27 April 2022, the EU activated the Rule of Law Conditionality Mechanism against Hungary. One major aspect of the rule of law violations was the

1. Press Release by the European Commission https://ec.europa.eu/commission/presscorner/detail/en/ip_21_3668.
2. 2021 Rule of Law Report Country Chapter on the rule of law situation in Hungary. SWD(2021) 714 final. https://eur-lex.europa.eu/legal-content/EN/TXT/PDF/?uri=CELEX:52021SC0714&from=EN.

government-controlled media system, besides the anti-LGBT law and the 'Stop Soros' anti-migration and anti-NGO law. The Council decided to suspend EUR 6.3 billion on 12 December 2022.[3]

On 15 July 2022, the European Commission referred Hungary to the Court of Justice because of the anti-LGBT law that prohibits content that depicts homosexuality or transsexuality.[4]

Several of the tools that the Orbán Government used to acquire control over the media landscape and the Hungarian economy and society in general were either non-legal tools (like using state advertising, informal pressures, and clientelism) or were laws that had been enacted through a seemingly proper legislative procedure, sometimes with a qualified majority (The Orbán Government has been winning two-thirds majority of the parliamentary seats in the fourth election in a row in 2022). This book also describes how the entire system of public administration was transformed in Hungary in 2011. This transformation served a few key aims: (1) effectively centralized the public administration; (2) enabled the replacement of persons in positions with persons loyal to Orbán and the Fidesz party; (3) practically deconstructed the system of checks and balances. This transformation allowed the Orbán Government to realize its goals without any consultation with the opposition or with civil society. It used legislation for these purposes, and the gradually transformed Constitutional Court to approve its laws when challenged. While the surface shows that the transformation was lawful, the real meaning of democracy, division of powers, observing checks and balances, and protecting minorities was thwarted and mocked. This delusion has misled the EU for several years. It has seemed impossible to grasp the essence of the rule of law and of media freedom or pluralism and to translate them into solid rules.

In 2022, the EU also issued a proposal for a Regulation on the European Media Freedom Act. It would raise the principles and safeguards against political interference, pluralism, and transparency of ownership at the level of European law. Having a legal instrument in this subject matter will make it more straightforward to formulate the anomalies in the context of the law and create concrete expectations supported by the legal principles that the Regulation is to provide. Nevertheless, the law would by far not offer a panacea to these problems: it cannot eliminate mere procedural legality with empty or misinterpreted meaning. However, we would be one step further to point out abuse of law, our back being had by law, providing objectivity to what has been so long dismissed as a political value judgment. Existence of a common European law would also invite dialogue, interpretation and judicial assessment of the content of the law, thereby promoting the development of commonly accepted and agreed values on media freedom and pluralism.

We hope that in the next volume of this book, we authors will be able to discuss compliance with the European Media Freedom Act and further the comparative analysis of EU Member States.

---

3. Press Release by the Council of the EU. https://www.consilium.europa.eu/en/press/press-releases/2022/12/12/rule-of-law-conditionality-mechanism/.
4. Press Release of the EC. https://ec.europa.eu/commission/presscorner/detail/en/IP_22_2689.

General Introduction

§1. General Background of the Country

I. Political and Legal System of the Country

1. Hungary is a republic. Its name has been changed from the 'Hungarian Republic' to 'Hungary' in the new Basic Law.[5] Hungary has been a member of the European Union (EU) since 2004.

A. New Public Order from 2010

2. The Fidesz Government, which won a two-thirds majority of the seats in Parliament in 2010, profoundly changed the public law system of the country, both in terms of institutions and regulations. Within an unusually short time, the government drafted and pushed through Parliament a new Basic Law in the spring of 2011 to replace the Constitution.[6] Criticism was expressed by the opposition because the constitutional principle behind the requirement of a two-thirds majority vote was to ensure a consensus between the government and the opposition parties.[7] The government's parliamentary majority also changed almost all fundamental laws that required a two-thirds majority, including the media and press laws. All legal changes that were introduced during 2010–2011, including the Basic Law, stepped into effect not later than 1 January 2012.

B. The Parliament

3. The legislative power is possessed by the Parliament, which has one chamber. The new law on elections changed the system of parliamentary elections, redrew the

5. Basic Law, Arts A, B.
6. Act XX of 1949 on the Constitution of the Hungarian Republic. The content of the act went through a total transformation in 1989.
7. For example, in 1994 the Hungarian Socialist Party (MSZP) with its coalition partner Alliance of Liberal Democrats (SZDSZ) possessed even more seats in Parliament than today's governmental majority, but exercised self-restraint in its legislative decisions, for example by declaring that a consensus of five parliamentary parties were necessary to amend the Constitution.

election districts and decreased the number of representatives to 199.[8] The Parliament is often overshadowed by the strong government and its Prime Minister.

C. The Government

4. The head of the executive power is the Prime Minister, who is elected by the Parliament. The Prime Minister is entitled to appoint his ministers who are responsible to him. Removing the Prime Minister is possible only by electing his or her successor at the same time (constructive no-confidence motion).

D. The President of the Republic

5. The President of the Republic fulfils mainly symbolic and representative functions but has a supervisory role in the legislative process as well. The president signs and promulgates the laws passed by Parliament and has two types of veto rights. First, if he does not agree with the law's content, he may send it back to the Parliament for reconsideration. If the Parliament passes the law again and sends it for signature, the president is obliged to sign and promulgate it urgently. Second, if he deems the law's content unconstitutional, he may send it to the Constitutional Court for constitutional review. Some previous presidents, like László Sólyom, exercised their rights in legislation very actively, often debating with the Parliament (or rather with its majority, the government and the Prime Minister). Other presidents, like Ferenc Mádl, were less combative. Pál Schmitt, appointed by Orbán Viktor as Prime Minister in 2010, declared that he would like to act as the 'motor of legislation' and so he acted. His cooperation was indispensable to have the whole public law system of Hungary changed. After his doctoral thesis was found to have been plagiarized, he resigned on 2 April 2012. His successor is János Áder, a member and previously executive leader of the Fidesz party and member of the European Parliament between 2009 and 2012, in the faction of the European People's Party.

6. Rules on the election and rights of the president have not changed – the president is nominated by the Prime Minister and elected by the Parliament's two-thirds majority. Unsuccessful voting may be repeated, and if the same person still does not receive the necessary majority in the second turn, then in a third round, a simple majority is enough. This procedure allows the Prime Minister's appointee to receive the position in the end, but the dynamics of the voting are a reflection of the president's legitimacy in Parliament.

E. The Parliamentary Commissioners

7. The system of Parliamentary Commissioners has been changed by the new government in 2011. According to law CXI of 2011, the old ombudsmen lost their

8. Act CCIII of 2011 on the Election of Parliamentary Representatives, effective from 1 Jan. 2012.

mandates and their offices ceased to exist.[9] The three offices (Office of the Parliamentary Commissioner for Minorities, Office of the Parliamentary Commissioner for Civil Rights and Office of the Parliamentary Commissioner for Future Generations) were replaced by one Commissioner for Fundamental Rights on 1 January 2012. This commissioner, however, may have vice commissioners, also elected by the Parliament. One of the vice commissioners is responsible for minorities and the other for future generations. The commissioner is nominated by the President of the Republic, while the vice commissioners are nominated by the commissioner. The commissioner is elected by a two-thirds majority in Parliament for a term of six years and can be re-elected once. The commissioner and his or her vice commissioners cannot be members of any political party and may not pursue political activity.[10]

8. The Parliamentary Commissioner for Data Protection and Access to Public Information also lost his mandate, and his office was replaced by a governmental Authority for Data Protection and Access to Public Information.[11] The latter movement generated an investigation and the launching of an accelerated infringement proceeding by the EU.[12] Finally, the EU found a breach of European law (*see* paragraph 257).

F. Local Governments

9. The system of local governments was transformed in 2013. The main element of the reform is the centralization of tasks and powers. As a first step, local administrative tasks were centralized into governmental offices (from 1 January 2011), which also perform the legal supervision of local governments. Governmental offices closely supervise the local municipalities with extensive powers.[13] Among others, governmental offices are entitled to request the State Treasury to withhold or withdraw part of the central subsidies or impose a fine on the local government for several reasons, including delay in communication with the governmental office.[14] Governmental offices may make recommendations on the operation, structure and decision-making process of the local governments; their recommendations must be discussed and voted about, and in case they get rejected, the local government is

---

9. Act CXI of 2011 on the Commissioner of Fundamental Rights, effective from 1 Jan. 2012.
10. Basic Law Art. 30(3).
11. *See* Infotv. (Act CXII of 2011 on informational self-determination and freedom of information).
12. European Commission launches accelerated infringement proceedings against Hungary over the independence of its central bank and data protection authorities as well as over measures affecting the judiciary, http://europa.eu/rapid/pressReleasesAction.do?reference=IP/12/24 (17 Jan. 2012). Hungary – infringements: Commission takes further legal steps on measures affecting the judiciary and the independence of the data protection authority, notes some progress on central bank independence, but further evidence and clarification needed, http://europa.eu/rapid/pressReleasesAction.do?reference=MEMO/12/165 (7 Mar. 2012).
13. §12(2), 51(2), 127 of the Act CLXXXIX of 2011 on the local governments of Hungary, effective from 1 Jan. 2012 (hereinafter: Ötv.).
14. §132(a-l) Ötv.

obliged to give the reasons for rejection to the governmental office.[15] The government is entitled to recommend the Parliament to dissolute a local government's representative body if it operates contrary to the Basic Law. In this case, the head of the respective governmental office would take over the powers of the local government temporarily.[16]

10. As a second step, several tasks were transferred to the central administration from the local municipalities, among others, education and health care (this became effective from 1 January 2012). Financial self-determination of the local governments will also be limited, but they receive the right to impose local taxes.

11. As a final step, new administrative units will be developed between the level of local municipalities and counties, called *járás* (hereinafter translated as 'shire') (effective from 1 January 2013). Shires will perform the lowest territorial-level administrative function and territorial representation of county offices. County offices will largely lose their functions, and administrative tasks of the local governments will be transferred to the shires. According to plans, 168 shires will be in the countryside and twenty-three in the capital. Borders of shire territories will be defined in governmental decrees after the law was passed in 2012. Heads of the shires will be appointed by the government, contrary to the representatives of county offices or of local governments and the mayor, who are elected by the people. A person will not be allowed to be Member of Parliament (MP) and mayor at the same time. This double function was very popular among MPs and clearly was detrimental to public matters.[17]

G. State Audit Office

12. The public law transformation did not leave the State Audit Office (SAO) untouched, although the changes are minor compared to other institutions. The new regulation emphasizes the helping and consultative role of the SAO rather than its controlling one, leaving its sanctioning power relatively weak.[18] Its president is elected for twelve years by Parliament with two-thirds of the votes, like before, but the mandate is renewable for an unlimited number of times. If, after the lapse of time, the Parliament is unable to elect a new president (because none of the nominees would receive two-thirds of the votes), the previous president remains in office until the new president is elected successfully – this period is unlimited. The nomination is made by a Parliamentary committee (the committee's membership constituency is not detailed in the law).[19] The new president elected in 2010 was an MP of the Fidesz party between 1998 and 2010.

15. §133 Ötv.
16. §125(2), §126b Ötv.
17. However, Members of Parliament may become heads of shires (Act XCIII of 2012 on shires (*járások*)).
18. Act LXVI of 2011 on the State Audit Office, effective from 1 Jul. 2011 (hereinafter: Ásztv.).
19. §9 Ásztv.

13. The new law provides important powers and competences to the president, making the structure more centralized than before, for example, the right to nominate the vice president.[20] The international non-governmental organization (NGO) Transparency International criticized the law because the Office has strong investigative rights towards civil organizations and against private secrets.[21]

H. National Bank

14. The new law on the National Bank was also heavily criticized by the European Commission and launched an accelerated infringement procedure.[22] The main point of disagreement is the constitution of the new Monetary Council and the salary of the President of the National Bank which was dramatically decreased.[23] The EU objected to the possibility of government influence on the Monetary Council. The government amended the law several times in response to criticism, and further amendments are in progress. The latest amendment affects dismissal of members of the Monetary Council – this would be laid in the hands of Parliament and of the President of the National Bank.

15. Since 2013, the National Bank has also carried out the tasks of the (terminated) State Supervision of Financial Institutions (*Pénzügyi Szervezetek Állami Felügyelete*).

I. Constitutional Court

16. The second Orbán Government introduced important changes in the election of Constitutional Court judges and restricted its power. One important curtail of the Constitutional Court's role was the elimination of the *actio popularis*, the right to submit petitions to the court claiming unconstitutionality of any existing law.

17. The number of the Constitutional Court judges was raised from eleven to fifteen. The judges are elected by two-thirds of the votes in Parliament, as before, but their president is now also elected by the Parliament rather than by the court itself. The mandate lasts for twelve years rather than nine and is renewable for an unlimited number of times (rather than only once, as previously).[24] The new members that were elected to raise the number of judges to fifteen were criticized for being close to the government parties. The first two members in 2010 were widely criticized for

20. §13(2)a–m Ásztv.
21. *Korlátlanul ellenőrizhet az állami számvevőszék az 1%-os támogatásban részesülő szervezeteknél?* https://transparency.hu/hirek/korlatlanul-ellenorizhet-az-allami-szamvevoszek-az-1-os-tamogatas ban-reszesulo-szervezeteknel/ (24 May 2011).
22. European Commission launches accelerated infringement proceedings against Hungary over the independence of its central bank and data protection authorities as well as over measures affecting the judiciary, http://europa.eu/rapid/pressReleasesAction.do?reference=IP/12/24 (17 Jan. 2012).
23. §46(3–4), §51(1) Act CCVIII of 2011 on the Hungarian National Bank, effective from 1 Jan. 2012.
24. Article 24(4) Basic Law.

lacking relevant legal experience – as they were political scientists – and one of them for also having been a minister of the cabinet in the first Orbán Government (1998–2002).

18. The Basic Law lists the competences of the Constitutional Court. These are as follows:

- examine passed, but not promulgated, laws, if initiated by the president, the Parliament,[25] or the Parliamentary Commissioner for Fundamental Rights, whether they are consistent with the Basic Law;
- examine legal rules that are to be applied in individual cases, if initiated by ordinary courts, whether they are consistent with the Basic Law;
- examine legal rules that are applied in individual cases, whether they are consistent with the Basic Law – this examination may be initiated by any affected person or organization;
- examine court decisions on whether they are consistent with the Basic Law – this examination may be initiated by any affected person or organization;
- examine legal rules whether they are consistent with the Basic Law, if initiated by the government, one-quarter of parliamentary representatives or the Parliamentary Commissioner for Fundamental Rights;
- examine legal rules' consistency with international contracts;
- impeachment of the President of the Republic;
- examination of a parliamentary resolution about holding a referendum or about denying to hold a referendum;
- giving opinions to the government about the dissolution of a local government's representative body because of its operation contrary to the Basic Law upon request of the government;
- giving opinions to the government about the dissolution of a church, if its operation is contrary to the law on churches, upon request of the government;
- solving collision problems between State organs or between State organs and local governments;
- interpretation of the Basic Law;
- examination of local government decrees and other tools of regulation.[26]

19. The Basic Law restricts the right of the Constitutional Court to examine and annul laws that relate to the central budget, the implementation of the central budget, the central taxes, duties and rates, customs and the central conditions of local taxes. The court may examine such laws only in relation to the rights to life and human dignity, protection of personal data, right to the freedom of conscience and religion, and to Hungarian citizenship, and may annul these only because of an injury to these rights and freedoms. As an exception, the court is entitled to annul

25. Even though the chances appear low that Parliament would initiate an examination against a law it has just passed.
26. Article 24 Basic Law, and §§23–38 of Act CLI of 2011 on the Constitutional Court, effective from 1 Jan. 2012.

these laws without limitation if the procedural requirements for passing and promulgating laws were not fulfilled according to the Basic Law.[27]

20. The Constitutional Court had a great role in transforming the Hungarian legal system into a liberal democracy from 1989 until 2010. Its landmark decisions set firm bans against governmental attempts to limit press freedom or other freedoms. Its activity usually did not reflect political interest, being one of the very few such independent institutions serving as checks and balances.

J. The Judicial System

21. The new government changed the administrative supervision of the court system. The National Judicial Council (*Országos Igazságszolgáltatási Tanács*, (OIT)), the self-regulatory authority of the court system was terminated and its tasks were taken over by the new National Judicial Council (*Országos Bírói Tanács* (OBT)) and the new National Office of the Judiciary (*Országos Bírói Hivatal*, OBH), both operative from 1 January 2012. The President of the OBH is elected by Parliament for nine years with a two-thirds majority (upon the recommendation of the President of the Republic).[28] The President of the OBH fulfils his or her position until a new president's election is successful. The president has a wide scope of competences, for example, transferring a judge to another place of service; appointing another court for the procedure instead of the one where the case started; recommending the appointing and dismissing of judges to the President of the Republic; appointing, dismissing and controlling the presidents, vice presidents and leaders of departments (*kollégiumvezető*). The Orbán Government was criticized for filling this position through the wife of a European Parliament representative of the Fidesz party and a close friend of the Prime Minister.

22. A OBT consists of the president of the Supreme Court and fourteen other judges.[29] In theory, it has been created to supervise the activity of the OBH. It gives opinions and recommendations, but its operation is maintained by the OBH.[30] In all of its sessions – including closed sessions – the president of the OBH, OBH's minute-keeper, and the minister responsible for the judiciary are present.[31] Minutes of the sessions are kept by the OBH.[32] As it can be concluded from these rules, OBH's effective supervision by OBT is at least questionable. The regulation may be reviewed upon pressure from the Venice Commission and the European Network of Judicial Councils, but no plans are known at the time of writing.

---

27. Article 37(4) Basic Law, §41(2) Act CLI of 2011 on the Constitutional Court.
28. §66–67 of Act CLXI of 2011 on the organization and administration of courts, effective from 3 Dec. 2011 (hereinafter: Bszitv.).
29. §88(1–3) Bszitv.
30. §103–104 Bszitv.
31. §106 Bszitv.
32. §107(1) Bszitv.

23. The Basic Law lowered the age limit for judges to the general age limit of 62 years instead of the previous 70 years.[33] This measurement is also subject to the accelerated infringement procedure at the European Commission.[34] While university professors and similar professions are also subject to the 70-year age limit, their age limit has not been lowered. Effect of this measurement has been the removal of 7% of the judges, many of them fulfilling leader positions. For example, in the Supreme Court (*Kúria*), a quarter of the judges were affected. The affected judges left their offices in two waves, the older from 30 June 2012, while those who fulfilled age 62 in 2012 left on 31 December 2012. The European Court of Justice (ECJ) found that Hungary breached its obligations under Council Directive 2000/78/EC on equal treatment in employment and occupation.[35] In November 2013, Brussels terminated the infringement procedure after a new law provided adequate remedy to the judges. Some of the illegally removed judges got back their offices, but the majority asked for compensation.[36]

24. The court system did not change substantially; only the names of the courts were changed to reflect traditions. New administrative courts are to be created. Previously, administrative courts were only separate departments of ordinary courts. The changes have become effective from 1 January 2013.

25. The judicial system theoretically has two instances, and one extraordinary legal remedy is possible, called a supervisory procedure. Cases may start at the shire courts (*járásbíróság,* previously called local courts) or at the courthouses (*törvényszék*, previously called county courts). Appeals are decided in the courthouses, the High Courts (*ítélőtábla*) or the Supreme Court which is now called *Kúria*.[37] There are five High Courts in the country in the towns of Budapest, Pécs, Debrecen, Győr and Szeged.

26. The Supreme Court analyses decisions and examines and digests judicial practice. It passes decisions for the unification of law (*jogegységi határozat*) which are compulsory in all courts. Beyond this, it publishes principle court decisions and resolutions. The Basic Law defines a new competence of the courts – to annul decrees of local governments in case they are contrary to another law or to declare that a local government breached the Basic Law by not passing a decree (unconstitutionality by omission, *mulasztásos alkotmánysértés*).[38] The President of the Supreme Court is elected by the Parliament with a two-thirds majority of the votes, upon the recommendation of the President of the Republic.

---

33. Article 26(2) of Basic Law.
34. Hungary: Commission continues accelerated infringement procedure on independence of the data protection supervisor and measures affecting the judiciary and asks additional information on central bank's independence, http://europa.eu/rapid/pressReleasesAction.do?reference=IP/12/222 (7 Mar. 2012).
35. http://curia.europa.eu/jcms/upload/docs/application/pdf/2012-11/cp120139en.pdf.
36. http://hvg.hu/itthon/20130507_56_kirgutott_biro_folytathatja_a_munkajat.
37. §16 Bszitv.
38. Article 25(2) Basic Law.

K. Public Prosecutor

27. The system of public prosecution is an independent system directed by the public prosecutor. Under the new law, the public prosecutor is entitled to define the structure of the prosecutor's system. The public prosecutor is entitled to participate in the sessions of the Supreme Court, take into the prosecution's competence the investigation of any crime, file an appeal or a supervisory initiative to the Supreme Court, initiate a procedure for unification of law at the Supreme Court and express his position in the case, initiate procedures at the Constitutional Court, and exercise further rights like initiating or expressing his opinion related to legal rules, representing the accusation in criminal procedures, supervising the enforcement of sentences.

28. The public prosecutor is elected by the Parliament with a two-thirds majority of the votes, upon the recommendation of the President of the Republic. Prosecutors may not pursue any political activity or be members of a political party.[39]

II. Geography and Population

29. Hungary lies in the Carpathian Basin, between the Carpathian Mountains from the east and the north, the Alps from the west and the Dinaric Alps from the south. Its territory is 93,030 km^2 and its population is 9.9 million.[40] The biggest lake in Hungary is Lake Balaton with a surface area of 593 km^2. Almost three-quarters of the country's territory is low plain, with low mountains in the north and northeast (only 5% of the total territory of the country is between 400 and 1,000 m in height).

30. Hungary is administratively divided into twenty units – nineteen counties (*megye*) and the capital (*főváros*), Budapest. The nineteen counties and the capital were maintained as administrative units, but new units of territorial administration were created below the level of counties – shires (*járás*) which overtake the administrative powers of local authorities (of the notaries) and of the sub-regions.[41] There are also 173 sub-regions (*kistérségek*), with Budapest comprising its own sub-region. There are twenty-three towns with county rights (*megyei jogú város*). The local authorities of these towns have extended powers, but they are not independent county-level territorial units. Since 1996, the counties and the City of Budapest have been grouped into seven regions for statistical and development purposes.

III. Demographic and Cultural Composition

31. The official language of the country is Hungarian, which is part of the Finno-Ugric language family. It is one of four official languages of the EU which are not of Indo-European origin.

39. Article 29(2), (4), (6) Basic Law.
40. Central Statistical Office of Hungary. Data of the census of 1 Oct. 2011, http://www.nepszamlalas.hu/files/sharedUploads/Anyagok/2012/04_ho/nepszelo2011.pdf, March 2012.
41. *See* Governmental Decree 1299/2011. (IX. 1) and Bill T/6590 submitted to the Parliament.

32. Besides Hungarians, several ethnic minorities live in Hungary. Act LXXVII of 1993 on the Rights of National and Ethnic Minorities (Minority Act) states the following: 'It is the individual's exclusive and inalienable right to take on and declare their affiliation to a national or ethnic group or a minority. Nobody is obliged to proclaim that they belong to a minority group.' Under The Minority Act, Hungary officially recognizes thirteen national and ethnic minorities (listed in alphabetic order): Armenian, Bulgarian, Croatian, German, Greek, Polish, Roma, Romanian, Ruthenian, Serbian, Slovak, Slovenian and Ukrainian. Data from the 2011 census showed that 644,524 claimed to belong to one of the thirteen listed national and ethnic minorities out of the then 9.9 million population. However, only 148,155 people chose a minority language as their mother tongue, and further 228,353 used the minority language in close family and friendship relationships. Ahead of Germans, Slovaks and Croats, the biggest minority is the Roma community, numbering more than 190,000 people. Nevertheless, researchers and minority organizations consider that the real number of national and ethnic minorities is greater: estimates usually talk about more than half a million (570,000–600,000), but some surveys set forth that the number of Roma people in Hungary is in itself around 800,000–1,000,000. According to these estimates, today, ethnic minorities make up some 10% of the total population.

IV. Social and Cultural Values

33. Hungary transformed in 1989 from a soft communist regime to a transitional democracy. Social circumstances have deeply changed in the period between 1989 and 2010. A considerable social restructuring happened, as well as a re-ordering of social values. The transformation left large social classes disappointed. The decades of communist ruling (with its constrained etatism and paternalism) destroyed civil society and values like civil self-determination. The informal social structures and mechanisms, including those within State administration, economy, and judiciary, that existed under socialism, remained largely untouched in the democratic transition.[42] Sociological studies have revealed the value crisis of the Hungarian society at the beginning of the millennium.[43] These studies without exception argue that society is characterized by a lack of trust, disbelief in self-determination, scepticism in merit-based careers and preference for security to the detriment of freedoms.[44]

42. *See* Zoltán Fleck, *Változások és változatlanságok: A magyar jogrendszer a rendszerváltozás után* 164 (Napvilág Kiadó 2010).
43. Csepeli et al., examined trust and suspect in Hungarian society from an economic aspect, surveying attitudes towards economic actors, and the economic system, and they found the existence of envy, while the lack of trust. Envy is based on the lack of recognition of individual effort, which erodes legitimacy of legal rules and the system. György Csepeli et al., *Tisztesség és bizalom a posztszocialista átmenet fényében* (Kornai & Rose-Ackerman ed., Nemzeti Tankönyvkiadó 2005). *See also*, Zoltán Fleck & Csemáné Dr Váradi Erika (ed.), *Társadalmi zavarok – jegyzetek egy kutatási jelentéshez: VI. Országos kriminológiai Vándorgyűlés* (Bíbor Kiadó 2009).
44. Two Decades After the Wall's Fall (The Pew Global Attitudes Project. 2 Nov. 2009).

34. For example, it is widely held that family ties and social relationships are more influential on one's career than individual talent and effort.[45] Success is typically explained by external factors, similar to other post-communist countries.[46] Personal relations, corruption and informal agreements are the tools to get ahead in almost all fields of life, leading, among others, to the flourishing of black labour. There are several semi-legal or legal forms of corruption or tax evasion (secret tips in the public healthcare system (*hálapénz),* off-shore companies).

35. The Orbán Government exacerbated and reinforced these traditional social structures. It built its rhetoric on traditional christian-conservative values while, at the same time, pursuing a left-radical governance style, characterized by extreme centralization. In its political and economy policy strategy, it has leveraged informal ties (clientelism) and reorganized the national economy along these lines, creating a feudal-style system of dependencies. The contradiction between the declared values and the followed values creates a political neurosis. This treacherous political tactic leaves uneducated people captured, believing the rhetoric, but at the same time being exploited by the system. People who are educated and follow the government line have a good chance of being beneficiaries of the system.

36. Today, more than ever, social mobility is unlikely as social injustices are reproduced. School systems and geographic distribution of workplaces reinforce the advantages or disadvantages of the families. Geographical mobility within the country has also been scarce in the past decades, probably because of the legal and emotional status of the real estate property system. A considerable number of people emigrate or work abroad, but the exact numbers are not known.[47] According to polls, 25–34% of respondents planned to leave the country in 2022 if Orbán won again on the 2022 elections (which he did, acquiring a two-third majority). This illustrates the deep polarization of the society between those who believe in the governmental rhetoric and those who are nervous about the political hypocrisy, leaving only a handful of people who would support a moderate right-wing government. Characteristic of the new age of political communication, the disagreement is not between opinions on governance but between parallel, perceived realities. The discord between the perception of reality makes dialogue futile.

37. The media scene has become dominated by government-friendly media, a significant part of which is closely related to the Prime Minister through proxy ownership (*see* paragraphs 46–47). Some independent critical journals remained in the weekly newspaper market and in the online sphere. Until 2015, the national private electronic media typically avoided political topics. This changed in 2015 when RTL Klub responded to the unfriendly advertising tax rule – which targeted solely this company with a 40% addition taxation of its pre-taxed revenues – by becoming more critical to the government. In 2015, a cabinet minister, Andy Vajna's company, bought RTL Klub's only competitor, TV2 and changed it to become an open

45. Európai Társadalmi Jelentés (TÁRKI, 2009), Chapter 8.4, pp. 150–154.
46. World Social Values Report 2009.
47. https://index.hu/gazdasag/2022/04/20/kivandorlas-ausztria-lakashelyzet-fiatalok/.

supporter of the government. Public service broadcasting has been a propaganda instrument of the government, not shying away from imparting disinformation.

38. Orbán Viktor's government of 2010, 2014, 2018 and 2022 induced significant changes in the media field both in terms of legal regulation and economic influence. These changes were manufactured by the regulation scheme, the frequency distribution decisions of the Media Council, the editorial policy of public service media and the national TV2, and by the domination of the media landscape through State advertising and proxy ownership,[48] as well as by the aggressive political campaigns on television, online and through outdoor billboards.

39. In the 2011 census, 39% declared themselves as belonging to the Catholic Church, 11% to the Reformist Church, 18% confessed to not belong to any religion, and 27% refused to respond.[49] However, the number of those who actively practice the religion is around 10–20%.[50] The governmental rhetoric emphasized that the Christian 'majority' is to be represented in the media and the education system. This is reflected in the high number of religious representatives in the Public Service Body,[51] prohibiting advertisements from interrupting religious programmes[52] and obliging public service media to show respect for the institutes of marriage and family.[53] Since 2018, anti-LGBT rhetoric and measurements have been added to this pseudo-christian political line.

40. Hungary has a strong intellectual tradition, with its human intellectuals traditionally having participated in political debates. However, polarization is apparent between the average people's cultural habits and that of the intellectual elite, and there is no dialogue between the two groups. While there is a tiny but strong liberal elite in the country, liberal values are not embraced by the rest of the population. Freedom of expression is in high esteem in the Hungarian culture, but democratic values do not enjoy a long tradition. This is one of the explanations why the general public did not protest against the policy of the Orbán Government which hastily disassembled the constitutional system and did not observe the rule of law. Still, the media reform was the first issue which led to public demonstrations, especially by young people and students, and which generated the first civil group that aimed to step up against the governmental policy (1 Million People for Press Freedom, *Egymillióan a Sajtószabadságért Mozgalom).*

---

48. *See* more in: Bárd, P. & Bayer, J. *A Comparative Analysis of Media Freedom and Pluralism in the EU Member States.* Research paper for the Policy Department C: Citizens' Rights and Constitutional Affairs. http://www.europarl.europa.eu/RegData/etudes/STUD/2016/571376/IPOL_STU(2016)571376_EN.pdf.
49. KSH: Népszámlálás 2011. https://www.ksh.hu/nepszamlalas/docs/tablak/vallas/10_01_01.xls.
50. Kolozsi, Á. *A többség hisz Istenben, de templomba már sokkal kevesebben járnak Magyarországon.* Társadalmi Riport, G7. https://g7.hu/adat/20230101/a-tobbseg-hisz-istenben-de-templomba-mar-sokkal-kevesebben-jarnak-magyarorszagon/.
51. Annex I of the Mttv.
52. §33(3)d; 33(6)d Mttv.
53. §83(1)c Mttv.

41. Freedom of the press has a special place in Hungarian history because in the 1948 revolution it was the first among the twelve claims submitted to the Habsburg Court.[54] The special importance is also emphasized by the role that Hungarian poets and writers played in Hungary's historical events, especially in the nineteenth century and up to the 1920s. A third element to support the attachment to this specific freedom is the bad memories of the suppression of freedom of expression during the communist era. Therefore, an open suppression of press products would probably destroy Orbán's popularity, even among his followers.

§2. The Media Landscape

I. Overview of Media Markets and Main Actors

Ágnes Urbán

A. *Introduction*

42. Since the beginning of the 1990s, the Hungarian media scene has been governed by market forces. The shift from the state-owned media system to a market-driven sector lasted for years; companies were privatized and foreign investors entered the market. Content scarcity of communism disappeared soon; new titles were launched on the newspaper and magazine market, and the Act I of 1996 on Radio and Television created the legal background of commercial broadcasting. In this period, broadcasting infrastructure developed quickly – multichannel television became widespread based on cable and satellite transmission. From the end of the 1990s, Internet penetration increased and online content services emerged.

43. In the first decade of the new millennium, the changes were less dramatic, but market evolution was continuous. Content supply available for consumers was broader than ever before, and Hungarian investors also entered the market. Domestic companies gained interests in newspaper publishing, television and radio broadcasting and online content service markets. At the same time, markets witnessed a horizontal, vertical and cross-media integration process; enlarged and diversified media groups were more resistant to the global crisis, which started in 2008, than the smaller companies. In the 2010s, most foreign investors left the Hungarian media market; Hungary was not so attractive for investors anymore because of economic and regulatory circumstances. The market share of Hungarian-owned media companies increased significantly after 2010.

---

54. We demand freedom of the press and abolition of censorship. *See*: Mit kíván a magyar nemzet? http://tortenelemportal.hu/2010/03/%E2%80%9Emit-kivan-a-magyar-nemzet-%E2%80%9D/ (15 Mar. 2010).

B. Advertising Revenues

44. The advertising trend follows the general economic trends. In 2022, the advertising revenues of the media companies increased by 2.8% at nominal prices compared to the previous year, but this was a 10.8% decrease in real terms.[55]

45. The Internet generates the most advertising revenues, followed by television and print media. Radio broadcasting is marginal from this point of view. Two-third of the internet revenues went to global internet players in 2022.

C. Newspaper and Magazine Publishing

46. There are three major print media publishers in Hungary. Mediaworks is owned by a pro-government investor, Central Media Group is owned by an independent Hungarian investor, and Ringier is foreign-owned. Other international and domestic investors are less significant in economic terms. The newspaper market is dominated by Mediaworks, although, Ringier publishes the most popular tabloid newspaper. In October 2022, the sports daily (Nemzeti Sport) was bought up by the state, so it became a state-owned newspaper (Table 1).

Table 1 Main Hungarian Newspapers

	Type	*Publisher*	*Readership (2021)*
Blikk	Tabloid	Blikk Kft (Ringier AG)	489,738
Bors	Tabloid	Mediaworks	210,403
Nemzeti Sport	Sport	N.S. Media es Vagyonkezelo Kft (State)	170,294
Kisalföld	Regional	Mediaworks	105,821
Kelet-Magyarország	Regional	Mediaworks	100,132

Source: NMHH (2022): Médiapiaci jelentés https://nmhh.hu/cikk/234337/Mediapiaci_Jelentes_2022.

47. The ownership structure of the Hungarian print media market transformed dramatically in the 2010s. The most important reason is that some foreign investors have withdrawn from the market and their place was taken by domestic investors. The

55. MRSZ (Hungarian Advertising Association): Figures of the spendings in media and communication markets. https://mrsz.hu/cmsfiles/57/c4/2022_MRSZ_media_komm_torta_hosszu_v6_FINAL.pdf.

other important turning point was the creation of the Central and Eastern European Media Foundation (abbreviated as KESMA in Hungarian) in 2018. On 28 November, almost all media owners related to ruling party transferred the ownership rights of their media holdings to KESMA. Their companies joined the foundation, all of them without any type of compensation for the owners.

48. In October 2016, Hungary's highest-circulation political daily, *Népszabadság*, was shut down. This was an emblematic event in the Orban-regime, since Népszabadság was the biggest political newspaper in the country. The owner of the *Mediaworks* publishing house, the Austrian businessman Heinrich Pecina, cited business reasons for the decision, but the way the process was implemented (taking the newspaper's Internet archive offline, humiliating employees and keeping them in a state of uncertainty) strongly suggested political motives. The political background became obvious when a few weeks later it was announced that *Mediaworks'* Hungarian holdings would be taken over by Opimus Press. This company had ties to Lőrinc Mészáros, an oligarch who is a personal friend of the Prime Minister and who then entered the media business. Later, the Mediaworks publishing house became part of the KESMA.

49. The regional newspaper market became extremely concentrated. With the creation of KESMA, a monopoly was created in the regional newspaper market. All newspapers are published by Mediaworks, which is part of KESMA. Previously, four international investors shared this market, but all the foreign owners' stakes have been bought up by the pro-government company. The one region–one paper model prevails in Hungary, and each of the regions has its own newspaper. However, these newspapers have the same owner, so they have become a monopoly market which is also reflected in their content.

50. There are some political weeklies, and this segment is quite pluralistic. Some small independent Hungarian publishers entered this segment. With the exception of one (HVG), these are very small-circulation papers, and publishers are essentially struggling to survive.

51. The consumer magazine market is segmented, and the number of titles is dynamically changing. The pro-government Mediaworks has no dominant position in this market. The Hungarian-owned independent Central Media has a strong position in this market, just like two foreign-owned companies, Ringier and Marquard Media.

52. Altogether, the structure of the publishing sector has substantially changed during the last decade. Some new titles were launched, other titles disappeared, and the share of foreign investors dramatically decreased in the daily newspaper market. The biggest market player is close to the ruling party.

D. Television

53. Watching television is the most popular free time activity in Hungary, the average viewing time being 295 minutes in 2022[56] Programme choice is stable; currently, more than 100 channels are available in Hungarian. Due to the deployment of broadcasting infrastructure, multichannel television became widespread; based on the estimations of the National Media and Infocommunications Authority, 3.6 million households had a television subscription in August 2021.[57]

54. Public service broadcasting was restructured at the end of 2010, and a new institution was created called the Hungarian Media Service Support and Asset Management Fund (*Médiaszolgáltatás Támogató és Vagyonkezelő Alap*, (MTVA)) (*see* more on this topic in Part III below, paragraphs 344–362). MTVA supervises the operation of public television, public radio and national news agencies. There are six public television channels in Hungary. Public service broadcasting channels are not really popular; the audience share of the public channels was only 10.8% among the 4+ population in 2021.[58]

55. The two national commercial television channels were launched in 1997 and rapidly became dominant players. RTL Hungary is owned by the RTL Group, while the second biggest commercial company, TV2, is owned by a Hungarian investor close to the ruling party. Both broadcasters offer a broad range of channels.

56. Multichannel television is widespread, and the number of thematic channels (sport, music, movies, etc.) is high. These channels fulfil market niches; therefore, the television market is becoming more and more fragmented, and audience shares are decreasing.

57. Despite the high number of channels, political content is relatively poor on television. Public television channels have political programmes and news affairs, but these are heavily criticized because of their pro-government bias. The two national commercial channels also have news programmes, but these cover a lot of tabloid and celebrity news. There are three politically themed channels that are important forums for political debate. *ATV* is owned by *Hungarian Hit Gyülekezete* (Faith Church Hungary), an evangelical congregation. ATV is generally regarded as a left-wing channel that is critical of the government, but – undoubtedly due to its ownership background – on some major issues, it shares a platform with the government. The right-wing *Hír TV* is owned by KESMA, and its editorial line is heavily biased to the governing party. *Euronews* news channel is available in Hungarian, but it mainly covers international developments.

56. Newsletter of Nielsen Audience Research, 31 Jan. 2023 (Nielsen_TV_market_snapshot_2022_HUN.pdf).
57. NMHH (2021): Televíziós piac gyorsjelentés. Augusztus. https://nmhh.hu/dokumentum/224300/tvgyorsjelentes_2021_augusztus_hu.pdf.
58. https://mtva.hu/wp-content/uploads/sites/17/2022/05/2021_%C3%A9vi-besz%C3%A1mol%C3%B3_MTVA_30_k%C3%BCldhet%C5%91_d%C3%B6nt%C3%A9ssel.pdf.

58. Mainstreaming services (Netflix, HBO Max, Amazon Prime Video, Disney+, Apple TV+, Skyshowtime) are available in Hungary. They have a growing popularity, especially among younger viewers. RTL and TV2 also launched their catch-up television services.

E. Radio

59. Concerning the market size, radio broadcasting is less significant than television or print media, as the revenue-generating role of radio is relatively poor in Hungary. The public service broadcaster has four channels: one is dedicated to talk programmes, another to popular music, a third to classical music and the fourth one to traditional Hungarian music.

60. Retro Radio, the only national commercial radio station in Hungary, is the market leader. It is part of the pro-government KESMA Foundation.

61. The regional and local radio market is changing as the Media Council completes the tender procedures for frequencies. In recent years, the biggest winner of these tenders was the music radio station Rádió 1, which practically built up a national network. It is the second most popular radio in the country.

62. Karc FM, a right-wing talk radio station, has also been successful on the frequency tenders. It is part of the pro-government KESMA. There is another right-wing talk radio station, Inforadio, but it is only available in and around the capital. The internationally known Klubradio, which is critical of the government, could not win the media authority's frequency tender, so it has been operating as an online radio station since February 2021.

63. An analysis examined the radio frequency-tenders initiated and adjudicated by the media authority between January 2018 and April 2021. In this period, the Media Council closed a total of seventy-seven tenders. A quarter (24.4%) of the closed bids were won by the KESMA-affiliated pro-government political talk radio station Karc FM. The winner of 18% of the bids was Radio 1, another pro-government music radio network, while another 26% of the bids went to religious radio stations. Another pro-government music radio network, Best FM, acquired four frequencies, while KESMA-affiliated Gong Radio gained three frequencies in the same period, extending its network to a total of seven cities. Only 15.4% of the applications – twelve frequencies – were won by applicants not belonging to any network.[59]

59. Polyák, G. (ed.), *Four Shades of Censorship: State Intervention in the Central Eastern European Media Markets*. Mérték Médiaelemző Műhely 353 (Budapest 2021). https://mertek.eu/wp-content/uploads/2021/10/Mertek-fuzetek_19.pdf.

F. Internet

64. Internet penetration in Hungary was 83% in 2021 in the 16+ age group;[60] it is an important source of content consumption.

65. The news portal market is rather colourful with pro-government and independent market players. *Origo.hu* is part of KESMA and *index.hu* was acquired by a pro-government investor which led to the mass resignation of the journalists. There are also independent news portals, *24.hu* and *hvg.hu* are the most influential.

66. A negative development of the last decade was the migration of users and advertisers to digital platforms, like Google, Facebook or YouTube. The revenues of Hungarian content providers are decreasing since these huge aggregator sites can reach even more users and offer well-targeted advertising possibilities.

G. Cross-Media Ownership

67. The ownership structure of the Hungarian media market has significantly changed in the last decades. The dominance of foreign investors in the nineties has ceased in the first decade of the new millennium. Hungarian ownership became more significant, and cross-media ownership also occurred.

68. The creation of the KESMA in 2018 significantly increased the ownership concentration in Hungary. (For its legal solution, *see* §531 and 194) The KESMA owns almost 500 media brands and its dominance is especially strong in the print media market. Radio, television and online brands are also significant.

69. There are no regulatory constraints for a further increase in cross-media ownership. Strategic decisions are not foreseen; therefore, it is possible that cross-media concentration will increase in the future. There is fact-based evidence that pro-government media companies are partly financed by state advertisements.[61]

II. Broadcasting Infrastructure

Ágnes Urbán

70. The television broadcasting infrastructure is well-developed in Hungary. Competition between cable, satellite and Internet Protocol Television (IPTV) operators has resulted in declining prices. The latest television market report is available for

60. NMHH (2022): Az elektronikus hírközlési piac fogyasztóinak vizsgálata. Internetes felmérés – 2021, https://nmhh.hu/dokumentum/228626/elektronikus_hirkozlesi_piaci_fogyasztonak_vizsgalata_internethasznalok_2021.pdf.
61. Bátorfy, A. & Urbán, Á., *State Advertising as an Instrument of Transformation of the Media Market in Hungary*, East European Politics, 36:1, 44–65, (2020). DOI: 10.1080/21599165.2019.1662398.

August 2021. According to the data, more than 3.6 million households subscribed to television services and 82.4% of all television subscriptions were digital.[62]

71. The digital satellite broadcasting market has been competitive with three operators before Sat TV ceased to exist in 2022.[63] In August 2021, the DirectOne platform of Canal+ Luxemburg was the market leader in this segment, sharing the market with Digi TV satellite service and then still with Sat TV (owned by Magyar Telekom). Official data was not provided in 2022 and in 2023 by the Media Authority.

72. The cable market is more fragmented with a lot of small municipality-owned local operators. The level of concentration is high, with the top ten players covering more than 90% of subscribers. In January 2023, the biggest Hungarian telecommunication company, 4iG, bought up the Hungarian affiliation of Vodafone. Since 4iG previously had stakes in the cable market, it became far the biggest cable operator in the country after this transaction. The state bought a 49% ownership stake in the company, and the pro-government 4iG bought the 51% stake. Analysts and journalists question the rationality of the deal from the point of view of the state.[64]

73. *Antenna Hungária* (AH), the Hungarian broadcasting company, launched its DVB-T service (MindigTV) in 2008. It has a free service with twelve television channels. Its paid service includes fifty-two channels. The analogue switch-off date was October 2013.

74. IPTV has also been available since November 2006; Magyar Telekom was the first entrant.

Two big companies share the Hungarian distribution market:

- Magyar Telekom (owned by Deutsche Telekom) is an ex-incumbent telco; besides voice and data services, it has interests in cable, satellite and IPTV markets.
- 4iG, which merged with Vodafone in 2023 and got renamed as ‘One’. This is a market leader in cable television and a relevant player in the digital satellite market; data and voice services are also available.[65]

III. Technological and Economic Developments on the Media Markets

Gábor Polyák

75. The liberalization of the Hungarian electronic media market took off after Parliament adopted Act I of 1996 on Radio and Television Broadcasting, also

62. NMHH (2021): Televíziós piac gyorsjelentés. Augusztus. https://nmhh.hu/dokumentum/224300/tvgyorsjelentes_2021_augusztus_hu.pdf.
63. https://www.hwsw.hu/hirek/64181/telekom-sat-tv-muhold-teve-interaktiv-iptv.html.
64. https://g7.hu/vallalat/20230109/olcsobb-lett-a-vodafone-igy-vajon-mar-megeri/.
65. https://www.4ig.hu/uj-szakaszba-lep-a-4ig-csoport-integracioja.

known as 'Rttv.'.[66] By permitting market access for commercial radio and television stations, this law in effect brought about a dualistic media scheme in the country. Actually, the public broadcasters had enjoyed a less than complete monopoly even before the first Media Act, Rttv. entered into force. Local cable providers had been transmitting Hungarian language channels since 1994, the year that also saw the launch of HBO in Hungary.

76. While Rttv. enabled a variety of television and radio services to enter the market regardless of their means of transmission (terrestrial, satellite, or cable); it assigned remarkably strict limits to the economic manoeuvring space available to media enterprises. Despite certain regulatory difficulties, the Hungarian media market offered an increasingly varied selection of radio and television programming to the public in the 2000s.

A. *The Distribution of Terrestrial Capacities*

77. The law made the market entry of terrestrial radio and television stations subject to a tendering process administered by the National Radio and Television Body (*Országos Rádió és Televízió Testület*, (ORTT)). Nevertheless, rather than being retained as the privilege of the authority, an announcement of tender was permitted to be proposed by individual media enterprises as well. Rttv. allowed providers to design the technical parameters of the broadcasting themselves in consultation with the communications authority. In such cases, the frequency was allocated in a simplified process – a rather market-friendly legal scheme of which many local radio stations took advantage to establish themselves.

78. However, the tender rules and the tendering practices of the ORTT soon became a source of proliferating problems. In 2007 and 2008, deciding on petitions submitted nearly a decade earlier, the Constitutional Court ruled the tendering rules unconstitutional almost in their entirety. The Constitutional Court found that the law 'failed to implement a transparent tendering system' by neglecting to provide for evaluation criteria, a deadline for evaluating bids, the authority's liability to explain its decision, and the option for losing tender participants to initiate a comprehensive … parties to bring a comprehensive court review of the results on the merits of the case. The Constitutional Court also ruled the regulation of the so-called broadcasting fee unconstitutional in return for the opportunity to broadcast because the law failed to establish criteria to determine the rate of the fee. In short, the emergence of the Hungarian media market took place in a regulatory environment riddled with gaps, and the Parliament did not address the Constitutional Court's objections before 2010 when it passed a new Media Act – and even then, it did so in part only.

79. This regulatory environment paved the way for a murky, unpredictable and arbitrary tendering routine in which unverifiable subjective criteria weighed far too

66. This title has been partially updated in 2017.

heavily in the evaluation of individual bids. In fact, there was not a single nationwide radio or television tender administered by the ORTT that did not raise massive legal concerns. The results of the 1996 nationwide commercial television tender, as well as those of the 2010 rerun of the tender for nationwide commercial radio permits, were found to have been in violation of applicable rules by court judgments that are now final and non-appealable. In 1997, during the first bidding of nationwide commercial radio services, the authority had announced such irrational media market expectations that by 2002, it became inevitable to revise the terms of broadcasting contracts across the board. Equally serious legal concerns were voiced in connection with the 2007 renewal of the broadcasting contracts of the commercial television stations. Finally, the allocation of local radio and television frequencies has been frequently accompanied by heated legal and political debate.

B. Tendering of Nationwide Commercial Television Stations

80. The most important milestone of liberalization, the tendering of nationwide commercial television stations, determined the key parameters of the media market for the long haul. The two nationwide television licences advertised by the ORTT in November 1996 elicited three bids – one each from MTM-SBS Rt. (in the majority ownership of SBS Broadcasting S.A.) and Magyar RTL Klub (in the majority ownership of CLT-Ufa S.A., itself controlled by Bertelsmann A.G. as the largest owner), while Írisz TV Rt. (in the majority ownership of the U.S.-invested Central European Media Enterprises Ltd., CME) filed bids for both licences. In both cases, Írisz TV Rt. came out as the highest bidder and even upped the ante in the second round of the tender. Although Magyar RTL Rt. had failed to enclose some of the mandatory statements, the commission refrained from disqualifying its incomplete bid in recognition of the less-than-fully unambiguous rules. Ultimately, the licences were awarded to MTM-SBS Rt. (TV2) and Magyar RTL Rt. (RTL Klub) in June 1997 as the winning bidders.

81. Írisz TV Rt. then contested the commission's decision and asked the court to invalidate the tender, on the grounds that, by accepting Magyar RTL Rt.'s bid, the ORTT had violated the declared terms and evaluation criteria of the tender announcement. The Court of First Instance dismissed the suit, but upon appeal, in February 1999, the Supreme Court ruled that ORTT had indeed violated the law. However, this court judgment did not affect the validity of the contract awarded to the winning bidder because the rules of the tender prevented that contract from being voided by any entity other than the authority itself as a result of a public administrative rather than judicial review. In its turn, ORTT lodged a request for a review with the Supreme Court. In February 2000, two days before the judgment was to be passed, SBS Broadcasting S.A. joined forces with CLT-Ufa and bought out TV3, the Hungarian subsidiary of CME. In the wake of this transaction, Írisz TV Rt. withdrew its claim.

82. In 2006, the licences of RTL Klub and TV2, which were originally approved for a term of ten years, were renewed by ORTT for another five years with identical conditions. Subsequently, the Deputy Parliamentary Commissioner for Civil Rights lodged an appeal against this decision with the Attorney General. The Attorney General found that the extension of the contract was against the law on two counts – first, because the ORTT resolved to renew the licences before the lapse of the legally stipulated deadline, and second because it disregarded the mandate to deny such renewal if the broadcaster has committed a material or repeated legal violation – which both commercial channels in question had. When contested by the ORTT over his findings, the Attorney General refrained from taking further steps in the matter, citing a lack of competence.

83. The digital transition ended on 31 October 2013, when analogue broadcasting was switched off. The Authority is responsible for registering audiovisual services, managing frequencies and distributing the remaining licences.

C. Tendering of Nationwide Radio Stations

84. In announcing the tender for nationwide commercial radio licences, the ORTT stipulated a broadcasting licence fee nearly equal to the fee charged for commercial television stations. The winning bidders were Sláger Radio, an affiliate of the American Emmis Communication, and Danubius Radio, originally owned by DMG Radio and then, following a series of ownership changes, by Accession Mezzanine Capital. Formerly, Danubius had operated under the aegis of Hungarian Public Radio, providing essentially commercial programmes in German aimed at tourists.

85. As local radios entered the market and local stations began to organize themselves in networks, it soon became apparent that the two big ones would not be able to fulfil their undertaken commitments. In the outcome of a dispute between Sláger Radio and the ORTT, which comprised several legal processes, the authority finally extended the licences of both nationwide commercial stations by five years, limiting their broadcasting fee obligation to the full term of the original contract.

86. In 2008, the National Assembly passed an amendment to Rttv. (the previous Media Act) to the effect of enabling Sláger Radio and Danubius Radio to have their licences further renewed until the date of the digital switchover. In 2009, the Constitutional Court ruled this amendment unconstitutional and abolished it, arguing that it would have excluded all other potential service providers from the national radio market and would, therefore, have constituted a violation of freedom of enterprise. Moreover, because the date of the digital switchover is entirely uncertain, the amendment would have virtually extended the exclusive licences of the existing two majors for an indefinite period.

87. In the next step, the ORTT announced a new tender for the frequencies of the two national commercial stations. Bids were submitted, besides Sláger Radio and Danubius Radio, by four ventures – Advenio Zrt., Zene Radio Zrt., Radio Juventus Zrt., and FM1 Consortium – all of which had a background in operating local radio stations. Three of the bidders (Advenio Zrt., Zene Radio Zrt., and FM1 Consortium) offered approximately half of their annual revenues by way of a broadcasting fee. According to the Office of the ORTT and its president, the published rules of the tender would call for the disqualification of any bidder undertaking a commitment based on such an unfounded business plan. Advenio Zrt., whose owner runs a local Budapest station (Lánchíd Radio), also violated the tender requirements by neglecting to file a declaration of commitment to eliminate conflict of ownership interests. These irregularities notwithstanding, the majority of ORTT members deemed the bids of Advenio Zrt. and FM1 Consortium valid, only disqualifying Zene Radio Zrt. Finally, the tender was awarded to Advenio Zrt. (Class FM) and FM1 Consortium (Neo FM).

88. The owners of Sláger Radio and Danubius Radio filed suit. In a final and non-appealable decision, the court ruled that both tender procedures had been conducted in violation of the law. According to the explanation attached to the judgment, Rttv. did not authorize ORTT to waive ownership-related restrictions of eligibility, even for the duration of the tendering process. In this way, no enterprise already in possession of a single local radio licence should have been allowed to file a bid. The judgment, however, was not followed by the appropriate consequences because the new Parliament, formed in the interim in 2010, amended Rttv. to the effect of ruling out the termination of a programme provider's contract whenever the given breach did not exclusively arise from the fault of that provider. Now, the court took the view that, in this case, the tender announcement itself had been against the law. The ORTT then filed a petition for a review of the final and non-appealable judgment. The appellate court overturned the judgment and ruled each of the bids valid, except for that submitted by Advenio Zrt., due to the absence of the declaration concerning conflict of interest.

89. Ironically, the valid winner, Neo FM, got its licence withdrawn by the Media Council on 20 June 2012 for not being able to pay the licence fee. After its bankruptcy, Neo FM was bought by a new investor who was devoted to continuing the broadcast with a new team. However, at the appellate level, the court announced the withdrawal of licence valid, and the radio terminated its broadcast. It continued its programme online, under the name Neo World Radio, with sporadic breaks until about 2016, when it stopped operating for no apparent reason.

D. The Market of Cable and Satellite Media Providers

90. The market of cable and satellite television (and radio) services was fully liberalized by the Rttv., which stipulated a simple registration process as the sole condition for market access. However, these providers remained subject to the broadcasting fee payment obligation as well as certain structural programming requirements depending on their range of reception.

91. With the adoption of the Rttv., the number of households with cable, satellite and IPTV access entered a period of dramatic growth. At present, some 600,000 out of the 3.8 million households in the country (approx. 16%) have the ability to watch free access – analogue or digital – terrestrial broadcasts or free-access satellite programmes. The rest of the households subscribe to one of the several multichannel platforms.

92. The multichannel households have access to some 80–90 Hungarian language channels, excluding local stations, with the number of channels and the composition of the package depending on the provider. In other words, the selection of content on offer would seem sufficiently rich and diversified from the consumer's perspective.

93. At the same time, the overwhelming majority of television stations are not settled in Hungary and are, therefore, not subject to Hungarian laws and regulations. Indeed, the emigration of stations has been the single most decisive attribute of the multichannel television market in Hungary since the country joined the EU. Taking advantage of certain media-rights provisions of the EU, in particular the principle of country of origin and technical capacities, a large number of media ventures have set up or relocated their businesses outside the borders of Hungary. While Romania and the Czech Republic have proved to be particularly attractive in this regard, Viasat3, a channel with some of the best ratings in Hungary, has moved to the United Kingdom (UK). Many of these channels target audiences in Hungary exclusively or for the most part. The authority currently keeps on file a total of seventeen nationwide cable or satellite television services with reception not limited to foreign countries that are non-public in nature and are actually featured in the selection offered by one broadcaster or another. Of these, only one (Channel 4) has made it to the top ten television stations in terms of ratings.

94. The exodus of television programme processes is mainly rooted in regulatory problems. For one thing, Rttv. and the ORTT's practice have prescribed a broadcasting fee that is excessive compared to that charged in other Member States and is applied even to ventures that do not use a terrestrial frequency. Furthermore, Rttv. has made it mandatory for providers to reach more than half of the residents of the country to air newscasts and other public service programmes. The authority has applied the least favourable commercial-break calculation, and the stipulations aimed at preventing the concentration of media capacities have effectively prevented nationwide stations from launching new channels. All of these hindrances have been compounded by a rather unpredictable official routine as regards the monitoring of legal requirements. Even though Act CLXXXV of 2010 on media services and mass communication (Mttv.) (the new Media Act of 2010) has brought about conditions more favourable for enterprises and abolished a number of unreasonable restrictions, this will not be sufficient to accomplish great things beyond keeping services that presently operate under Hungarian law in the country. In fact, the new law incorporates several features that would seem to perpetuate the lack of allure that has characterized the Hungarian market.

E. Local Media Markets

95. Local media markets have availed themselves of the opportunities of both terrestrial and cable broadcasting. Despite the economic difficulties and frequent dependence on municipalities, it is safe to say that a colourful selection of local media has sprung up in Hungary. According to NMHH's records, local media markets currently comprise some thirty terrestrial television stations, nearly 500 cable television stations (many of which only broadcast still image news, though), and more than 200 radio stations. One thing that was instrumental in the development of local radio markets was the fact that under the Rttv., media enterprises were allowed to have a local tender conducted at their own initiative.

96. Local radio markets were particularly amenable to being shaped by the tendering practices of the ORTT. When it took off in 1998, tendering initially opened up each local market based on uniform criteria, mostly favouring the launch of local radio stations airing music and local news. In the 2000s, however, tendering began to afford more room for specialist topic orientations. Even so, call-in radio talk shows have fundamentally remained a market exception and continue to be confined to Budapest and an organized network run by a Budapest-based station.

97. Being linked to a network is a key feature of local media markets. While some local television stations, such as Hálózat Television, have also evolved their own networks, they have not made a noticeable market impact. By contrast, some major music radio networks – Juventus and Rádió 1, for example – have risen to nationwide significance, and new networks have emerged recently that focus on themes such as public affairs or religion (Klubradio, Lánchíd Radio, Mária Radio).

98. The re-tendering of a number of local radio licences is now under way, in a process that is likely – in view of the routine followed by the Media Council to date – to shake out the market.

99. The financial position of local media is shaped by three basic factors. First, programme broadcasters owned by local municipalities are particularly dominant in television markets. These stations rely on a more or less stable financial base, although municipal ownership does pose a threat to editorial independence. Second, local advertising markets are rather narrow, a fact aggravated by the lack of capacity – particularly of television channels – to produce credible ratings data. Third, support funds awarded by the Media Authority by tender have been an important source of financing for years. Local radio and television stations may use these resources to finance their costs of operation. However, the media service revenues that have been the source of such support are expected to drop significantly in the future, in particular owing to fees missed from nationwide television stations due to the digital switchover.

100. A proposed amendment to the law on programme distribution and digital switchover was submitted to the Parliament on 21 November 2017, with the proposed effect of allowing local linear media service providers to have their interim licence valid until 2020 to be extended for another twelve years without a tender. The request is to be made to the Head of the Media Authority.[67]

F. Digital Switchover

101. The digital switchover has not materially changed the media market in Hungary, at least as regards terrestrial broadcasting, which tends to be the most sensitive to the regulatory environment. The largest cable providers (UPC and Magyar Telekom) began to digitalize the cable network in 2007 and 2008, while the first IPTV service was launched in 2007 (Magyar Telekom). The same year also saw the first steps toward the construction of optical networks (Magyar Telekom, DigiTV). Building on these platforms, digitalization has further diversified the channel selection and enabled new Hungarian language channels to emerge. However, the channels that have appeared on terrestrial digital platforms to date have been invariably available on other platforms before.

102. The terrestrial digital television platform was launched in December 2008, with the MindigTV service, run by Antenna Hungaria, initially limited to the channels of Duna TV, one of the country's public service stations. At present, the service provides free access to all of the public channels, the two nationwide commercial channels and Euronews. An additional twenty-three television channels are available in a paid package.

103. From the outset, the Digital Terrestrial Television (DTT) platform encountered a remarkably competitive environment, which previously – particularly since the 2006 launch of the satellite service of DigiTV – had been characterized by the emergence of new actors and platforms as well as plummeting prices. Already at launch, households limited to terrestrial reception accounted for no more than 20% of the total. The strengthening of the new platform was hindered by regulation, which not only delayed the launch but also stipulated ill-conceived terms of operation.

104. The allocation of terrestrial capacities and their respective positions within the digital media system are determined by the Strategy of Digital Switchover and the severally amended Act LXXIV of 2007, known as the Digital Switchover Act.

105. The legally stipulated deadline for the digital switchover on the television market was 31 December 2014. As a condition for analogue switch-off of television broadcasting, terrestrial digital transmission of public television channels had to reach at least 94% of the population, and reception equipment had to be available in the retail trade. Uncharacteristically, legislators changed the switchover deadline three times in the course of a single year without explaining the considerations of media policy necessitating each revision. The initial deadline of 31 December 2011

---

67. T18566. http://www.parlament.hu/irom40/18566/18566.pdf.

was amended by Mttv. to 31 December 2014. In the summer of 2011, this was brought forward to 31 December 2012. Then, on 1 January 2012, the deadline was re-established as 31 December 2014.

106. In regulating market access, the Digital Switchover Act places the emphasis on electing the operator of the digital terrestrial platform. The operation of individual media services is merely subject to a simple licence of the authority. The platform operator is free to choose the media services to be transmitted at its own discretion and is also free to decide the terms of transmission. Nevertheless, the law imposes restrictions on the platform operator by stipulating 'must-carry' requirements more stringent than those applied to other broadcasters.

107. The tender for electing the platform operator was conducted by the National Telecommunications Authority (NHH *(Nemzeti Hírközlési Hatóság)*), transformed into National Media and Telecommunications Authority (NMHH *(Nemzeti Média és Hírközlési Hatóság)*) in 2010. Published in August 2007, the draft announcement of the tender solicited bids for the operation of the five nationwide digital television broadcasting networks and a single nationwide digital radio broadcasting network. Finally, the tender was officially announced in March 2008 and eventually led to the establishment of a monopoly in the Hungarian digital broadcasting market.

108. The Digital Switchover Act defined the major substantive elements of the announcement and provided for a detailed list of eligibility criteria. The NHH published the tender results in September 2008. The announced winner and thus the new operator of both the television and radio multiplex networks was Antenna Hungaria Zrt., the company also in charge of analogue broadcasting, defeating the Slovakian-owned Digital Broadcasting Kft. in the television tender, and Hungarian Radio Zrt. in the radio tender.

109. The winning bidder undertook the commitment to apply MPEG-4 compression, which enables the transmission of several channels, launch a mobile television service, and, as a 'bonus option', introduce Multimedia Home (MHP)-based receiver-decoders. Today, it has become obvious that mobile television is unfeasible, and there is a lack of demand for MHP decoders. Nonetheless, the application of the MPEG-4 standard has enabled the DTT platform to be implemented as a genuine multichannel platform and compete meaningfully with other multichannel systems.

110. Under the law, the winning bidder was free to make decisions about communicating the digital switchover virtually without restrictions and devising forms of support on its own. However, the decree on the uses and means of public funds allocated for the digital switchover is yet to be enacted.

111. Under the new regulations, the switchover of non-nationwide television broadcasts is essentially subject to the same rules as those governing broadcasting on the nationwide level. The provisions adopted in conjunction with Mttv. fail to make it clear what kind of business model for local switchover is being envisioned. Apparently, an independent platform operator will be allowed to enter the market in each reception district, although it remains highly doubtful whether sufficient content will be available to fill existing capacities.

112. The condition for the analogue switch-off in the radio market is that at least 94% of the population must be able to access public service media via digital, and a minimum of 75% of the population must have equipment in place for receiving digital broadcasts. Even though in 2008, the NHH conducted a tender for the operation of a nationwide digital radio broadcasting network, and the winner, AH, did commence operating the DAB+ (Digital Audio Broadcasting) network, the future of digital radio in Hungary remains very uncertain. Currently, availability of the service is confined to the capital city of Budapest and its surroundings, comprising about 38% of the population.

§3. Sources of Media Law

I. Legislation of Hungary

113. Hungarian laws are published in the *Magyar Közlöny,* the Official Gazette. There is an official online database of effective legal regulations at https://njt.hu.

A. *Constitutional Provisions*

114. The Basic Law of Hungary (*Magyarország Alaptörvénye)* does not have a number, only the date of the promulgation by which it is defined: *2011 április 25.* The Basic Law is effective from 1 January 2012. Its Article IX of Chapter 'Freedom and Responsibility' (*Szabadság és felelősség*) deals with freedom of expression. The right of access to information is Article VI(2) of the Basic Law. Prior to passing the Basic Law, the Constitution was amended several times in 2010, and so were its regulations on freedom of expression and the media.

B. *Legal Rules*

1. Media Law Reform in 2010 and 2011

115. The legal background of media regulation was fully changed in 2010 after the landslide victory of the Fidesz-KDNP (*Keresztény Demokrata Néppárt*, Christian Democratic People's Party) party alliance. The second Orbán Government which – together with its allied party KDNP – won more than two-thirds of parliamentary mandates, framed its election victory as a revolution and started to transform key areas of public law without delay. In Hungary, a two-thirds majority is enough to amend any laws of the country, including the Constitution. The government did not hesitate to exploit this opportunity and pass key laws that otherwise required political consensus, including a new Basic Law in place of the Constitution.

116. The previous media law (the Rttv., Act I of 1996) had been outdated due to the rapid technological and market development. There had been plans to pass a new media law, but the necessary consensus-seeking process between the political parties remained unsuccessful again and again.

117. In 2010, while the political consensus of more parties was still missing, the necessary majority existed. The media reform package was prepared secretly in the summer of 2010, and all stages of legislation were rushed through within a few weeks, lacking substantial public discussion. Both the laws' content and the method of legislation attracted worldwide criticism. Severe disapproval was expressed by the European Commission,[68] the European Parliament,[69] the Organization for Security and Co-operation in Europe (OSCE) representative on freedom of the media,[70] the United Nations Special Rapporteur,[71] the Council of Europe,[72] and international

---

68. Neelie Kroes, *Hungary's New Media Law Open Hearing on Freedom of the Press in Hungary European Parliament*, Brussels 11 Jan. 2011, http://europa.eu/rapid/pressReleasesAction.do?reference=SPEECH/11/6&format=HTML&aged=0&language=EN&guiLanguage=en.
69. European Parliament Resolution of 10 Mar. 2011 on Media Law in Hungary, http://www.europarl.europa.eu/sides/getDoc.do?pubRef=-//EP//TEXT+TA+P7-TA-2011-0094+0+DOC+XML+V0//EN.
70. OSCE Media Freedom Representative Calls on Hungarian Government to Halt Media Legislation Package, Start Public Consultations, http://www.osce.org/fom/69491 (24 Jun. 2010); Karol Jakubowicz, *Analysis and Assessment of a Package of Hungarian Legislation and Draft Legislation on Media and Telecommunications*, http://www.osce.org/fom/71218 (7 Sep. 2010); Hungarian Media Legislation Severely Contradicts International Standards of Media Freedom, Says OSCE Media Freedom Representative, http://www.osce.org/fom/72229 (7 Sep. 2010); Hungarian Media Law Further Endangers Media Freedom, Says OSCE Media Freedom Representative, http://www.osce.org/fom/74687 (22 Dec. 2010); Despite Adjustments, Hungary's Media Law Continues to Violate OSCE Commitments, Says OSCE Representative on Freedom of the Media, http://www.osce.org/fom/75999 (8 Mar. 2011).
71. United Nations Special Rapporteur: UN Expert Still Concerned Despite Moves on Controversial Media Legislation, http://www.ohchr.org/en/NewsEvents/Pages/DisplayNews.aspx?NewsID=10916&LangID=E (5 Apr. 2011); Ban Encourages Hungary to Address Concerns Over Constitution and Media Laws, https://news.un.org/en/story/2011/04/372682 (18 Apr. 2011).
72. Commissioner Hammarberg Initiates Dialogue and Calls on the Authorities to Ensure Freedom of Expression and Media Pluralism, https://www.coe.int/ro/web/commissioner/-/hungary-commissioner-hammarberg-initiates-dialogue-and-calls-on-the-authorities-to-ensure-freedom-of-expression-and-media-pluralism (1 Feb. 2011); Hungary Should Use the Council of Europe's Standards to Guarantee Freedom of Expression and Media Pluralism Strasbourg, https://www.coe.int/en/web/commissioner/-/hungary-should-use-the-council-of-europe-s-standards-to-guarantee-freedom-of-expression-and-media-pluralism (25 Feb. 2011); Opinion of the Commissioner for Human Rights on Hungary's Media Legislation in Light of Council of Europe Standards on Freedom of the Media, Strasbourg (25 Feb. 2011), CommDH(2011)10; Recommendation 1950 (2011) on the protection of journalists' sources (born with reference to the new Hungarian legislation); Legislative Changes Threaten Democracy and Human Rights, https://www.coe.int/uk/web/commissioner/country-monitoring/hungary/-/asset_publisher/hKTqZqCwoY6P/content/hungary-legislative-changes-threaten-democracy-and-human-rights (12 Jan. 2012).

NGOs such as Article XIX,[73] Amnesty International,[74] the European Federation of Journalists,[75] the Human Rights Watch,[76] the Open Society Foundations,[77] the Freedom House,[78] the European Broadcasting Union,[79] the Committee to Protect Journalists,[80] the Reporters Without Borders,[81] and so forth.

118. The media law was, in fact, the first key area to be changed by the new Parliament, followed by several others. In June 2010, three reform bills were submitted formally by two Members of Parliament, among them an amendment to the Constitution's section about freedom of expression (section 61). Submissions by MPs do not have to go through the same transparent legislative process as governmental

73. Article 19, Hungary: Art. 19 Calls for Comprehensive Media Law Reform, http://www.unhcr.org/refworld/docid/4d6f3b182.html, 1 Mar. 2011 (accessed 2 Apr. 2012); *see also*: Art. 19 and the Hungarian Civil Liberties Union (TASZ), Hungarian Media Laws Q & A, http://www.article19.org/data/files/medialibrary/2714/11-09-01-REPORT-hungary.pdf, August 2011.
74. Sweeping New Media Law Threatens Freedom of Expression in Hungary, https://www.amnesty.org/en/latest/news/2010/12/sweeping-new-media-law-threatens-freedom-expression-hungary-2/ (23 Dec. 2010); Freedom of Expression Under Fire – Briefing to the Hungarian Government on the New Media Legislation, https://www.amnesty.org/en/documents/eur27/004/2011/en/.
75. European Journalists Reject the New Hungarian Media Bill and Call for New Talks, https://www.ifj.org/media-centre/news/detail/article/european-journalists-reject-the-new-hungarian-media-bill-and-call-for-new-talks (23 Jun. 2010); Journalists Question Hungary's Leadership of Europe as Media Law Provokes Outrage, https://ifex.org/journalists-question-hungarys-leadership-of-europe-as-media-law-provokes-outrage/ (23 Dec. 2010); EFJ Tells Barroso: Defend Free Speech and Media Rights in Hungary, https://www.ifj.org/media-centre/news/detail/article/efj-tells-barroso-defend-free-speech-and-media-rights-in-hungary (6 Jan. 2011); Change the Law Now Says EFJ as Hungary Targets Bloggers, https://ifex.org/change-the-law-now-says-ifj-as-government-targets-bloggers/ (11 Feb. 2011); EFJ Calls for 'Radical Surgery' Not Cosmetics on Hungary's Media Law, https://ifex.org/ifj-calls-for-radical-surgery-not-cosmetic-changes-in-media-law/ (18 Feb. 2011); EFJ Warns of Collapse of Journalism as a Public Good in Hungary, https://www.ifj.org/media-centre/news/detail/category/asia-pacific/article/efj-warns-of-collapse-of-journalism-as-a-public-good-in-hungary (4 Oct. 2011); Statement of the International Press Freedom Mission to Hungary, https://cpj.org/wp-content/uploads/2012/01/Hungary_Press_Freedom_Mission_report.pdf (17 Nov. 2011).
76. Hungary: Media Law Endangers Press Freedom, https://www.hrw.org/news/2011/01/07/hungary-media-law-endangers-press-freedom h (7 Jan. 2011); Pulling Punches on Hungary Media Law, https://www.hrw.org/news/2011/03/25/pulling-punches-hungary-media-law (25 Mar. 2011); Memorandum to the European Union on Media Freedom in Hungary, http://www.hrw.org/node/105200 (16 Feb. 2012).
77. Borbála Tóth, Mapping Digital Media: Hungary, https://www.opensocietyfoundations.org/publications/mapping-digital-media-hungary, February 2012.
78. Hungarian Media Law: International Mission Condemns Chilling Effect and Calls for Change, https://www.mediasupport.org/hungarian-media-law-international-mission-condemns-chilling-effect-and-calls-for-change/ (21 Nov. 2011).
79. EBU Appeals to Hungarian Prime Minister to Ensure Media Pluralism, https://www.ebu.ch/news/2011/ebu-appeals-to-hungarian-prime-m (14 Jan. 2011).
80. Hungary Must Repeal Repressive New Media Law (a Letter to Prime Minister Viktor Orbán), https://cpj.org/2011/01/hungary-must-repeal-repressive-new-media-law/ (10 Jan. 2011); Fundamental Changes Still Needed in Hungary Media Law, https://cpj.org/2011/03/fundamental-changes-still-needed-in-hungary-media/ (11 Mar. 2011).
81. European Parliament Urged to Pass Resolution Condemning Hungary's New Media Law, https://rsf.org/en/european-parliament-urged-pass-resolution-condemning-hungary-s-new-media-law (31 Dec. 2011); Hungary's Media Law Is Unacceptable Despite Amendments, https://rsf.org/en/hungary-s-media-law-unacceptable-despite-amendments (8 Mar. 2011).

submissions.[82] Two of the three bills (one of them the amendment to the Constitution) were passed within only six weeks, then signed and promulgated by the newly elected President of the Republic, Pál Schmitt. Pál Schmitt had been Speaker of the House when the bills were passed. In his role as speaker, he delayed signature of the law until the legal maximum (fifteen days) to be able to sign and promulgate it himself as newly elected president.[83]

119. The media reform package consisted of the following bills: a bill amending the Constitution; Bill T/360, which amended the Act on Radio and Television and modified the structure of the supervisory bodies and the supervisory authority, was passed on 22 July and promulgated on 10 August (Act LXXXII of 2010). The third bill with the title 'T/363 on Press Freedom and Basic Rules of Media Content' was passed on 2 November and promulgated on 11 November (Act CIV of 2010). In addition, two parliamentary resolutions were submitted by the same two MPs, and they were passed on 15 September. One of them provided for the consolidation of the properties of the three public service media foundations and the Hungarian News Agency.[84] The other set up an ad hoc committee to appoint members of the National Media and Telecommunication Authority.[85]

120. In the autumn legislative period, on 4 October, the same two MPs submitted yet another amendment to the still-existing Act on Radio and Television and the law on *telecommunication* (Bill T/1268 on Amendment of Certain Laws on Media and Telecommunication), which was passed on 25 October and promulgated on 2 November. However, on 22 November, a whole new law was submitted again to change the existing Act on Radio and Television: the Act on the Hungarian News Agency and the Press Law (Bill T/1747 sz., submitted by the same two MP's together with a third individual MP). It was passed on 21 December 2010, promulgated on 31 December 2010 and is effective as of 1 January 2011. The law applied to pending cases as well. This legislative wave was severely criticized by civil organizations for lack of transparency and lack of public consultancy. It was without precedent that such a complex regulatory area was changed with immediate effect.

121. On 11 December, another amendment to the Constitution was submitted, and they were passed on 23 December 2010.[86] This amendment incorporated a new chapter into the Constitution about the National Media and Telecommunication Authority, with the main purpose of empowering the Media Council and its president to issue decrees. The act entered into effect on 2 January. Later, the Orbán Government passed a new constitution, the Basic Law, in April 2011, which entered into effect on 1 January 2012.[87] The Basic Law does not contain this section but grants

82. §98–111 of Act CXXX of 2010 on legislation.
83. The previous President of the Republic, Sólyom László, was a constitutional lawyer and would have submitted the law to the Constitutional Court, using his constitutional right of veto, it was supposed.
84. 80/2010. (IX. 15) OGY határozat.
85. 81/2010. (IX. 15) OGY határozat.
86. Act CLXIII of 2010.
87. Basic Law, Art. 23(4).

the right to issue decrees to all heads of independent regulatory bodies.[88] With an amendment, the Authority was included in the range of independent regulatory bodies: organs whose head was appointed by the President of the Republic; after an amendment, organs whose head was appointed by the Prime Minister were also included.[89]

122. The new Mttv. has been amended several times in 2011 – in February, in July, and in December. The amending act, passed on 11 July 2011, modified 196 elements of the Mttv.[90] Several further amendments have been added since then. The amendments have been incorporated into the relevant paragraphs of this book. This manuscript was closed on 2 March 2023 and uses a version of the law effective at that date.

2. Relevant Laws Governing the Field of Media

123. Acts passed by Parliament are as follows:

- Act CIV of 2010 on press freedom and the fundamental rules on media content *(2010. évi CIV. törvény a sajtószabadságról és a médiatartalmak alapvető szabályairól, hereinafter: Smtv.)*.
- Act CLXXXV of 2010 on media services and mass communication (*2010. évi CLXXXV. törvény a médiaszolgáltatásokról és a tömegkommunikációról*).
- Act C of 2003 on electronic telecommunication *(2003. évi C. törvény az elektronikus hírközlésről)* (Eht.).
- Act LXXIV of 2007 on programme distribution and digital transition *(2007. évi LXXIV. törvény a műsorterjesztés és a digitális átállás szabályairól)* (Dtv.).
- Act CVIII of 2001 on electronic commercial services and certain questions relating to the information society *(2001. évi CVIII. törvény az elektronikus kereskedelmi szolgáltatásokról és az információs társadalommal kapcsolatos egyes kérdésekről)*.
- Act XIX of 1998 on Criminal Procedure (*1998. évi XIX. törvény a Büntető Eljárásról*).
- Act C of 2012 on the Criminal Code (*2012. évi C. törvény a Büntető Törvénykönyvről*) (Criminal Code).
- Act V of 2013 on the Civil Code (*2013. évi V. törvény a Polgári Törvénykönyvről*) (Civil Code).
- Act CXL of 2004 on the general rules of administrative procedure and services (*2004. évi CXL. törvény a a közigazgatási hatósági eljárás és szolgáltatás általános szabályairól, hereinafter: Ket.*).
- Act III of 1952 on Civil Procedures (*1952. évi III. törvény a Polgári Perrendtartásról, hereinafter Pp.*).

88. Article T(2) and Art. 23(4) Basic Law.
89. T/2627/158, http://www.parlament.hu/irom39/02627/02627-0158.pdf.
90. Act CVII of 2011 on amendments of telecommunication laws, effective from 20 Jul. 2011, find at: http://mediajogfigyelo.hu/index.php?do=a&id=1691.

- Act XC of 2005 on electronic freedom of information *(2005. évi XC. törvény az elektronikus információszabadságról)*.
- Act CXII of 2011 on informational self-determination and freedom of information (effective from 27 July 2011) *(2011. évi CXII. törvény az információs önrendelkezésről és az információszabadságról, hereinafter: Infotv.)*.
- Act II of 2004 on movies *(2004. évi II. törvény a mozgóképről)*.
- Act XLVIII of 2008 on economic advertising and its certain limits *(2008. évi XLVIII. törvény a gazdasági reklámtevékenység alapvető feltételeiről és egyes korlátairól)*.
- Act CLV of 1997 on the protection of consumers *(1997. évi CLV. törvény a fogyasztóvédelemről)*.
- Act LXXVI of 1999 on authors' rights (intellectual property) *(1999. évi LXXVI. törvény a szerzői jogról)*.
- Act CLV of 2009 on the protection of qualified data (State and official secrets) *(2009. évi CLV. törvény a minősített adat védelméről)*.
- Act LVII of 1996 on the prohibition of unfair market behaviour and limitation of competition *(1996. évi LVII. törvény a tisztességtelen piaci magatartás és a versenykorlátozás tilalmáról)*.
- Act CXXXI of 2009 on promulgating the Convention of the Council of Europe on access to documents containing data of public interest *(2009. évi CXXXI. törvény az Európa Tanács közérdekű adatot tartalmazó iratokhoz való hozzáférésről szóló Egyezményének kihirdetéséről)*.
- Act CI of 2007 on ensuring the access of data necessary to prepare decisions *(2007. évi CI. törvény a döntéselőkészítéshez szükséges adatok hozzáférhetőségének biztosításáról)*.
- Act LIII of 2005 on the promulgation of the Additional Protocol of 8 November 2008 in Strasbourg about the supervisory authorities and the flow of personal data through national borders, attached to Convention of 28 January 1981 on the protection of persons during the automatic processing of personal data (*2005. évi LIII. törvény az egyének védelméről a személyes adatok gépi feldolgozása során, Strasbourgban, 1981. január 28-án kelt Egyezménynek a felügyelő hatóságokról és a személyes adatok országhatárokat átlépő áramlásáról szóló, Strasbourgban, 2001. november 8-án kelt Kiegészítő Jegyzőkönyve kihirdetéséről*).
- Act XLVII of 1997 on the protection and treatment of health information and related personal data (*1997. évi XLVII. törvény az egészségügyi és a hozzájuk kapcsolódó személyes adatok kezeléséről és védelméről*).
- Act VI of 1998 on promulgating the Convention of 28 January 1981 in Strasbourt about the protection of persons during the automatic processing of personal data (*1998. évi VI. törvény az egyének védelméről a személyes adatok gépi feldolgozása során, Strasbourgban, 1981. január 28. napján kelt Egyezmény kihirdetéséről*).
- Act LXVI of 1992 on the register of addresses and personal data of citizens, consolidated with the 146/1993 (X. 26) Gov. Decree on its execution (*1992. évi LXVI. törvény a polgárok személyi adatainak és lakcímének nyilvántartásáról, a végrehajtásáról kiadott 146/1993. (X. 26) Korm. rendelettel egységes szerkezetben*).

– Act XXII of 2014 about advertising tax (*2014. évi XXII. törvény a reklámadóról*).

124. Decrees of the NMHH:

– 10/2012. (III. 28) NMHH Decree on the conditions of labelling movies according to age limits, the ways of representation of age limit categories, and about how to define costs of movie production for the purpose of application for State subsidies (*NMHH rendelet A filmalkotások korhatár szerinti megjelölésének feltételeiről és a korhatár besorolási kategóriák feltüntetésének módjairól, valamint az állami támogatás igénybevételének alapjául szolgáló filmgyártási költségek megállapításáról*).
– 9/2012. (III. 28) NMHH Decree on the quantity of the supervisory fee and the obligation to provide data relating to the supervisory fee and official tasks related to it (*NMHH rendelet A felügyeleti díj mértékéről, valamint a felügyeleti díjjal kapcsolatos adatszolgáltatásról és hatósági feladatokról*).
– 8/2012. (I. 26) NMHH Decree on the defence, access to telecommunication edifices, and their crossing by other types of edifices using tracks (*NMHH rendelet Az elektronikus hírközlési építmények egyéb nyomvonalas építményfajtákkal való keresztezéséről, megközelítéséről és védelméről*).
– 7/2012. (I. 26) NMHH Decree on certain official procedures of civil frequency management (*NMHH rendelet A polgári frekvenciagazdálkodás egyes hatósági eljárásairól*).
– 6/2012. (I. 26) NMHH Decree on the measurements necessary to ensure the compatibility of equipment capable to receive digital television services (*NMHH rendelet a A digitális televízió-médiaszolgáltatások vételére alkalmas készülékek együttműködő képessége érdekében szükséges intézkedésekről*).
– 5/2012. (I. 24) NMHH Decree on the fees of using and binding identifiers necessary to provide electronic telecommunication services (*NMHH rendelet Az elektronikus hírközlési szolgáltatásokhoz szükséges azonosítók lekötésének és használatának díjáról*).
– 4/2012. (I. 24) NMHH Decree on the obligation of keeping the secrets and protecting the personal data relating to public electronic telecommunication services, the special conditions of data management and secret protection, the integrity and safety of networks, the management of traffic and billing data, and the rules on call transfers and displaying identifiers (*NMHH rendelet A nyilvános elektronikus hírközlési szolgáltatáshoz kapcsolódó adatvédelmi és titoktartási kötelezettségre, az adatkezelés és a titokvédelem különleges feltételeire, a hálózatok és a szolgáltatások biztonságára és integritására, a forgalmi és számlázási adatok kezelésére, valamint az azonosítókijelzésre és hívásátirányításra vonatkozó szabályokról*).
– 3/2012. (I. 24) NMHH Decree on the technological requirements of the publicly available telephone services in the interest of supporting emergency calls directed at the unified European emergency call number and the national emergency call numbers (*NMHH rendelet Az egységes európai segélyhívószámra és a nemzeti segélyhívó számokra irányuló segélyhívások támogatása érdekében a nyilvánosan elérhető telefonszolgáltatásra vonatkozó műszaki követelményekről*).

- 2/2012. (I. 24) NMHH Decree on the detailed rules of number carrying (*A számhordozás részletes szabályairól*).
- 1/2012. (I. 3) NMHH Decree on the amendment of certain NMHH decrees related to identifier management (*NMHH rendelet Egyes azonosítógazdálkodással összefüggő NMHH rendeletek módosításáról*).
- 9/2011. (XII. 14) NMHH Decree on amending 6/2011 (X. 6) NMHH Decree on the detailed rules of contracts of electronic telecommunication subscribers (*NMHH rendelet Az elektronikus hírközlési előfizetői szerződések részletes szabályairól szóló 6/2011. (X. 6) NMHH rendelet módosításáról*).
- 14/2011. (XII. 27) NMHH Decree about labelling certain technological means as capable to receive terrestrial digital programmes (*NMHH rendelet Az egyes műszaki eszközök földfelszíni digitális műsorok vételére való alkalmasságának megjelöléséről*).
- 13/2011. (XII. 27) NMHH Decree about the quality requirements of electronic telecommunication services relating to the protection of subscribers and users, and authenticity of fee-setting (*NMHH rendelet Az elektronikus hírközlési szolgáltatás minőségének az előfizetők és felhasználók védelmével összefüggő követelményeiről, valamint a díjazás hitelességéről*).
- 12/2011. (XII. 16) NMHH Decree about the order of non-civil frequency management and the organizations in the field of non-civil frequency management (*NMHH rendelet a nem polgári célú frekvenciagazdálkodás rendjéről, valamint a nem polgári célú frekvenciagazdálkodás körébe tartozó szervezetekről*).
- 11/2011. (XII. 16) NMHH Decree about certain official procedures of non-civil frequency management (*NMHH rendelet A nem polgári célú frekvenciagazdálkodás egyes hatósági eljárásairól*).
- 10/2011. (XII. 16) NMHH Decree about the domestic trade of radio equipment belonging to non-civil frequency management and the proof of their adequacy (*NMHH rendelet A nem polgári célú frekvenciagazdálkodás körébe tartozó rádióberendezések belföldi forgalomba hozataláról és megfelelőségének igazolásáról*).
- 9/2011. (XII. 14) NMHH Decree amending 6/2011. (X. 6) NMHH Decree on the detailed rules of electronic telecommunication subscribers' contracts (*9/2011. (XII. 14) NMHH rendelet Az elektronikus hírközlési előfizetői szerződések részletes szabályairól szóló 6/2011. (X. 6) NMHH rendelet módosításáról*).
- 8/2011. (XI. 3) NMHH Decree on the amendment of 1/2011. (III. 31) NMHH Decree on fees of frequency bindings and usage (*NMHH rendelet A frekvencialekötés és – használat díjáról szóló 1/2011. (III. 31) NMHH rendelet módosításáról*).
- 7/2011. (X. 6) NMHH Decree about setting the rules on the use of frequency bands (*NMHH rendelet A frekvenciasávok felhasználási szabályainak megállapításáról*).
- 6/2011. (X. 6) NMHH Decree on the detailed rules of electronic telecommunication subscribers' contracts (*NMHH rendelet Az elektronikus hírközlési előfizetői szerződések részletes szabályairól*).
- 5/2011. (X. 6) NMHH Decree on administrative service fees of certain procedures of the National Media and Telecommunication Authority and the ways of

paying the fee (*NMHH rendelet A Nemzeti Média – és Hírközlési Hatóság egyes eljárásainak igazgatási szolgáltatási díjairól és a díjfizetés módjáról*).
- 4/2011. (X. 6) NMHH Decree on rules of the auction and tender for acquiring entitlement to frequency usage (*NMHH rendelet A frekvenciahasználati jogosultság megszerzését szolgáló árverés és pályázat szabályairól*).
- 3/2011. (IX. 26) NMHH Decree about the national distribution plan of identifiers of national electronic telecommunication networks (*NMHH rendelet az elektronikus hírközlő hálózatok azonosítóinak nemzeti felosztási tervéről*).
- 2/2011. (IX. 26) NMHH Decree on the management of the identifiers of electronic telecommunications networks (*NMHH rendelet az elektronikus hírközlő hálózatok azonosítóival kapcsolatos gazdálkodás rendjéről*).
- 1/2011. (III. 31) NMHH Decree on the fees of frequencies reservation and usage (*NMHH rendelet A frekvencialekötés és – használat díjáról*).

125. Governmental Decrees:

- Government Decree No 521/2020 (XI. 25.) on the derogation from certain provisions on data requests in times of emergency.
- 161/2010. (V. 6) Gov. Decree about electronic safety of qualified data and the detailed rules of licensing and supervising ciphering activity (*Korm. rendelet a minősített adat elektronikus biztonságának, valamint a rejtjeltevékenység engedélyezésének és hatósági felügyeletének részletes szabályairól*).
- 90/2010. (III. 26) Gov. Decree about the rules of operation of the National Security Supervision and the management of qualified data (*Korm. rendelet a Nemzeti Biztonsági Felügyelet működésének, valamint a minősített adat kezelésének rendjéről*).
- 311/2005. (XII. 25) Gov. Decree about the rules on access to information about the environment (*Korm. rendelet a nyilvánosság környezeti információkhoz való hozzáférésének rendjéről*).
- 9/2005. (I. 19) Gov. Decree about the detailed rules on cooperation between postal service providers, postal contributors, and organs entitled to secret information and data collection (*Korm. rendelet a postai szolgáltatók, a postai közreműködők és a titkos információgyűjtésre, illetve titkos adatszerzésre felhatalmazott szervezetek együttműködésének részletes szabályairól*).
- 180/2004. (V. 26) Governmental Decree on the cooperation of the organizations performing electronic telecommunication and the organs entitled to secret information and data collection (*Korm. rendelet az elektronikus hírközlési feladatokat ellátó szervezetek és a titkos információgyűjtésre, illetve titkos adatszerzésre felhatalmazott szervezetek együttműködésének rendjéről*).
- 97/2010. (III. 31) Gov. Decree about the detailed financial and technological conditions and requirements of providing universal electronic telecommunication services (*Korm. rendelet az egyetemes elektronikus hírközlési szolgáltatás nyújtásának részletes pénzügyi és műszaki feltételeiről és követelményeiről*).
- 362/2008. (XII. 31) Gov. Decree about the appointment of the expert authorities cooperating in the procedures of the NHH, and the termination or amendment of certain expert authority cooperations (*Korm. rendelet a Nemzeti Hírközlési Hatóság eljárásában közreműködő szakhatóságok kijelöléséről, valamint egyes*

szakhatósági közreműködések megszüntetéséről és módosításáról).
- 229/2008. (IX. 12) Gov. Decree on the quality requirements of electronic telecommunication services relating to the protection of consumers (*Korm. rendelet az elektronikus hírközlési szolgáltatás minőségének a fogyasztók védelmével összefüggő követelményeiről*).
- 45/2005. (III. 11) Gov. Decree on the tasks and competences of the National Telecommunication Authority related to electronic signature, and the detailed rules of its procedure (*Korm. rendelet a Nemzeti Hírközlési Hatóságnak az elektronikus aláírással kapcsolatos feladat – és hatásköréről, valamint eljárásának részletes szabályairól*).
- 180/2004. (V. 26) Gov. Decree on the cooperation rules between organizations performing electronic telecommunication tasks, and the organs entitled to secret information and data collection (*Korm. rendelet az elektronikus hírközlési feladatokat ellátó szervezetek és a titkos információgyűjtésre, illetve titkos adatszerzésre felhatalmazott szervezetek együttműködésének rendjéről*).
- 134/2004. (IV. 29) Gov. Decree on the detailed rules of operating, supervising, expending, terminating and sources of the Universal Electronic Telecommunication Budget (*Korm. rendelet az Egyetemes Elektronikus Hírközlési Támogatási Kassza működésére, felügyeletére, felhasználására, megszüntetésére és forrásaira vonatkozó részletes szabályokról*).
- 100/2004. (IV. 27) Gov. Decree on the system of preparing the electronic telecommunication system ready for emergency and qualified periods, the tasks of the State organs, and ensuring the conditions of their operation (*Korm. rendelet az elektronikus hírközlés veszélyhelyzeti és minősített időszaki felkészítésének rendszeréről, az államigazgatási szervek feladatairól, működésük feltételeinek biztosításáról*).
- 73/2004. (IV. 15) Gov. Decree on choosing interim service providers during the use of electronic telecommunication services (*Korm. rendelet az elektronikus hírközlési szolgáltatás igénybevétele során alkalmazható közvetítőválasztásról*).

C. *Case Law*

1. Constitutional Court Decisions

126. The Basic Law of Hungary now replaces the Constitution of the Hungarian Republic, and it is not officially declared whether the case law of the Constitutional Court will apply in future. Without reference to the contrary, it is reasonable to assume that it will be so. Below, decisions of the previous Constitutional Court's case law relevant to press freedom and media regulation are listed:

- 3350/2022. (VII. 25.) AB határozat.
- 3064/2022. (II. 25.) AB határozat (Klubrádió).
- 22/2021. (VII. 13.) AB határozat.
- 16/2020. (VII. 8.) AB határozat (KESMA).

- 15/2020. (VII. 8.) AB határozat (scaremongering).
- 8/2018. (VII. 5.) AB határozat.
- 3145/2018. (V. 7.) AB határozat.
- 34/2017. (XII. 11.) AB határozat.
- 17/2016. (X. 20) AB határozat.
- 28/2014. (IX. 29.) AB határozat.
- 7/2014 (III. 7.) AB határozat.
- 165/2011. (XII. 20.) AB határozat (*Smtv. hatálya sajtótermékre*).
- 34/2009. (III. 27.) AB határozat (*sajtótermék nyilvántartásba vétele*).
- 96/2008. (VII. 3.) AB határozat (*közösségek becsületvédelme*).
- 95/2008. (VII. 3.) AB határozat (*gyalázkodás új büntetőjogi tényállása – előzetes normakontroll*).
- 46/2007. (VI. 27.) AB határozat (*Médiatörvénnyel kapcsolatos kérdések*).
- 37/2008. (IV. 8.) AB határozat – *műsorszolgáltatási díj mértékéről*.
- 20/2007. (III. 29.) AB határozat (*parlamenti ülések televíziós közvetítése*).
- 6/2007. (II. 27.) AB határozat (*a kampánycsend intézménye és a közvélemény-kutatási eredmények közzétételére vonatkozó tilalom*).
- 1/2007. (I. 18.) AB határozat (*kiegyensúlyozottság követelményének érvényesülése – Médiatörvény*).
- 20/2006. (V. 31.) AB határozat (*harci szellem bomlasztása bűntette*).
- 12/2006. (IV. 24.) AB határozat (*képviselői felszólalói jog – országgyűlési házszabály*).
- 34/2004. (IX. 28.) AB határozat (*országgyűlési képviselő felelőssége rágalmazás, becsületsértés miatt*).
- 18/2004. (V. 25.) AB határozat (*közösség elleni izgatás*).
- 60/2003. (XI. 26.) AB határozat (*választási kampány idején pártok reklámfilmjeinek sugárzása*).
- 50/2003. (XI. 5.) AB határozat (*országgyűlési bizottsági vizsgálatok – közügyek megvitatásának szabadsága*).
- 39/2002. (IX. 25.) AB határozat (*kampánycsend*).
- 57/2001. (XII. 5.) AB határozat (*válaszadás joga, lex Répássy*).
- 13/2001. (V. 14.) AB határozat (*elkövető sajtó útján nyilatkozik*).
- 18/2000. (VI. 6.) AB határozat (*rémhírterjesztés*).
- 14/2000. (V. 12.) AB határozat (*önkényuralmi jelkép*).
- 13/2000. (V. 12.) AB határozat (*nemzeti jelkép*).
- 12/1999. (V. 21.) AB határozat (*gyűlöletbeszéd*).
- 20/1997. (III. 19.) AB határozat (*sajtótermék ügyészi betiltása*).
- 47/1994. (X. 21.) AB határozat (*MR-MTV költségvetését kormány ne befolyásolhassa*).
- 36/1994. (VI. 24.) AB határozat (*hivatalos személy becsülete*).
- 37/1992. (VI. 10.) AB határozat (*média*).
- 36/1992. (VI. 10.) AB határozat (*kinevezés*).
- 30/1992. (V. 26.) AB határozat (*közösség elleni izgatás*).

D. *Co-regulation*

127. A limited co-regulation was imposed by the new media law. *See* details in Part II. The public contracts concluded between the co-regulative bodies and the Media Council are:

- Contract between the Association of Hungarian Content Providers (*Magyar Tartalomszolgáltatók Egyesülete*, (MTE)) and the Media Council.[91]
- Public contract between the Association of Hungarian Journal Publishers (*Magyar Lapkiadók Egyesülete*, MLE) and the Media Council.[92]
- Public contract between the Hungarian Electronic Programme Providers' Association (*Magyar Elektronikus Műsorszolgáltatók Egyesülete*) and the Media Council.[93]
- Public contract between the Self-Regulative Advertisement Body (*Önszabályozó Reklámtestület*) and the Media Council.[94]

E. *Self-Regulation, Codes of Ethics*

128. The following codes of the journalistic and media associations are in existence:

- Ethical Code of the Association of Hungarian Journalists (MÚOSZ).[95]
- Ethical Code of the Association of Hungarian Catholic Journalists (MAKUSZ).[96]
- Code of Protection of the Interests of Journalists in Hungarian Journalism Organizations (*A magyar újságíró-szervezetek Érdekvédelmi Kódexe*).[97]
- Ethical Code of the Community of Hungarian Journalists (MÚK).[98]
- Ethical Code of Advertising.[99]
- Ethical Code of Providing Content of the Hungarian Content Providers' Association.[100]

---

91. *Társszabályozási szerződés a Magyar Elektronikus Műsorszolgáltatók Egyesülete és a Médiatanács között*, 20 Jul. 2011, http://mediatanacs.hu/dokumentum/1745/magyar_elektronikus_musorszolgaltatok_egyesulete.pdf.
92. *Társszabályozási szerződés a Magyar Lapkiadók Egyesülete és a Médiatanács között*, 8 Jul. 2011, http://mediatanacs.hu/dokumentum/1742/magyar_lapkiadok_egyesulete.pdf.
93. *Társszabályozási szerződés az önszabályozó Reklámtestület és a Médiatanács között*, 6 Jul. 2011, http://mediatanacs.hu/dokumentum/1741/onszabalyzo_reklam_testulet.pdf.
94. *Társszabályozási szerződés a Magyarországi Tartalomszolgáltatók Egyesülete és a Médiatanács között*, 29 Jun. 2011, http://mediatanacs.hu/dokumentum/1743/magyarorszagi_tartalomszolgaltatok_egyesulete.pdf.
95. *Újságírói Etikai Kódex*, Hungarian National Association of Journalists, https://muosz.hu/kodexek/ujsagiroi-etikai-kodex/#.
96. *Etikai Kódex*, Association of Hungarian Catholic Journalists, http://makusz.hu/etikai-kodex.
97. *A magyar újságíró-szervezetek Érdekvédelmi Kódexe és érdekvédelmi szervezetei*, Press Trade Union, http://sajtoszakszervezet.hu. The Press Trade Union has no longer an Ethical Code.
98. Community of Hungarian Journalists, http://muk-press.hu/?page_id=26.
99. *Reklámetikai Kódex*, Self-regulatory Association of Advertisers, https://www.ort.hu/kodex/.
100. *Tartalomszolgáltatási Kódex*, Association of Hungarian Content Providers, http://www.mte.hu/etikaikodex.html.

II. International Sources of Law

A. *European Directives*

129. Television without Frontiers Directive:

Council Directive 89/552/EEC of 3 October 1989 on the coordination of certain provisions laid down by law, regulation or administrative action in Member States concerning the pursuit of television broadcasting activities. *OJ* (1989) L 298/23. Amended by: Directive 97/36/EC of the European Parliament and of the Council of 30 June 1997. *OJ* (1997) L 202/60; and Directive 2007/65/EC of the European Parliament and of the Council of 11 December 2007. *OJ* (2007) L 332/27 *(infra)*
Codified by: Directive 2010/13/EU of 10 March 2010 *(infra)* amended by Directive 2018/1808 of 14 November 2018.
Directive 97/36/EC of the European Parliament and of the Council of 30 June 1997 amending Council Directive 89/552/EEC on the coordination of certain provisions laid down by law, regulation or administrative action in Member States concerning the pursuit of television broadcasting activities, *OJ L* 202, 30 July 1997, 60.
Directive 2007/65/EC of the European Parliament and of the Council of 11 December 2007 amending Council Directive 89/552/EEC on the coordination of certain provisions laid down by law, regulation or administrative action in Member States concerning the pursuit of television broadcasting activities, *OJ L* 332, 18 December 2007, 27.
Audiovisual Media Services Directive: Directive 2010/13/EU of the European Parliament and of the Council of 10 March 2010 on the coordination of certain provisions laid down by law, regulation or administrative action in Member States concerning the provision of audiovisual media services (Audiovisual Media Services Directive). *OJ* (2010) L 95/1.
Directive on electronic commerce: Directive 2000/31/EC of the European Parliament and of the Council of 8 June 2000 on certain legal aspects of information society services, in particular electronic commerce, in the Internal Market (Directive on electronic commerce), *OJ L* 178, 17 July 2000, 1.
Universal Service Directive: Directive 2002/22/EC of the European Parliament and of the Council of 7 March 2002 on universal service and users' rights relating to electronic communications networks and services, *OJ L* 108, 24 April 2002, 51.
Privacy in Electronic Communications Directive: Directive 2002/58/EC of the European Parliament and of the Council of 12 July 2002 concerning the processing of personal data and the protection of privacy in the electronic communications sector, *OJ L* 201, 31 July 2002, 37.
Better Regulation Directive: Directive 2009/140/EC of 25 November 2009 amending Directives 2002/21/EC on a common regulatory framework for electronic communications networks and services, 2002/19/EC on access to, and interconnection of, electronic communications networks

and services, and 2002/20/EC on the authorization of electronic communications networks and services, *OJ L* 337, 18 December 2009, 37.
Directive (EU) 2018/1972 of thc European Parliament and of the Council of 11 December 2018, establishing the European Electronic Communications Code (Recast)
Online searchable database: <http://eur-lex.europa.eu/nl/index.htm>.

B. International Documents on Press Freedom

130.
- The United Nations' Universal Declaration of Human Rights (Article XIX).
- European Charter of the Fundamental Rights (Article 11).

1. Conventions, Recommendations, and Declarations of the Council of Europe

131.
- European Convention on Human Rights (ECHR) (Article 10).
- Council of Europe Convention on Transfrontier Television.
- Council of Europe Convention on Cybercrime.
- Council of Europe Protocol on Xenophobia and Racism.
- Council of Europe Convention for the Protection of Individuals with Regard to Automatic Processing of Personal Data.
- Recommendation 1805 (2007) on blasphemy, religious insults and hate speech against persons on grounds of their religion.
- Recommendation 1641 (2004) on public service broadcasting.
- Recommendation CM/Rec (2011) seven of the Committee of Ministers to Member States on a new notion of media, adopted on 21 September 2011.
- Recommendation CM/Rec (2011) eight of the Committee of Ministers to Member States on the protection and promotion of the universality, integrity and openness of the Internet, adopted on 21 September 2011.
- Declaration of the Committee of Ministers on measures to promote the respect of Article 10 of the ECHR, adopted on 13 January 2010.
- Recommendation CM/Rec (2009) five of the Committee of Ministers to Member States on measures to protect children against harmful content and behaviour and to promote their active participation in the new information and communications environment, adopted on 8 July 2009.
- Recommendation CM/Rec (2008) six of the Committee of Ministers to Member States on measures to promote the respect for freedom of expression and information with regard to Internet filters, adopted on 26 March 2008.
- Recommendation CM/Rec (2007) sixteen of the Committee of Ministers to Member States on measures to promote the public service value of the Internet, adopted on 7 November 2007.
- Recommendation CM/Rec (2007) fifteen of the Committee of Ministers to Member States on measures concerning media coverage of election campaigns, adopted on 7 November 2007.

- Recommendation CM/Rec (2007) eleven of the Committee of Ministers to Member States on promoting freedom of expression and information in the new information and communications environment, adopted on 26 September 2007.
- Guidelines of the Committee of Ministers of the Council of Europe on protecting freedom of expression and information in times of crisis, adopted on 26 September 2007.
- Declaration by the Committee of Ministers on the protection and promotion of investigative journalism, adopted on 26 September 2007.
- Recommendation Rec (2007) three of the Committee of Ministers to Member States on the remit of public service media in the information society, adopted on 31 January 2007.
- Recommendation Rec (2007) two of the Committee of Ministers to Member States on media pluralism and diversity of media content, adopted on 31 January 2007.
- Declaration of the Committee of Ministers on protecting the role of the media in democracy in the context of media concentration, adopted on 31 January 2007.
- Recommendation Rec (2006) twelve of the Committee of Ministers to Member States on empowering children in the new information and communications environment, adopted by the Committee of Ministers on 27 September 2006.
- Declaration of the Committee of Ministers on the guarantee of the independence of public service broadcasting in the Member States, adopted on 27 September 2006.
- Declaration of the Committee of Ministers on human rights and the rule of law in the Information Society (CM(2005) fifty-six final).
- Recommendation Rec (2006) three of the Committee of Ministers to Member States on the United Nations Educational, Scientific and Cultural Organization Convention on the protection and promotion of the diversity of cultural expressions.
- Declaration on freedom of expression and information in the media in the context of the fight against terrorism, adopted on 2 March 2005.
- Recommendation Rec (2004) sixteen of the Committee of Ministers to Member States on the right of reply in the new media environment.
- Declaration on freedom of political debate in the media, adopted on 12 February 2004.
- Recommendation No. R (2003) thirteen on the provision of information through the media in relation to criminal proceedings.
- Declaration on the provision of information through the media in relation to criminal proceedings adopted on 10 July 2003.
- Political message from the Committee of Ministers to the World Summit on the Information Society.
- Declaration on freedom of communication on the Internet, adopted on 28 May 2003 (PDF version, including explanatory note).
- Recommendation No. R (2003) nine on measures to promote the democratic and social contribution of digital broadcasting.
- Recommendation No. R (2002) seven on measures to enhance the protection of the neighbouring rights of broadcasting organizations.

– Recommendation No. R (2002) two on access to official documents (PDF version including Explanatory Memorandum).
– Recommendation No. R (2001) eight on self-regulation concerning cyber content and its Explanatory Memorandum.
– Recommendation No. R (2001) seven on measures to protect copyright and neighbouring rights and combat piracy, especially in the digital environment.
– Recommendation No. R (2000) twenty-three on the independence and functions of regulatory authorities for the broadcasting sector and its Explanatory Memorandum.
– Recommendation No. R (2000) seven on the right of journalists not to disclose their sources of information and its Explanatory Memorandum.
– Declaration on cultural diversity adopted on 7 December 2000.
– Recommendation No. R (99) fifteen on measures concerning media coverage of election campaigns and its Explanatory Memorandum.
– Council of Europe Convention on the Legal Protection of Services based on, or consisting of, Conditional Access http://conventions.coe.int/Treaty/en/Treaties/Html/178.htm.
– *See* more Council of Europe Recommendations at http://www.coe.int/t/dghl/standardsetting/media/Doc/CM_en.asp.

2. Recommendations and Declarations Passed with Reference to the New Hungarian Legislation

132.
– Expertise by Council of Europe Experts on Hungarian Media Legislation: Act CIV of 2010 on the freedom of the press and the fundamental rules on media content and Act CLXXXV of 2010 on media services and mass media, 11 May 2012.[101]
– Recommendation 1950 (2011) on the protection of journalists' sources.
– Declaration of the Committee of Ministers on Public Service Media Governance (Adopted by the Committee of Ministers on 15 February 2012 at the 1134th meeting of the Ministers' Deputies).
– Recommendation of the Committee of Ministers to Member States on Public Service Media Governance (Adopted by the Committee of Ministers on 15 February 2012 at the 1134th meeting of the Ministers' Deputies).

C. Case Law of the European Court of Human Rights

133. Searchable database: http://cmiskp.echr.coe.int/tkp197/search.asp?skin=hudoc-en.

– *Kenedi v. Hungary* (31475/05, 26 May 2009).
– *Vajnai v. Hungary* (33629/06, 8 July 2008).

101. Although this piece of document is neither recommendation nor declaration, it is the most current and relevant document by the Council of Europe targeting Hungarian media legislation.

- *Csanics v. Hungary* (12188/06, 20 January 2009).
- *TASZ v. Hungary* (37374/05, 14 April 2009).
- *Karsai v. Hungary* (5380/07, 1 December 2009).
- *Uj v. Hungary* (23954/10, 19 June 2011).
- *MTE and Index v. Hungary* (22947/13, 2 February 2016) *see* more in paragraph 185.
- *Karácsony and Szél and Others v. Hungary*: (*42461/13, 44357/13, 17/05/2016,* 17, May 2016.) At a plenary session of the Parliament, during a discussion of the alleged corruption relating to the tobacco market, while the Secretary of State for National Economy was responding to the allegations, opposition MPs Mr Karácsony and Mr Szilágyi carried into the centre of the chamber a large placard displaying the words 'FIDESZ You steal, you cheat, and you lie.' They were fined for their action. The European Court of Human Rights (ECtHR) found that the interference with the applicants' right to freedom of expression was not proportionate to the legitimate aims pursued because it was not accompanied by adequate procedural safeguards.
- *Hungarian Helsinki Commisssion v. Hungary* (*18030/11*, 8 November 2016). The Hungarian Helsinki Commission requested data about public defenders, suspecting discrepancies in police departments' practice in appointing defence counsel. Seventeen police departments complied with the request, five departments disclosed the requested information following a legal challenge, and one police department refused the request. The ECtHR first instance passed the case to the Grand Chamber, which held that refusing the request was not necessary in a democratic society.
- *Szanyi v. Hungary* (*35493/13*, 8 November 2016.) At a plenary session of the Parliament, during a discussion, MP Szanyi showed his left middle finger in the direction of the Jobbik MPs after he finished talking and sat down. He was fined for his expression. The ECtHR found that the interests of the order in Parliament were not demonstrated to be seriously affected, nor was it shown that these interests were weightier than the right to freedom of expression of the opposition. In addition, the procedural guarantees were insufficient. It established a violation of Article 10 of the Convention in respect of the fine imposed on the applicant and the banning of the applicant's interpellations.

D. Case Law of the ECJ

134. There are no cases where Hungary would be an applicant or a respondent in this field of law.[102] An infringement procedure is about to start against Hungary in a related field of law – the Hungarian government introduced a special 'crisis tax' on telecommunication operators in 2010 (among others). Such a tax probably violates

102. Please note that since the Lisbon Treaty entered into force on 1 Dec. 2009, the official name of the ECJ is now the 'Court of Justice of the European Union', comprising the Court of Justice, the General Court (formerly the Court of First Instance) and the Civil Service Tribunal.

the European rules on telecommunications which allow sector-specific charges only to cover the specific costs of regulating the sector and not generate additional revenue for the central budget.[103]

103. Commission Refers Hungary to Court for Failure to End Special Tax on Telecom Operators, IP/12/286, http://ec.europa.eu/information_society/newsroom/cf/itemdetail.cfm?item_id=7927 (22 Mar. 2012).

Part I. Freedom of Speech

Chapter 1. Recent Acts Affecting the Freedom of Speech

§1. The Legislative Package Against LGBT Minorities

135. In 2021, an amending legislative package was passed by the Parliament. The legislative package law carried the title: 'on tougher action against paedophile offenders and amending certain laws to protect children'. Part of the legislative package was indeed addressed at strengthening criminal rules on child pornography and sexual violence against children. However, several other laws were amended, prohibiting the depiction and promotion of homosexuality, gender non-conformity, or gender re-assignment. These words were inserted into the Media Law (*see* below, §372) and the Advertising Act, the Education Act, the Act on the protection of families and the Act on protection of children and administration of child custody.

136. The amendment in the Education Act included that when providing education on 'sexual culture, sexual life, sexual orientation and sexual development to pupils, special attention shall be paid to the provisions of Article XVI (1) of the Basic Law.[104] These educational lessons shall not be aimed at promoting gender non-conformity, gender reassignment or homosexuality'. The other amendment to the Education Act restricted the providing of information on a programme on 'sexual culture, sex life, sexual orientation, sexual development, the harmful effects of drug use, the dangers of the Internet and other physical and mental health promotion' to registered entities. Violation of this rule shall be an offence by both the school principal and the said entity.[105] Generally, this means that the government would control which NGOs and experts may provide such information in schools.

137. The amendment to the Family Protection Act implies that even parents are prohibited from making available content to children which depicts or promotes the deviation from the sex assigned at birth, gender reassignment, or homosexuality. This means that books, films and all other content that include an element of homosexuality or transsexuality are banned from private homes.

104. Article XVI. (1) of the Basic Law says: 'Hungary protects the right of children to an identity corresponding to their sex assigned at birth and ensures an education based on the constitutional identity of our country and its Christian culture.'
105. New §9(12), §9/A, §79(8), §94(1)j) of the Act of CXC of 2011 on Public Education.

§2. The Misimplementation of the Whistleblower Directive

138. With the purpose of implementing the Whistleblower Directive,[106] the vice-Prime Minister submitted a proposal for an act on Complaints, Whistleblowing and Rules on reporting abuse.[107] The proposal contains the possibility to report if someone 'puts into doubt' Hungarian values, such as the constitutionally recognized role of marriage and family, the protection of children necessary for their physical, mental and moral development, and their right to identification with their natural-born gender identity.[108] Besides, anyone can be reported who puts into doubt that nationalities who live with us (sic) are parts of the Hungarian political community and integral parts of the state; who engages in any activity that systematically mitigates or exonerates the crimes committed during national socialist and communist dictatorships, and any action directed at hindering the respect and use of our national symbols.[109]

139. The said reportable actions are 'speech-actions' (putting into doubt, mitigating); therefore, the law indirectly limits freedom of expression, by exercising a chilling effect on expression. In a homophobic atmosphere as the one in Hungary caused by the governmental anti-LGBT policy and propaganda campaign (*see* paragraph 135), human rights activists fear that the law can lead to aggressive attacks against sexual minorities, especially same-sex families.[110]

140. The Proposal can hardly be regarded as an honest implementation attempt of the Directive for two reasons. First, the Directive focuses on reporting breaches against Union law, whereas the action of 'raising doubt' as such would never constitute a breach of Union law. Second, Hungary already had an Act on Public Interest Notification, which 'draws attention to a circumstance, the remedying or removal of which is in the interest of the community or society as a whole. A public interest notification may also contain a proposal'.[111] This law has a wider scope than the Directive, but the protection that it provides is somewhat weaker than that of the Directive. Some experts also criticize the implementation of creating a separate law rather than amalgamating the two laws, which may cause confusion among citizens and legal professionals.[112]

106. Directive (EU) 2019/1937 of the European Parliament and of the Council of 23 Oct. 2019 on the protection of persons who report breaches of Union law – Whistleblower Directive.
107. https://www.parlament.hu/irom42/03089/03089.pdf.
108. §50d) of the Proposal.
109. §50a)–b)–c).
110. https://magyarnarancs.hu/belpol/barki-tehet-majd-bejelentest-panaszt-a-genderpropaganda-ellen-es-a-magyar-eletmod-vedelmeben-256777.
111. §13.1(3) Act CLXV of 2013 on complaints and notifications of public interest.
112. https://tasz.hu/cikkek/uj-bejelentovedelmi-torvenyjavaslat-a-kormany-a-minimumot-surolja-alulrol.

Chapter 2. Relevant Constitutional Provisions Protecting Freedom of Expression and the Press

§1. The New Basic Law

141. Hungary has a new Basic Law effective from 1 January 2012. This was passed by the two-third parliamentary majority of the second Orbán Government with its allied party KDNP in April 2011, in order to change the Constitution which had originated in 1949 and – although transformed completely – was declared 'temporary' in 1989.[113]

142. Article IX of the Chapter 'Freedoms and Responsibilities' discusses freedom of expression. It says:[114]

Article IX. Basic Law

1. Everybody has the right to freedom of expression.
2. Hungary acknowledges and protects freedom and pluralism of the press and ensures the conditions of providing free information that is necessary for the formation of a democratic public opinion.
3. In the interest of providing information in election campaigns necessary for a democratic public opinion, political advertisements may only be published in media service without charge, on conditions that ensure equal treatment, defined in fundamental (*sarkalatos*) law.
4. Exercising press freedom may not be directed to harm the human dignity of others.
5. Exercising press freedom may not be directed to harm the dignity of the Hungarian nation, or national, ethnic, racial or religious communities. Persons belonging to such communities are entitled – as defined in law – to enforce their claims in court against expressions of opinion which hurt their community, their human dignity.

---

113. The new Basic Law was criticized by the Hungarian opposition and civil organizations like the Hungarian Civil Liberties Union (TASZ), the Eötvös Károly Public Policy Institute (EKINT) and the Hungarian Helsinki Committee (Magyar Helsinki Bizottság) (https://helsinki.hu/wp-content/uploads/Comments_on_the_Process_of_Framing_the_New_Constitution_of_Hungary_EKI_HCLU_HHC.pdf), the Venice Commission CDL-AD(2011)016-e.

    Opinion on the new Constitution of Hungary adopted by the Venice Commission at its 87th Plenary Session (Venice, 17–18 Jun. 2011), https://www.venice.coe.int/webforms/documents/CDL-AD(2011)016-E.aspx and Amnesty International: AI Index: EUR 27/006/2011 20 Apr. 2011 Hungary: Newly adopted Constitution at odds with human rights. https://www.amnesty.org/fr/wp-content/uploads/2021/07/eur270062011en.pdf because of the lack of social and political consensus, the rapid time (approx. three months) within which it was passed, and the unsatisfactory treatment of human rights.

114. The original text in Hungarian: *IX. cikk (1) Mindenkinek joga van a véleménynyilvánítás szabadságához. (2) Magyarország elismeri és védi a sajtó szabadságát és sokszínűségét, biztosítja a demokratikus közvélemény kialakulásához szükséges szabad tájékoztatás feltételeit. (3) A sajtószabadságra, valamint a médiaszolgáltatások, a sajtótermékek és a hírközlési piac felügyeletét ellátó szervre vonatkozó részletes szabályokat sarkalatos törvény határozza meg.*

6. Detailed rules on freedom of the press, and the body supervising media services, press products and the telecommunications market shall be defined by a fundamental (*sarkalatos*) law.[115]

§2. Differences from the Previous Constitution

143. The previous Constitution was changed numerous times by the second Orbán Government in 2010 and 2011, and so was its provision for freedom of expression, specifically. This section discusses only the differences between the last version of section 61 of the Constitution and Article IX of the Basic Law.

144. The title of the chapter about rights pairs responsibilities with freedoms. This recalls the socialist constitutions, where human rights (then called civil rights) were seen as granted by the State and could be suspended if civil duties were not fulfilled. The duties listed in this Basic Law under Articles XXX and XXXI. Article XXX prescribe the obligations of contribution to the coverage of common needs and of defence of the homeland.

145. The Basic Law returned to the 1989 version of declaring freedom of expression, abandoning reference to 'free speech' (inserted in 2010) after public discussion criticized the latter for being narrower than 'freedom of expression'.

146. Contrary to the previous Constitution, this Basic Law discusses access to public information and protection of personal data separately from freedom of expression in Article VI. This Article also establishes a new authority to supervise the rights of access to public data and privacy, replacing the ombudsman's office. This movement has also been criticized by human rights lawyers and activists because the new authority may not be politically as independent as the ombudsman's office (which has often been critical of the government). The European Commission started an infringement procedure against Hungary, among others, for this reason.[116] More information on the new law on freedom of information (FOI) and data protection can be found in Part II.

147. Paragraph (2) of Article IX maintains a reference to pluralism, which was inserted in 2010. This was also criticized because pluralism is not supposed to be protected by governments, but rather, its conditions should be ensured. Maintaining

115. Fundamental laws are laws that require two-thirds majority of the MPs present to be passed or modified. Article Q(4) of the Basic Law defines fundamental laws.

116. European Commission launches accelerated infringement proceedings against Hungary over the independence of its central bank and data protection authorities as well as over measures affecting the judiciary, http://europa.eu/rapid/pressReleasesAction.do?reference=IP/12/24. *See* an analysis about the new situation: M. Szabó, *Az adatvédelmi ombudsman hiánya*, http://www.szuveren.hu/vendeglap/szabo-mate-daniel/az-adatvedelmi-ombudsman-hianya (23 Feb. 2012). *See* the positions of the affected persons: *Eltérő álláspontok az új adatvédelmi hatóság függetlenségéről. Eltér Dr Pétefalvi Attila, illetve Dr Jóri András, véleménye az új adatvédelmi hatóság függetlensége tekintetében*, http://www.jogiforum.hu/hirek/27099 (30 Jan. 2012).

pluralism has often been interpreted in the new Hungarian democracy as the expectation of equal political representation in the media content and equal political influence in the media market. The second part of paragraph (2) (*... ensures the conditions of providing free information that is necessary for the formation of a democratic public opinion*) was praised for its first part which declares ensuring the conditions of free information providing. However, it was criticized for its second part, which narrows the cases of providing legitimate information to those that are 'necessary in the formation of democratic public opinion', leaving information that is deemed unnecessary, unprotected.

148. The Basic Law gives a list of regulated areas that require a two-thirds majority. The list omits the area of privacy and access to public information, which is a meaningful change. The restriction of media monopolies was not included in the list – although it was part of it under the previous Constitution.

149. The Basic Law abandoned the declaration that 'everybody has the right to be properly informed'. This section was inserted in 2010 and was often criticized because of the word 'properly' and because it created a vague obligation for the media to provide 'proper' information.[117]

150. Probably the most meaningful change is the complete omission of any reference to public service media. This terminates the constitutional obligation of the State to maintain public service media.[118] The amendments in 2010 gave a detailed description of the duties of the public service media and incorporated a detailed reference to its supervisory bodies – all these were omitted in the Basic Law.

151. The Basic Law was amended five times between January 2011 and September 2014. The fourth and the fifth amendments affected the media: the fourth amendment (among others) ordered that political advertisements in a national election campaign, or the European parliamentary elections, could be published only by public service television. Private televisions could publish only advertisements of candidates of those parties which were not able to run a national list, and only without charge. This provision was ensued by great political and international controversy;[119] therefore, it was changed by the fifth amendment, which eliminated the

117. However, a similar provision is included in Smtv. (§13) and in the Mttv. (§12). After many improvements, the obligation applies only to linear media service providers and the only sanction for its breach is obligation to publish a statement.

118. 61/1995. (X. 6) Constitutional Court Decision, at 317 p. declared that 'as long as s 61(4) of the Constitution explicitly defines public service news agency, it is a constitutional obligation to maintain such an institution'. Since the Constitution defined public service radio and television in the same section, it can be concluded that the maintenance of those is also a constitutional obligation. *See* more in: Judit Bayer et al., *A közszolgálati média és az európai versenyjog. Közszolgálatiság a változó világban* 68 (L'Harmattan 2010). *See also* Gábor Polyák, *A közszolgálati médiaszolgáltatás alkotmányjogi pozíciói*, 2 Jura 133–143 (2007).

119. http://www.venice.coe.int/webforms/documents/default.aspx?pdffile=CDL-AD(2013)012-e; https://www.amnesty.eu/news/amnesty-internationals-concerns-about-the-fourth-amendment-to-hungarys/; http://helsinki.hu/en/newest-amendment-to-the-fundamental-law-of-hungary-would-seriously-undermine-the-rule-of-law. Links accessed 26 Sep. 2014.

rule that only public service media may publish advertisements but retained the provision that commercial media services may publish those only free of charge. Other rules affecting the media in the fourth amendment prepared the new Civil Code's provision on civil claims in the case of hate speech against national, ethnic, racial or religious communities.[120]

§3. Conditions for Public Authorities to Restrict Freedom of Speech

152. Restriction of speech must be based on laws, as freedom of expression is a basic constitutional right (*alapvető jog*). According to Article 1 of the Basic Law, rules related to basic rights and obligations must be defined by laws (*törvény* – a law passed by Parliament). Further, as the Basic Law sets out, basic rights may be restricted only in the interest of another basic right or for the protection of constitutional values, to the extent absolutely necessary, proportionally to the purpose to be achieved, and respecting the substantial content of the basic right.[121] This latter sentence did not appear in the previous Constitution; however, that one was more firm in stating that 'even law cannot restrict the substantial content of a basic right'.[122]

153. The new National Media and Telecommunication Authority (established in 2010) received extensive powers under the new law. It has the constitutional entitlement to issue decrees.[123] It is responsible for printed press, online journals and audiovisual media. Its rights and duties will be discussed in full detail in Part V below.

---

120. Article IX Basic Law, (4–5), *see* above at para. 136.
121. Article 1(3) Basic Law, in Chapter Freedom and Responsibility, (*Az alapvető jogokra és kötelezettségekre vonatkozó szabályokat törvény állapítja meg. Alapvető jog más alapvető jog érvényesülése vagy valamely alkotmányos érték védelme érdekében, a feltétlenül szükséges mértékben, az elérni kívánt céllal arányosan, az alapvető jog lényeges tartalmának tiszteletben tartásával korlátozható*).
122. §8(2) of the Act XX of 1949 on the Constitution of the Hungarian Republic (hereinafter: Constitution): (*A Magyar Köztársaságban az alapvető jogokra és kötelességekre vonatkozó szabályokat törvény állapítja meg, alapvető jog lényeges tartalmát azonban nem korlátozhatja*).
123. Articles T2 and 23(4) of the Basic Law.

Chapter 3. Special Duties of the State in Relation to Freedom of Expression

§1. Constitutional Obligations

154. According to constitutional legal theory, freedom of expression demands primarily passivity, i.e., non-interference from the State. Based on the previous Constitution, the Constitutional Court declared that the State also had the obligation to pass the necessary laws to govern the area. This obligation was not always easy because a two-thirds parliamentary majority was required to regulate this field of law, and the political consensus could not be reached often for years.[124] The Basic Law explicitly provides for a duty of the State in paragraph (2) Article IX by prescribing that the State should ensure the conditions of free information provision. As this section did not exist earlier, there is no case law or established theory on how this should be interpreted.

155. From the Constitution, it could be derived that it was the duty of the State to maintain at least one public service medium because they were mentioned in the Constitution. The Basic Law does not mention the public service media, and the old constitutional case law probably would not apply any more. However, both the Smtv. and Mttv. mention and regulate public service media, and both require a two-thirds majority for their amendment, just like the Basic Law.

156. In constitutional jurisprudence, based upon the case law of the Constitutional Court, an institutional-protective obligation (*intézményvédelmi kötelezettség*) of the State became known. The State's obligation to respect and protect fundamental rights includes more than just refraining from violating them – it must ensure the conditions necessary for their realization.[125]

157. Because of the removal of the constitutional reference to regulation of privacy and access to public information, it could be debated whether or not the regulation of these areas by law is still a constitutional duty of the State. However, international obligations still apply.[126]

158. The Basic Law also omitted the reference to the State's obligation to prevent media monopolies or to protect pluralism. This theoretically allows for laws governing the field of media to allow or even create information monopolies, without being unconstitutional. The Mttv. however, declares among its principles that

124. 37/1992. (VI. 10) ABh.
125. 64/1991. (XII. 17) ABh on abortion and following ABh-s: 30/1992. (V. 26), 37/1992. (VI. 10) ABh; 60/1993 (XI. 29) ABh; 32/1998. (VI. 25) ABh; 48/1998. (XI. 23) ABh; 8/2011. (II. 18) ABh; 37/2000. (X. 31) ABh; 42/2000. (XI. 8) ABh; 29/2011. (IV. 7) ABh; 37/2011. (V. 10) ABh; 165/ 2011. (XII. 20) ABh; 175/2011. (XII. 29) ABh; *see also* BVerfGE 74, 297 Baden-Württemberg (1987); BVerfGE 83, 238 WDR (1991).
126. Article 12 of the Universal Declaration of Human Rights, Art. 17 of the International Covenant of Civil and Political Rights, Art. 8 of the ECHR and Arts 7–8 of the Charter of the Fundamental Rights of the EU.

pluralism is an exceptionally important value, that its protection includes the prevention of ownership monopolies or unjustified limitation of the market competition and that the law shall be interpreted with respect to this value.[127]

§2. Legal Obligations

159. The State created obligations for the NMHH in the Mttv. – such as keeping a registry of all media outlets, deciding about frequency tenders and performing all other duties set out by law (in more detail, *see* Part V).[128]

160. The Smtv. sets out that public media services shall confirm and preserve the national and European identity, as well as national, family, ethnic and religious communities. Public media services should care for and enrich Hungarian and minority languages as well as their cultures and fulfil the informational and cultural needs of citizens.[129]

161. The same law also declares that the conditions of registration cannot restrict press freedom.[130] The Smtv. also sets out an obligation, the addressee of which is undefined – stating that 'everybody has the right to be properly informed about local, national and European public affairs, and events that are meaningful for the citizens of the Hungarian Republic and the Hungarian nation'.[131]

§3. International Obligations: ECHR

162. Further duties are created for the State by international obligations. As a Member State of the ECHR, it is an international obligation of Hungary to follow the principles of the Convention in both its legislation and case law. According to this Convention, freedom of expression may be restricted only if the restriction is prescribed by law, aims at a legitimate purpose that is listed in Article 10 of the Convention, is necessary in a democratic society and is proportionate to the goal that is to be achieved.

163. The following is a list of cases where the ECtHR found a violation of Article 10, with Hungary being the respondent State:

– In the case of *ATV Zrt. v. Hungary*, the applicant television station reported on a public matter related to a parliamentary speech of an MP, a member of the political party 'Jobbik'.[132] The MP stated: 'it is time … that we made an assessment

127. §4 Mttv.
128. §§109, 110, 132 Mttv.
129. §11 Smtv.
130. §5 Smtv.
131. §10 Smtv. This section has been criticized because of the expression 'be properly informed', especially as the word 'proper' gives way to subjective interpretation.
132. *ATV Zrt. v. Hungary* (Application No. 61178/14), 28 Apr. 2020.

how many persons of Jewish origin, especially members of Parliament and government, there are who pose a risk to national security … '. The news anchor presented the proposed demonstrations, stating that 'an unprecedented alliance is about to materialise on Sunday based on the biased remarks of the parliamentary far-right'. Jobbik complained about being called a 'parliamentary far-right' and reported to the Media Authority that the station violated Article 12(3) and (4) of Mttv., which prohibits media service providers from adding 'any opinion or evaluative explanation to the political news' without 'distinguishing it from the news [itself]'. The Court noted that the various levels of court decisions gave inconsistent assessments of what 'opinion' means as opposed to facts and concluded that the station could not have foreseen that the term 'far right' would qualify as an opinion. It considered that the context and factual elements were relevant for the contention that the term 'far right' did not concern an assessment of morality but described the position of a party within the political spectrum. It disagreed with the Constitutional Court which found the applicant's defence based on veracity and factual accuracy as irrelevant.[133]

- In the case of *Magyar Jeti Zrt. v. Hungary*, Roma children in their school were threatened by a group of drunken football fans who had just stopped at the school with their bus.[134] The victims wrongly attributed their actions to the political party 'Jobbik'. A journal reported about the incident and published a video interview with the mayor. The party sued for violation of good reputation. The journal argued that their action was in harmony with journalistic ethics and professional standards and that in the internet era, when news is very short-lived, it is not possible to check the veracity of every single factual claim immediately. They argued that the political party (Jobbik) is known for its anti-Roma, racist and inciting political stance and that the interview with the mayor reflected the opinion of the mayor.
- The Court found that posting a hyperlink does not automatically create liability for the linked content, recalling the *Jersild v. Denmark* case, among others. It recalled that to penalize a journalist on the ground that he is helping to disseminate a statement made by others in an interview would seriously undermine the contribution of the press to the discussion of public affairs and should therefore be applied only where there is an overriding reason to do so. It added that the range of acceptable criticism of politicians or political parties is wider. The key is marked as a 'key case' within the Strasbourg jurisprudence.
- In the case of *Mándli and others v. Hungary*, the applicants had attempted to interview MPs outside the areas designated for journalists.[135] The topic of these planned interviews would have been illicit payments linked to the National Bank, a matter of considerable public interest which had attracted significant media attention. The Parliament had withdrawn the accreditation of the journalists as a sanction against violating the rules for the press. The Court found that although

---

133. *See also*: Voorhoof, D., *European Court of Human Rights: ATV Zrt v. Hungary; and Nina de Puy Kamp, ATV Zrt v. Hungary*: A Missed Opportunity to Address Hungary's Oppressive Media Act (2020). 15 May 2020. https://strasbourgobservers.com/2020/05/15/atv-zrt-v-hungary-a-missed-opportunity-to-address-hungarys-oppressive-media-act/.
134. *Magyar Jeti Zrt. v. Hungary* (Application No. 11257/16), 4. Dec. 2018.
135. *Mándli and Others v. Hungary* (Application No. 63164/16), 26 May 2020.

the Parliament has the right to regulate journalistic activity on its territory, the right to appeal should be granted, and this was not the case.

- In the case of *Magyar Kétfarkú Kutya Párt (MKKP) v. Hungary*, the question in the case was whether the actions of MKKP were prohibited by the law on electoral procedure (EPA) or not.[136] MKKP is a mock party in Hungary, which aimed to use a mobile application for posting ballot photographs in an anonymous manner. The Court found that the law was not formulated with sufficient precision so as to rule out any arbitrariness and enable the MKKP to regulate its conduct accordingly, as the law conferred a very wide discretion on the electoral bodies and the domestic courts. The case is marked as a 'key case' in the database.
- In the case of *Szurovecz v. Hungary*, the applicant as a journalist was denied access to the refugee camp in Debrecen. The Court established that this prevented the applicant from reporting first-hand information and facts on a matter of considerable public interest. The authorities' reasoning was not specific and did not justify the restriction. The government's argumentation, namely that access would violate the safety and private life of the asylum-seekers, was relevant; however, the Court was not persuaded that it was carefully balanced and, therefore, whether the restriction was necessary to reach these goals.
- The Court emphasized the 'watchdog' role of the media that played particular importance in such contexts and concluded that the authorities' decision was reached without any sensible consideration of the public interest in receiving information on a matter of public interest.[137]
- In the case of *Herbai v. Hungary*, the applicant contributed to a website which represented educational and informative articles of professional practice (HR management).[138] The applicant published two articles for which he was fired for allegedly breaching confidentiality standards and violating the employer's financial interests. The Court found that the content in question formed part of a discussion on matters of public interest. They did not carry signs of personal grievance or antagonism. It found neither of the domestic courts had made any attempt to show how the content could have adversely affected the bank.
- In the case of *Karácsony and others v. Hungary*, MPs were fined for showing billboards during a plenary session. The court found that the interference with their freedom of expression was devoid of a compelling reason, and the sanctions were imposed without consideration of less intrusive measures, such as warnings or reprimands.[139] On the same day, a very similar case was decided. Three other MPs were fined for demonstrating their opinion during a plenary session, which the court found to be in violation of Article 10 because of the same reasons.[140]
- In the case of *Ungváry and Irodalom Kft. v. Hungary*, the court found that the domestic courts did not convincingly establish a proper balance between the personality rights of a public figure and the first applicant's right to freedom of expression. The historian Ungváry had presented a scholarly position using

---

136. *Magyar Kétfarkú Kutya Párt (MKKP) v. Hungary* (Application No. 201/17), 20 Jan. 2020.
137. *Szurovecz v. Hungary* (Application No. 15428/16), 8 Oct. 2019.
138. *Herbai v. Hungary* (Application No. 11608/15), 5 Nov. 2019.
139. *Karácsony and others v. Hungary* (Application No. 42461/13), 16 Sep. 2014.
140. *Szél and others v. Hungary* (Application No. 44357/13), 16 Sep. 2014.

excessive language, but without any sensationalism, related to Mr K., who was an elected deputy party secretary in 1983 in the People's Republic of Hungary, a totalitarian State.[141]

- In the case of *Tatár & Fáber v. Hungary*, the two applicants had made a public performance expressing political views to a few invited journalists in a public space. The performance lasted thirteen minutes, and the Hungarian authorities fined the persons for failing to notify the gathering. The court found that there was no gathering in this sense, and sanctioning such an expression of opinion would have a chilling effect on public speech.[142]
- In the case of *Baka v. Hungary*, early termination of the applicant's mandate as President of the Supreme Court was found to be a reaction against his criticism and publicly expressed views on judicial reforms and thereby constituted an interference with the exercise of his right to freedom of expression.[143]
- In the case of *Fáber v. Hungary*, the applicant raised a red-white striped flag, a symbol of Nazism in Hungary, during a demonstration against Nazism and hatred. Fáber was committed to a police station, held in custody, interrogated for six hours, and fined HUF 50,000. The court found a violation of Article 10.
- In the case of *Vajnai v. Hungary*, the applicant was a speaker at a lawful demonstration in central Budapest as vice president of the Workers' Party (*Munkáspárt*) – a registered left-wing political party. The demonstration took place at the former location of a statue of Karl Marx, which had been removed by the authorities. On his jacket, the applicant wore a five-pointed red star as a symbol of the international workers' movement. In the application of §269/B(1) of the (old) Criminal Code, a police patrol which was present called on the applicant to remove the star, which he did. Subsequently, the applicant was convicted for the use of a totalitarian symbol, with the sanction being suspended for a probationary period of one year. The appeals court, the Capital Court, referred the case to the ECtHR, which established a violation of Article 10 and ordered reimbursement of costs.[144]
- Subsequently, to the Vajnai decision, a regional appeal court (*Pécsi Ítélőtábla*) found Mr Fratanoló guilty under the same circumstances but applied only reprehension as a sanction (which does not have any further consequences but still is a criminal sanction). The ECtHR again established a violation of Article 1, awarded EUR 4,000 in damages and reimbursement of costs and called upon Hungary to change its law.[145] The Hungarian government refused to enforce the judgment and to change the law.[146]
- A journalist described the quality of a bottle of Hungarian speciality wine Tokaji Aszú as being very bad, using the word 'shit'. Hungarian courts found him guilty

141. *Ungváry & Irodalom Kft. v. Hungary* (Application No. 64520/10), 3 Dec. 2013.
142. *Tatár & Fáber v. Hungary* (Application No. 26005/08 26160/08), 12 Jun. 2012.
143. *Baka v. Hungary* (Application No. 20261/12), 27 May 2014.
144. *Vajnai v. Hungary* (Application No. 33629/06), 8 Jul. 2008.
145. *Fratanoló v. Hungary* (Application No. 29459/10), 3 Nov. 2012.
146. http://www.parlament.hu/irom39/06853/06853.pdf, http://www.parlament.hu/irom39/06854/06854.pdf.

of criminal defamation and sentenced him to a reprehension.[147] The court established violation of Article 10; the applicant demanded no damages, only reimbursement of costs, which was awarded.

- In the case of *Kenedi v. Hungary*, a historian specialized in the functioning of the secret services of dictatorships requested the Ministry to grant him access to certain documents deposited with it, with a view to publishing a study concerning the functioning of the Hungarian State Security Service of the Ministry of the Interior in the 1960s, but his request was denied. The Ministry made reference to a decision of 29 October 1998 classifying the documents as State secrets until 2048. The ECtHR found a violation of Articles 6 and 10 and awarded EUR 6,000 in damages and EUR 7,000 in reimbursed costs.[148]
- In case of *Csánics v. Hungary*, the applicant, a former trade union leader, expressed that his previous workplace 'tramples constitutional and labour rights' and that '[b]ecause of the inhuman conduct of the management [the employees] should not have to stay in a place where they were called "criminals"'. The ECtHR found it 'striking that the domestic courts considered the manner in which the applicant expressed his statements "gratuitously insulting, offensive and harsh" and gave him no opportunity at all to prove the veracity of his assertions.' The court observed that the dispute at issue was a debate on matters of public interest, where there is little scope for restrictions and established violation of Article 10, awarding EUR 3,000 damages and EUR 1,000 for the costs.[149]
- Following a debate in connection with Hungary's facing up to its role in World War II and the Holocaust, the court found that applicant's – a historian, who published extensively on the Holocaust – argument was a value-laden factual statement that could not be considered excessive or devoid of factual basis. The debate was of utmost public interest, and the plaintiff voluntarily exposed himself to public criticism. The applicant's disagreement with plaintiff's views was formulated in indirect terms, but the court held that even harsh criticism in the present context would be protected by Article 10 of the Convention, whether expressed directly or indirectly. The sanction of an order to retract the statement affected the applicant's professional credibility as a historian, was capable of producing a chilling effect and was not 'necessary in a democratic society' within the meaning of Article 10 §2 of the Convention. The court ordered the payment of EUR 4,000 as damages and EUR 2,310 for costs.[150]
- In the case of *TASZ v. Hungary*, TASZ (the Hungarian Civil Liberties Union) requested access to a parliamentarian's complaint to the Constitutional Court. The court denied access to it, making reference to the personal rights of its author. The Civil Court approved this decision, arguing that the requested material was not 'data' under the Act on Data Protection and Access to Public Information. The court found that it would be fatal for freedom of expression in the sphere of politics if public figures could censor the press and public debate in the name of their

147. *Uj v. Hungary* (Application No. 23954/10), 19 Jun. 2011.
148. *Kenedi v. Hungary* (Application No. 31475/05), 26 Aug. 2009.
149. *Csanics v. Hungary* (Application No. 12188/06), 20 Jan. 2009.
150. *Karsai v. Hungary* (Application No. 5380/07), 1 Dec. 2009.

personality rights, alleging that their opinions on public matters are related to their person and therefore constitute private data which cannot be disclosed without consent.[151]

164. Hungary is one of the signatories to the United Nations' Covenant on Civil and Political Rights, and as such, assumed the obligation to respect and ensure the rights listed in the Covenant to all persons on its territory and jurisdiction, without discrimination, and to take the measures or pass the laws necessary to ensure these rights. Article XIX of the Covenant ensures the right to freedom of expression.

165. As a member of the EU, Hungary needs to harmonize its laws with European law in certain fields. Human rights, freedom of expression and media freedoms, in particular, have been considered a fundamental part of the EC legal framework (*acquis communautaire*) by the ECJ from the start[152] and have, since the adoption of the Lisbon Treaty, been part of EU primary law.[153] Nevertheless, the EU has always exercised its competences with much caution and great respect for the subsidiarity principle when it comes to media matters (because of the politically sensitive nature of many aspects related to media law).[154] Its intervention has mainly focused on the promotion of the internal market for and the trans-border flow of television broadcasting services. This was done first by the Television Without Frontiers Directive in 1989, which was amended in 1997 and later substantially reformed into the Audiovisual Media Services Directive (AVMS) Directive in 2007 (eventually codified in 2010). The directive's purpose is to ensure free transmission of audiovisual media services and harmonize minimum standards in relation to a number of legitimate restrictions on broadcasting freedom, such as regulation in the interest of protection of children, prohibition of hate speech, restrictions on advertising, granting access to major events and respect for copyright. In short, the Directive provides the following:[155]

151. *TASZ v. Hungary* (Application No. 37374/05), 14 Apr. 2009.
152. *See*, for instance, Case C-11/70, *Internationale Handelsgesellschaft mbH v. Einfuhr – und Vorratsstelle für Getreide und Futtermittel* [1970] E.C.R. 1125: 'Respect for fundamental rights forms an integral part of the general principles of law protected by the Court of Justice. The protection of such rights, whilst inspired by the constitutional traditions common to the Member States, must be ensured within the framework of the structure and objectives of the Community.' The Treaty on EU of February 1992 (Maastricht Treaty) inserted Art. F.2 which explicitly stated that, The Union shall respect fundamental rights, as guaranteed by the European Convention for the Protection of Human Rights and Fundamental Freedoms signed in Rome on 4 Nov. 1950 and as they result from the constitutional traditions common to the Member States, as general principles of Community law.
153. Freedom of expression and the freedom and pluralism of the media are explicitly affirmed in Art. 11 of the Charter of Fundamental Rights of the EU, OJ C 83/389 (2010).
154. Controversies around the Hungarian media regulation raised the need for more explicit and far-reaching EU competences in relation to the safeguarding of freedom of expression. *See* the High-Level Group on Media Freedom and Pluralism. http://ec.europa.eu/information_society/media_taskforce/pluralism/hlg/index_en.htm.
155. For more details, *see*, Valcke Peggy & Lefever Katrien, *International Encyclopaedia for Media Law* (Kluwer L. Intl. 2012).

- that audiovisual media services provided by media service providers under their jurisdiction do not contain any incitement to hatred based on race, sex, religion or nationality (Article 6);
- that media service providers under their jurisdiction do not transmit cinematographic works outside periods agreed with the rights holders (Article 8);
- that audiovisual commercial communications or sponsored programmes comply with the requirements set out in the directive (Articles 9–10, 19–24);
- that audiovisual media services which might seriously impair the physical, mental or moral development of minors are only made available in such a way as to ensure that minors will not normally hear or see such on-demand audiovisual media services (Articles 12, 27);
- that on-demand audiovisual media services promote the production of and access to European works (Article 13);
- that broadcasters do not deprive a substantial proportion of the public from following such events on free television (Article 14);
- that broadcasters reserve for European works a majority proportion of their transmission time and at least 10% of their programming time and budget for European works created by producers who are independent of the broadcasters (Articles 16–17); and
- that the right of reply is ensured (Article 28);
- in 2018, an important amendment of the AVMS Directive, included provisions for video-sharing platform providers (Article 28a–b). The rules include jurisdictional specifications and enforcement of the rules on the protection of minors, against incitement to violence or hatred, and against content the dissemination of which constitutes an activity which is a criminal offence under Union law, namely public provocation to commit a terrorist offence, offences concerning child and offences concerning racism and xenophobia;
- a further important amendment provided for the independence of national regulatory authorities. Unfortunately, the rules provided by the AVMS appear to be still insufficient to guarantee impartiality of a regulatory authority, as the example of Hungary shows. The AVMS rules on national regulatory authority were not addressed as Mttv. already laid down the conditions and procedures for the appointment and dismissal of the heads and members of the national regulatory authority, including the duration of the mandate. The Media Authority has strong competences and powers and adequate financial resources. It is also legally distinct from the government, and an effective appeal mechanism to courts also exists. However, some requirements of the Directive are still not ensured. It is not entirely clear how these requirements can be enforced, how they can be quantified, and how non-compliance can be proven. The following requirements are not fulfilled by the national regulatory authority:
  - be functionally independent of their respective governments;
  - exercise their powers impartially and transparently and in accordance with the objectives of this Directive, in particular media pluralism, [...] non-discrimination [...] and the promotion of fair competition;
  - not seek or take instructions from any other body;
  - the ways of making them accountable are clearly defined in law.

– the following signs show non-compliance (that the requirements are not fulfilled):
  – election of the Media Council members (*see* §548) and the Head of the Media Authority (§543–545) took place always with the votes of the governing party only, despite the idea of a multi-party coalition;
  – the objective of media pluralism was not observed when the Media Council assisted in the distribution of radio frequencies overwhelmingly to government-friendly and christian stations and depriving independent stations of their licences;
  – the Media Council not raising its voice against market processes that are clearly injurious to media freedom and pluralism, such as the KESMA merger;
  – the law does not define a procedure for making the head of the Media Authority and of the Media Council or the members of the latter accountable for their decisions.

§4. About the 2010 Media Legislation

166. It is widely held by legal experts and international organizations that the new Hungarian media legislation does not respect traditional European norms and principles on freedom of expression and the rule of law. The Hungarian media laws and the national regulatory authority are regarded as instruments for stifling media pluralism in Hungary. Naturally, the government and the national regulatory authority NMHH and its Media Council regularly represent their particular position in opposition to this view.[156]

167. This monograph aims to provide an objective presentation of Hungarian media law and its practice without giving an evaluation. It has not been ambitioned by this book to represent the opinion of its authors. Only objective accounts and references from external, recognized sources are included for the sake of providing

156. For example, *see* NMHH fighting back the statements of international monitoring organizations: NMHH (2023): *Médiaszabadság-jelentések értékelése*, https://nmhh.hu/dokumentum/241040/mediaszabadsag_jelentesek_ertekelese_NMHH.pdf. Besides, the Media Council runs a blog which consistently defends the law and its subsequent amendments, often trying to disqualify its critiques by alleging their ignorance regarding the media law. The style of the blog is well reflected by the titles of the blog entries, for example: 'MÚOSZ (the biggest journalism organization) in the labyrinth of the law' (*A MÚOSZ a jog útvesztőjében*); 'Adventures of the Central European University with Hungarian media regulation' (*A Közép-európai Egyetem kalandjai a magyar médiaszabályozással*); 'Intentional political provocation in the case of Klubradio' (*A Klubrádió ügyében tudatos politikai provokáció folyik*). The Media Council takes clear position in political debates, discussions (*see*, 'It is about the ideology, not press freedom', '*Az ideológiáról van szó, nem a sajtószabadságról*'). The president of the Authority wrote a reply to Kim Lane Scheppele in which she accused her with ignorance of the law, and demanded arguments from her regarding her opinion, for example why it is a problem that the media law protects 'majorities'. http://hunmedialaw.org/dokumentum/237/answer_Scheppele_20120320_final.pdf (the original Hungarian at: http://mediatanacs.blog.hu/2012/03/26/szalai_annamaria_levele_kim_lane_scheppele_reszere). Kim Lane Scheppele constitutional lawyer published several articles about Hungary, among others: Hungary's Free Media, in Krugman's blog at N.Y. Times (14 Mar. 2012), accessible at http://krugman.blogs.nytimes.com/2012/03/14/hungarys-free-media.

information for the reader. In the General Introduction, we referred to declarations of international governments and NGOs who expressed their concerns about the 2010 legislation (*see* above in paragraph 117). In this part, we will provide a short summary of the objections raised by experts, expert groups, researchers and of course by the mentioned organizations:

- The Media Council is part of the National Media and Telecommunication Authority (hereafter: Media Authority). Members of the Media Council are to be elected by the Parliament with a two-thirds majority, but until 2023, they have been appointed only by Fidesz, the governing party which held this majority. The president of the Authority – who is also president of the Media Council and is closely connected to the Fidesz party – was, for the first time, appointed by the Prime Minister.[157]
- In 2022, the law was amended so that a simple majority of the Cultural Committee of the Parliament can recommend the members of the Media Council, as opposed to an ad hoc committee that needed to vote with a two-thirds majority.[158]
- The mandate lasts for nine years and was originally renewable for an unlimited number of times.[159] In 2013, the law was amended so that the Head of the Authority is appointed by the President of the Republic upon the recommendation of the Prime Minister, and the post is non-renewable.[160]
- Even after the lapse of their mandate, members, as well as the president of the Media Council, stay in position until new members are elected by Parliament's two-thirds majority – this may be prevented even by a small opposition power. In this latter case, the president of the Authority appointed by the Prime Minister loses his or her position, and the president of the Media Council retains the role of president of the Authority.
- The Authority and the Media Council have overbroad competences in the field of telecommunication, media content regulation, supervision of printed press, frequency distribution and supervision of the public service media.
- Judicial control over the Media Council's decisions is limited to administrative courts, which cannot overrule the council's argumentation. In case the Council violated the law, the court can change the decision, but it cannot overrule the logic or evaluation of the Media Council's argumentation. For example, it could not state that the Council erroneously evaluated the facts or came to a wrong conclusion after balancing the facts and the contradicting interests.[161] A long debate

157. Annamária Szalai died in April 2013. Just before her death, rules on fulfilling the position were slightly amended.
158. §124(3) Mttv. amended and (4–9) abolished, effective since 1 Aug. 2022.
159. *See*: Jakubowicz Karol, *Analysis and Assessment of a Package of Hungarian Legislation and Draft Legislation on Media and Telecommunications*, http://www.osce.org/fom/71218, (September 2010), III. 2, III. 3.
160. §111/A(1) and §125(5) Mttv. amended by Act XXXIII of 2013, effective from 5 Apr. 2013.
161. §339/B of Act III of Pp.

has developed regarding the depth and extent of judicial supervision of Media Council decisions, and the least we can say is that the regulation is not entirely clear at this point.[162]

- The Media Council exercises an indirect influence on public service media through its appointing of the director and managing of the finances of the Media Property Management and Supporting Fund (hereinafter: MTVA), which holds assets, income and staff of the public service media. The Media Council may change the system of public media services.
- The public service media is limited to exclusively using the news service of the Hungarian News Agency, which is also part of the MTVA. The news agency provides its news for free to all other media, which creates a competitive disadvantage for all independent news agencies and the media outlets that pay for their services.[163]
- The Media Council has the right to impose prohibitive sanctions. In response to criticism, it expressed that it would not abuse its sanctioning power. However, a chilling effect is created by the possibility of sanctioning.
- Press products are part of the content regulation and are subject to the Media Council's jurisdiction. The Constitutional Court ordered the legislative to annul certain content provisions' effect on the printed and online press. Several provisions on content restriction were found constitutional, and the Media Council's jurisdiction over printed and online press was left intact.

---

162. Hungarian Media Law vs. Laws in Europe, Center for Media and Communication Studies, http://medialaws.ceu.hu/findings.html, 2012; on the other hand, *see*: *Miért nincs jogorvoslat, ha van*? http://mediatanacs.blog.hu/2012/01/17/miert_nincs_jogorvoslat_ha_van (17 Jan. 2012).
163. *See*: Karol Jakubowicz, *Analysis and Assessment of a Package of Hungarian Legislation and Draft Legislation on Media and Telecommunications*, http://www.osce.org/fom/71218 (September 2010), IV.

Chapter 4. Case Law of the Constitutional Court Affecting Freedom of Expression

168. The fourth amendment to the Basic Law of Hungary declared that all Constitutional Court decisions, which were passed before the Basic Law came into effect, were ineffective.[164] The Constitutional Court, however, in its decision on 11 June 2013, declared that it retains the right to refer to its previous decisions, provided that they are applicable based on the Basic Law's specific rule's similarity with the Constitution's specific rule, the similarity of the Basic Law's context, also considering the interpretation rules of the Basic Law and the circumstances of the case. The Constitutional Court also added that this – using the argumentation and principles of previous decisions – appears necessary.[165] In one of its following decisions, the Constitutional Court stated that the right to freedom of expression is basically identical in §61(1) of the Constitution and IX(1) of the Basic Law, and so is the right to press freedom in §61(2–3) of the Constitution and IX(2) of the Basic Law. Therefore, the Constitutional Court held that there is no reason not to apply the arguments from previous decisions.[166] Several of the previous Constitutional Court decisions – especially landmark decisions in the 1990s – were derived from the constitutional theory that the judges called 'the invisible constitution'. The decisions are meant to serve as measures of constitutionality, thus completing the text of the Constitution.[167] These were not based on the wording of the previous Constitution.[168]

§1. The Constitutional Court on the 2010 Legislation

169. The Constitutional Court delivered its decision on the new media laws on 19 December 2011. It brought changes in the following areas:[169]

- The court annulled the Smtv.'s effect on press products as of 31 May 2012 but allowed the legislative to reinstate it along the constitutional principles defined in the decision.
- The court annulled a part of the rules on journalistic sources, which prescribed that only information, the publication of which was in the public interest, deserves protection (with immediate effect).

---

164. Closing and Miscellaneous Provisions of the Basic Law, 5, effective from 1 Apr. 2013.
165. 13/2013. (VI. 17) Constitutional Court decision, at [30–32].
166. 19/2014. (V. 30) Constitutional Court decision at [48].
167. The notion 'invisible constitution' was introduced by Sólyom László, first chairman of the Constitutional Court and later President of the Republic: 'The Constitutional Court shall carry on to formulate the bases of the Constitution and the rights incorporated in it, and create a coherent system with its decisions, which serves as an "invisible constitution", a secure standard of constitutionalism – the Constitutional Court shall enjoy freedom in this action as long as it stays within the frames of constitutionalism'. (23/1990. (X. 31) ABh). *See* more: Illéssy István, *Az Alkotmánybíróság működésének kezdeti problémái*, 1 Jura (2001).
168. Also the landmark decision about the standards of hate speech: 30/1992. (V. 26) AB decision.
169. 165/2011. (XII. 20) AB decision at 1–6.

- The court declared it unconstitutional that no procedural guarantees ensured the protection of journalistic secrets in official procedures and called upon the Parliament to fulfil its duty until 31 May 2012.
- The court declared it unconstitutional that the Mttv. did not provide legal tools for media service providers to protect their sources of information and legal secrets in the course of fulfilling their obligation to reveal data to the Media Council under §155; and called upon the Parliament to fulfil its duty until 31 May 2012.
- The court annulled the section which allowed the Media Council to collect data outside of official procedures (§175) with immediate effect.
- The court annulled the part about the Media and Telecommunication Commissioner, who had the right to investigate and report to the Authority (and was employed by the president of the Authority) even in cases where no violation of the law could be suspected, effective from 31 May 2012, but allowed re-regulation along the constitutional principles.

170. However, the court rejected several parts of the submissions, among others, the unconstitutionality of the Mttv. as a whole; the assumption that the Mttv.'s stepping into effect from 1 January 2011 – without enough time for preparation – would violate the rule of law; the assumption that the Authority's right to investigate under §155 (discussed below in Part V, in paragraph 325) would violate the constitutional right to the protection of secrets, personal data and private house; the unconstitutionality of §5(1) of the Smtv. which allows laws to set as a condition for publication of media services or even of press products, official registration with an authority; the unconstitutionality of registration of press products by the Authority; that the confidentiality of journalistic sources does not extend to the identity of a source who passed on qualified secrets; and the unconstitutionality of allowing courts or investigative authorities to reveal journalistic sources.[170]

171. There were several other areas that were not examined by the court, specifically the appointment of the members of the Media Council, the appointment of the president of the Authority, the independence of public service media and the rules on tenders that provide wide powers of discretion to the Media Council.

172. The areas which the court decided on addressed a few of the most important concerns regarding the 2010 legislation: content requirements in connection to press products; unlimited right of investigative authorities to get access to journalistic sources; and the possibility of the Authority to gain access to journalistic sources and other confidential information through its unlimited right of investigation, and also by way of its commissioner.

173. However, the court left the door open for, and even encouraged, re-regulation in several cases. First of all, Smtv.'s effect on press products was allowed to be reinstated – the court declared that restrictions in the interest of protection of children, to prevent displaying persons in humiliating situations, or to

170. 165/2011. (XII. 20) AB decision at 7–10.

sanction hate speech are justified reasons to restrict freedom even in the case of press products. Although the commissioner's activity was found to be an unnecessary restriction of press freedom, the court set out the possibility of re-regulation, according to the principles in the decision (allowing interference by the commissioner in the field of telecommunication rather than the media).

§2. Constitutional Case Law Relating to Hate Speech

174. The 30/1992. (V. 26) AB határozat ('ABh') is one of the most influential decisions of the Constitutional Court, one that was reinforced several times and which exerted a significant effect on the Hungarian public sphere. In this case, the Constitutional Court analysed §269 of the (old) Criminal Code: incitement to hatred (§269(1), *gyűlöletre uszítás*) and racial insults (§269(2) *gyalázkodás).* It found that the latter was too broadly defined to be a proportionate limitation of freedom of expression, especially by means of criminal sanctions, and annulled it. While interpreting subsection (1) 'incitement to hatred', it found that the word 'hatred' described an extremely negative emotion and that the word 'incitement' meant an action that was capable of inflaming hatred in a greater mass of people, which could lead to the disturbance of peace and social order. This would mean a threat to individual rights: dignity, personal integrity, even life. Such a situation makes violation of these rights of individuals likely and would hinder individuals from exercising their rights (among others, free expression of their opinion).

175. This interpretation was later simply construed by courts as the level of 'clear and present danger' and resulted in this section hardly ever being applied in criminal procedure. Very few accusations were brought, and only one person was ever convicted for this crime.[171] While the presence of hate speech became more and more frequent and tolerated in the public sphere, the issue of regulation was raised from time to time in Parliament. But every time the Constitutional Court rejected the lowering of the constitutional limit of freedom of expression in relation to hate speech, relying on the same arguments (12/1999. (V. 21) ABh, 18/2004. (V. 25) ABh, 95/2008. (VII. 3) ABh, 96/2008. (VII. 3) ABh) (read more on hate speech in Part II, Chapter 3, §3 in paragraphs 265–270.)

§3. Case Law of the Constitutional Court Relating to the Control over Public Media (1992)

176. In its 37/1992. (VI. 10.) decision, the Constitutional Court passed a landmark decision on the independence of public service television and radio companies. It declared that the influence on public media content by either State organs (Parliament, government, local governments) or social groups (among them political parties) must be excluded by law. The examined piece of regulation was a

171. BH1999.6; 1998. 521; 1997. 165. (Various decisions of the same case).

remainder from the socialist times and provided for supervision by the government,[172] even though the Constitution implied that the law on public media shall be passed by the Parliament. Therefore, the rule was declared unconstitutional, and the Parliament was declared to be violating the Constitution by failing to have passed the necessary law on media. However, the Constitutional Court found that being supervised by the government was supposed to be a 'smaller threat on legal security (*jogbiztonság*)' than not being regulated at all therefore it did not annul the unconstitutional decree but kept it in place until Parliament would pass the necessary law (which, however, did not happen until December 1995).

§4. Case Law of the Constitutional Court on Defamation of Public Figures

177. A number of Constitutional Court decisions were issued in the same case related to depiction of a person in relation to a high-profile criminal financial fraud case which had a high number of victims and, therefore, was a case of extremely high public interest. The question in each case was whether the person was a public figure and what scope of personal information was of legitimate public interest. The Court found that previous work relationship and personal ties to the Chief Prosecutor are facts which affect the public matter of concern in the case and whose publication is regarded as neither arbitrary, nor unnecessary, nor unjustified. However, the full name of the applicant, names of previous workplaces, and the place of holiday were not necessary information, if the information relates to the matter of exceptional public interest, such as the fact that his previously direct colleague was a person who was a key figure in this matter of public interest. Revelation of family ties while maintaining anonymity was still in harmony with the Basic Law. [3210/2020. (VI. 19.) 3211/2020. (VI. 19.), 3212/2020. (VI. 19.), 3213/2020. (VI. 19.), 3214/2020. (VI. 19.), 3215/2020. (VI. 19.)].

178. In the case that served as a basis for the 26/2019 (VII. 23.) Constitutional Court decision, the press published photos and videos of the applicant in a bar in Ibiza. The video was a promo video of the bar in which the applicant was seen incidentally. The court found that the applicant works as a government consultant, regularly appears in the company of political leaders and persons close to the government, and, consequently, information about his lifestyle, which refers to his income situation, is of public interest. The Court recalled that without the freedom and diversity of public debate, there is no free public opinion and no democratic rule of law.[173] In its practice, the Constitutional Court has considered the free expression of public discourse of a political nature to be the most fundamental protection of freedom of expression.[174]

172. Section 6 of the decree of the Council of Ministers 1047/1974. (IX. 18) (MT határozat).
173. 7/2014. (7 Mar. 2014) Constitutional Court decision, at 39.
174. 5/2015. (25. II.) Constitutional Court decision, at 28.

179. Clickbait title: 8/2018. (VII. 5.) The clickbait title of the press article was defamatory, but the article's content was not. According to the Court, some church officeholders, by their own individual choice, leave the sphere more closely linked to the life of their religious community and take an active part in public debates and political events. In the latter case, the protection of their individual rights as regards freedom of expression and of the press is more important than that which would be justified by their ecclesiastical status alone. According to the Court, it must be decided in a new proceeding whether the overly simplistic negative content of the title was then balanced in the text or whether it was capable of misleading readers in a way that infringed the individual rights of the person concerned.

180. The decision 3145/2018 (V. 7.) pointed out that the scope of public figures is broader than the scope of persons exercising public authority and politicians acting in public, and no clear criteria have been developed to serve as a basis for determining the quality of public figures. However, the need to clarify this criterion for the application of the law is particularly justified by the fact that, as a result of changed social conditions, in particular the spread of telecommunications, the circle of public figures has widened. As a result of this trend, it is possible for persons who were not previously public figures, by virtue of their status, to become active participants in public debates. These persons are the so-called exceptional public actors because of their 'significant opinion-forming influence in public debates' [45–46]. This characterization applies not only to media actors but also to those who influence political decisions and the development of public life or who influence public opinion through their ownership of the media. The justification or refutation of the petitioner's exceptional status as a public figure is part of the free debate on public affairs. Their undisclosed activities not related to public affairs (a protected part of their private life) cannot be disclosed by the media on the basis of freedom of expression. If, however, it is precisely a part of private life that is the subject of public debate, then it is precisely in this area that freedom of expression should be given priority.

181. The Constitutional Court had two decisions in relation to the images of policemen. Before these, the Capital High Court (*Fővárosi Ítélőtábla*) consequently held that policemen are non-public figures, and the recording and publication of their images are subject to their individual consent.[175] In its 28/2014. (IX. 29.) decision, the Constitutional Court found that the lower court did not evaluate the freedom of the press and the right to be informed about the events of the present. It held that when policemen perform their duty during a public event, they should be allowed to be recorded and their picture published; however, when they are out of their official activity and no longer represent the State's legitimate power, then they deserve privacy similarly to other persons. (e.g., when they suffer in or after a violent action.)

182. In its 17/2016. (X. 20) decision, the Constitutional Court declared again that images of policemen in official duty are rightfully published in online journals.

175. Capital High Court (Fővárosi Ítélőtábla) Pf.20.656/2012/7.

In this specific case, the policeman was partly hidden in a police cap and sunglasses. The picture showed more than one person; it was neither degrading nor did it make an unpleasant impression, conveying an authentic image of the facts. The court decisions Kúria Pfv.IV.20.283/2015/4. and Capital High Court 2.Pf.20.186/2014/4. therefore were found to be unconstitutional and nullified.

183. Originally, the Criminal Code set a higher sanction for defaming official persons compared to ordinary persons. This undemocratic rule (§232) was annulled in Decision 36/1994. (VI. 24) ABh. Still, criminal defamation has remained part of the Criminal Code ever since, even after new codification, though it was renumbered to §226 and §227. The decision declared that the scope of freedom of expression is wider in the case of persons who exercise public power and politicians who are public figures, and even statement of untrue facts should be punishable only if the person who made the statement knew or – because of his or her profession – should have known that the statement was untrue. The court suggested that this principle should become part of the legal system through case law of the courts. However, this principle was not applied regularly by lower courts, and it was hardly transposed into civil law defamation (BH1998.270, BH1995.77).[176]

184. The decision 13/2014. (IV. 18) annulled decisions of two lower courts which found a journalist guilty of criminal defamation and sentenced him to a fine because of a critical article about the mayor's use of public money. The Constitutional Court declared that the courts interpreted the law contrary to the Basic Law.[177]

185. In the decision 34/2004. (IX. 28), the court declared that the immunity of Members of Parliament should extend to the defamation of other MPs, persons exercising public power or other politicians who are present in the public sphere. This was necessary because the law on the immunity of MPs set defamation (*rágalmazás és becsületsértés*) as an exception from the rule of immunity from criminal procedures.

186. In its decision 57/2001 (XII. 5.) on the right of reply to opinions, the Court examined an amendment to the Civil Code, that would have extended the existing right of reply to false facts to negative opinions as well. The court found that this law was unconstitutional because it did not define the limits of this right and because a compulsory fine was to be levied by the courts. It declared that protection of human dignity and reputation did not justify such an extensive restriction of free expression.

176. Lower court cases where the principle was not applied: 20.B.MV.35024/2008/12; 20.Bf.V.7908/2009/5; 20.B.24599/2007/14; 1.B.17/2009/8; 2.Bf.101/2009/6; 9.B.24.503/2007/18; 1.B.III.1770/2008/7; 14.Bf.521/2007/13. Decisions of higher courts reversing the previous decisions and applying the said principle while referring to this ABh or even the case law of ECHR: 3.Bhar.292/2009/10; 3.Bhar.341/2009/6, Bfv.II.699/2009/4.szám, 1.Bhar.339/2010/3.szám; 3.Bhar.32/2010/5; 3.Bhar.90/2008/7.szám. Other cases of higher courts, in line with the principle: 3.Bhar.232/2010/5, 3.Bhar.324/2009/4, 3.Bhar.2/2010/6, 5.Bhar.213/2008/12.szám; 5.Bhar.200/2008/5.szám.

177. 13/2014. (IV. 18) Constitutional Court decision.

§5. Case Law of the Constitutional Court on Pluralism and the Obligation to Provide Balanced Information

187. The complaint in the case 3350/2022. (VII. 25.) AB határozat was brought by the public service television MTVA, which was condemned in court for the following case: a youth association held a press conference in front of the office of an association for migrants, during which it stuck a sticker 'Organisation for the Support of Immigration' on the door of the association's office and made statements in its speech that were found defamatory by the association. The event was covered by several media outlets, including the ruling Fidesz party's website, and MTVA reported the event in its evening 18-hour news show. In its news, it republished the video by Fidesz. The association was not given an opportunity to respond, and its declaration was not covered later on either. The public broadcaster invoked freedom of expression and that the requirement of balanced information did not mean that it was obliged to include certain people in its programmes:

- The Constitutional Court gave a proper discussion of the justification of press freedom, citing, in particular, the previous decision 7/2014 (III. 7.) which held that the importance of press freedom is justified both as a fundamental subjective right and as a constitutional institution of democratic public opinion, and that Article IX(2) of the Fundamental Law, in addition to recognizing the freedom of the press, also orders the ensuring of the conditions necessary for the development of democratic public opinion.[178] It described clearly that information on issues that affect the public should always present opposing views, thus enabling the public to make informed decisions on the issue under discussion. However, the requirement of balance is not the same as pluralism: the former is an obligation that applies only to information programmes. The requirement of balanced information cannot therefore mean a second-by-second equality in the presentation of different opinions. The law cannot measure how the subjects of a report are treated or the tone of the reporter's voice or gesticulation. It is also important that the issue of balanced reporting is affected by the question of editorial freedom. In line with this, it is not possible to require that all opposing views must be presented in their entirety in every debate. Therefore, it will not in itself violate the requirement of balanced information if, in the course of the editorial process, a choice is made between the relevant views, represented with the necessary weight and in the appropriate proportion.
- The Court also referred to its decision 22/2021 (VII. 13.) in which it established that a linear television or radio programme may be considered balanced in accordance with Article IX(2) of the Fundamental Law if it meets, besides the general precondition that it is intended to discuss a matter of public interest, the following three criteria: (1) the programme clearly shows that there are several opposing views on the issue concerned; (2) it identifies which individuals or groups represent each position; (3) it makes it clear how the opposing views differ from the position set out in more detail in the programme (whether presented by the presenter, the interviewees or those who represent the position), exercising their

178. 7/2014. (III. 7.) Constitutional Court decision, at 40.

editorial freedom. It found that the case of press conferences was specific: the interest of the public debate requires the accurate publication of what is said in line with the topicality of the news.[179] The limitation of the responsibility of the press in reporting the statements of others is particularly relevant when the media disseminates statements by politicians at the forefront of public debate (as was the case in the present case). In this case, it cannot be ignored that 'what is said in public debate can be assessed by society with due care'.[180] It is an everyday part of this prudence that, following an incriminating statement by one of the participants in a political debate, those following the debate can safely rely on the response or refutation of the participant concerned, which will also appear in the public domain. Based on all the aspects and factors described, the report published by the applicant did not meet the requirement of balanced information.

188. The test developed in AB Decision 34/2017 (XII. 11.) (cited in the previous paragraph) has been further developed by the Constitutional Court in its subsequent practice. In its Decision 3217/2020 (19. VI.) AB, the Constitutional Court ruled that the content of a communication, including the content of a press article, must be assessed in its entirety, and its embeddedness in the political debate must also be taken into account.

189. Case 22/2021. (VII. 13.): On 16 December 2018, protests took place in front of the MTVA headquarters, demonstrating for an independent public media, among other things. Several MPs and MEPs entered the building, which led MTVA to initiate a property protection procedure with the district clerk. Following appeals, the case was upheld at the highest level of court. On the day of the ruling, the case was discussed with two lawyers in the MTVA evening studio meeting, and the opposition's opinion was not represented despite repeated inputs and prompts. The applicant submitted a complaint to the Media Authority for breach of balanced information, which was rejected (1292/2019 (XI. 12.)). Following different court judgments, at last, the Highest Court found against the plaintiff, who submitted a constitutional complaint against the final decision. The AB pointed out that, although the contested programme was a public service broadcaster, in the present case, there was no justification for examining the public service character of the programme and thus the public service criteria set out in Article 83(1) of the Mttv. because the judgments under appeal did not address that issue. Therefore, the Constitutional Court did not have to rule on the question of the balanced nature of the public service media but only on whether the Curia had assessed the balance of the specific programme and the requirement of balanced information in general in accordance with Article IX(2) (on freedom of expression) of the Fundamental Law. It found that: (1) although the invited guests expressed their own opinions on the judgment in the programme, the programme also clearly showed that there was a contrary position. The court established this based on the programme presenter presenting the court decision, which presupposes that there must have been an opposing party; (!) (2) it was clear from the programme which political parties took the

179. 34/2017. (XII. 11.) Constitutional Court decision, at 44.
180. 7/2014. (7 Mar. 2014) Constitutional Court decision, at 57.

opposite view; (3) although the programme in question did not indeed present the opposing positions in detail, the arguments of the interviewees in the programme, the references they made and the presented court decision showed the essential points on which the two positions differed. For these reasons, the Court rejected the complaint.

190. In the decision 16/2020. (VII. 8.), the Constitutional Court practically approved the creation of KESMA, the government-friendly press conglomerate that received more than 470 donated press outlets (*see* more on KESMA in Part I. Overview of Media Markets and Main Actors). This merger was extracted from the scope of the Competition Authority with a governmental decree that defined the merger as one with national importance. The Court found that the decision on whether a specific investment is of overriding public interest from a national economic point of view is a decision of economic policy decision, which is the political responsibility of the government. In its assessment of diversity as a constitutional value, the Constitutional Court held that the petition did not allege a restriction of fundamental rights, a violation of the substantive aspect of the fundamental right to diversity of the press, but a potential reduction of the related substantive aspect, the level of objective institutional protection, which creates a lower constitutional obligation to protect. The applicants have not referred to any other circumstances from which it could reasonably be inferred that the freedom and diversity of the press and the conditions for the free provision of information and information necessary for the development of a democratic public opinion are not generally guaranteed in Hungary.[181]

191. In the decision 1/2007 (I. 18), the Constitutional Court used the word 'pluralism' and the expression 'opinion pluralism' as the representation of several opinions in the media sphere, similar to the German expression '*Vielfaltigkeit*'. It stated that 'external pluralism' (*külső pluralizmus*) had been realized since the monopolistic situation of the public media had ceased and several private channels were accessible. However, it held that this does not eliminate the goal of 'internal pluralism' (*belső pluralizmus*) – this can be expected only from public service media or media outlets that have a significant influence on public opinion. Preserving the pluralism of opinions (*véleménypluralizmus*) can be a legitimate goal of restricting freedom of editing. The petition challenged the practice of the Complaints Committee which decided complaints on the lack of pluralism of broadcast media. The court ruled that those complaints that fell out of the legally defined categories (called 'other complaints', *egyéb panasz*)[182] meant an unnecessary restriction of freedom

181. 16/2020. (VII. 8). Constitutional Court decision.

182. The Complaints Commission issued an 'opinion' (vélemény) in these cases. This was invented because a majority of the complaints did not fulfil the legal (thematic and procedural) requirements. Although the opinions did not contain any obligation, only advices or suggestions, they meant an unnecessary chilling effect on freedom of the press. *See* more in: Judit Bayer, *Kiegyensúlyozottság és kampány a médiában* 93–108 (Péter Bajomi-Lázár, Róbert Kotroczó & Miklós Sükösd (ed.), L'Harmattan 2007); Judit Bayer, *A Panaszbizottság ügyei*, 3 Médiakutató (2001); Judit Bayer, *Gondolatok a szólásszabadságról az ORTT Panaszbizottsága kapcsán*, *in ELTE* Annales December (1998).

of expression. Therefore, they were unconstitutional and section 48(3) of the Rttv. got annulled. But the existence and the legally regulated procedure of the Complaints Committee were otherwise held constitutional.[183]

192. In the Mttv., the requirement to impart balanced information (opinion pluralism) has remained similar to the previous regulation. It is now the Media Council that deals with complaints because of the breach of obligation to impart balanced information in case of media service providers which have Significant Influencing Power (hereinafter: SIP media service providers, *see* paragraphs 503–509) and of public service media. In case of other media service providers, the Office of the Authority deals with the cases.[184]

§6. The Constitutional Court on Dissemination of False Rumours

193. During the COVID-19 pandemic, the criminal prohibition of scaremongering was extended (*see* paragraphs 209, 215), and the constitutionality of this extension was contested for being insufficiently precise, violating the principle of *nullum crimen sine lege certa,* and threatening expressions on matters of public interest. The Constitutional Court found that because only intentional commitment is a crime, criminal liability can only be established if it can be proven that the perpetrator was fully aware of the untruthfulness or distortedness of the facts. The offender's state of mind is a relevant factor here. If the published facts were disputed at the time of the offence, then the perpetrator could not know that they were untrue or that they were true and therefore cannot be held liable.[185]

194. In 2018, the court found that the criminal prohibition on the dissemination of false rumours (*rémhírterjesztés*) was unconstitutional because it was not sufficiently narrowly tailored but gave suggestions on how it could be more precisely formulated, and the Parliament passed new sections according to the court's suggestions.[186]

§7. The Constitutional Court on Liability for Online Comments: 19/2014. (V. 30) ABh and the Following ECHR Judgment

195. MTE is a non-profit association and the self-regulatory body of Hungarian Internet content providers. On its website, it published an article under the title 'Another unethical commercial conduct on the net' about two website services of a real estate management company, which operated using misleading practices (also

183. The Complaints Committee discussed complaints submitted by the public (often political parties or politically biased organizations) because of the violation of the obligation to provide balanced information. If it found the complaint well founded, it could oblige the media service provider to issue a statement.
184. §181 Mttv.
185. 15/2020. (VII. 8.) Constitutional Court decision.
186. 18/2000. (VI. 6) Constitutional Court decision.

examined by the consumer protection authority). The article attracted user comments, among them one which called the company a 'sly, rubbish, mug company'. Index, a popular online news portal, republished the article in its consumer protection column. In the commenting section, one user comment read as: 'People like this should go and shit a hedgehog and spend all their money on their mothers' tombs until they drop dead.'[187]

196. The Budapest Regional Court held that Index and MTE violated the company's right to reputation and held that the comments constituted edited content, using the analogy of readers' letters and the respondents were liable for enabling their publication, notwithstanding the fact that later on, they had removed them (The affected company did not contact MTE or Index before initiating the legal procedure).

197. The Court of Appeal held that the analogy to readers' letters was incorrect, but still, the websites were liable for the comments. It argued that the E-Commerce Act,[188] transposing Directive 2000/31/EC on Electronic Commerce into Hungarian law, did not apply to the applicants' case since it only related to electronic services of commercial nature, in particular to purchases through the Internet, and it did not extend to expressions made by persons acting outside the sphere of economic or professional activities or public duties, whereas the comments were private utterances; hence, the Civil Code was applicable for them.

198. *Kúria*, the highest court, held that by enabling readers to make comments on their websites, the portals had assumed objective liability for any injurious or unlawful comments made by those readers.

199. The portals' owners turned to the Constitutional Court, which found that the portals were liable because the identities of the primarily responsible commenters were unknown. Although it declared that comments were indeed non-private but public communication, it found that holding the ISP liable could be regarded as necessary, provided that no other remedy was available for the defamed party. Further, the court found this to be a proportionate limitation of freedom of expression, based on the logic that if those Internet Service Providers (ISPs) which moderated comments were liable for those, then also ISPs which do not moderate comments should be liable.[189]

200. The portals' owners then applied to the ECtHR, which found a violation of Article 10. It distinguished the case from *Delfi v. Estonia*[190] and found that the rigid stance of the Hungarian courts reflected a notion of liability which precluded a balance between the competing rights. It established that the comments in question did

---

187. ('*Azért az ilyenek szarjanak sünt és költsék az összes bevételüket anyjuk sírjára, amíg meg nem dögölnek.*').
188. Act CVIII of 2001 on Electronic Commerce, based on the Directive on Electronic Commerce.
189. 9/2014. (V. 30) Constitutional Court decision at [67].
190. *Delfi v. Estonia*, 16 Jun. 2015, ECtHR No. 64669/09.

not amount to hate speech and violence; therefore, it found that the notice-and-take-down system would have been an appropriate legal tool to provide redress to the affected company.

§8. The Constitutional Court on the Definition of Governmental Advertisements: 20/2016. (X. 28) ABh and 19/2016. (X. 28) ABh

201. During 2016, the government organized a popular vote: the question was: 'Do you want that the European Union should be able to prescribe, without the approval of our Parliament, the compulsory settlement of non-Hungarian citizens to Hungary?'

202. The government published posters and television advertisements which asserted the threat of migration, emotionally campaigned against the European plan of 'forced settlement' and tried to raise Islamophobia. The alleged purpose of the advertisements was to urge the citizens to participate in the popular vote, whereas the opposition's campaign urged people to boycott the vote.

203. The emerging legal question was whether the government's advertisements were political advertisements – which on television are limited to campaign periods – or 'social purpose advertisements'. The National Election Commission (Nemzeti Választási Bizottság (NVB)) held that they were social purpose advertisements; the *Kúria* held they were political advertisements. The Constitutional Court annulled the *Kúria*'s decision and decided that it was not political advertising because the message did not try to influence the voters concerning how to answer the question.

§9. Other Constitutional Court Decisions Relating to Press Freedom

204. In the case initiated by Klubrádió for non-renewal of its frequency licence, the Constitutional Court rejected the complaint.[191] According to the petitioner, section 48(5) of the Mttv. violates the right to fair procedure under Article XXiV(1) of the Fundamental Law, as it grants the Council of the Media a discretionary power. This section orders that the licence cannot be renewed if the media service provider has repeatedly or seriously infringed the licence contract or the media laws, and this has been established in a final decision. The incriminate infringement was the failure to provide data in time. The petitioner cited an example where the Media Council had not interpreted the exclusion condition set out in section 48(7)a) of the Mttv. in such a strict manner in relation to other broadcasters. However, the Court found that the named sections should not be interpreted as obstacles to the freedom of the press or the development of democratic public opinion because those are content-neutral and apply equally to all broadcasters subject to the Mttv. It emphasized that

191. 3064/2022. (II. 25.) Constitutional Court Decision.

the previous courts correctly found that there was no possibility to review those earlier administrative decisions that were used as the basis for non-renewal of the licence.

205. The decision 3/2015. (II. 2) ABh was passed in relation to an alarming decision of the Capital Administrative and Labour Court which found[192] that an article had illegally interfered with the market, violating the principles of the Fair Competition Act (Tptv.) and scaring off investors. The article reported on news and possible outcomes of the events at the Norwegian oil fund and its effect on the Hungarian oil company MOL. The Constitutional Court established[193] that the prohibition of market influencing shall be interpreted so that it does not infringe on the freedom of the press, emphasizing that it is the press' duty to verify the veracity of the information published and to convey it without misleading the public. As there was no such misleadingness proven, and the facts were not contested, the decision unconstitutionally restricted the freedom of the press.

206. The NVB accepted a complaint on violation of fairness of political campaign and found that X had violated election principles. X turned to the Constitutional Court, which found[194] that negative allegations in an election campaign are protected by freedom of expression if they are made with the view of helping citizens make decisions. This decision also referred to 31/2014. (X. 9) ABh decision which had a similar content.

207. In its decision 20/2007. (III. 29.) on the telecasting of parliamentary sessions, the court found no violation of the constitutional right of freedom of expression in the fact that the sessions of the Parliament could be recorded only from certain places. The court found no violation of the constitutional right of freedom of expression. It held the following: 'This restriction was necessary to ensure the peace of the Parliament's work, and in the interest of objective and factual informing that ensures the development and prevailing of democratic public opinion. It is a proportionate restriction compared to the protection of fundamental rights and constitutional values.'

208. In two connected decisions (13/2000. (V. 12) and 14/2000. (V. 12) Constitutional Court decisions), the court found that it is not unconstitutional to prohibit the insult of national symbols (§269/A of old Criminal Code, §334 in new Criminal Code) because no other legal instrument could effectively achieve the same – legitimate – goal. Similarly, the court found that the prohibition of showing or using the symbols of the hammer and crescent, the red star, the swastika, the arrow and cross[195] and the SS badge did not violate the constitutional right of freedom of

192. Fővárosi Közigazgatási és Munkaügyi Bíróság 26.K.33.829/2013/6.
193. 3/2015. (II. 2) ABh.
194. 5/2015. (II. 25) ABh.
195. Symbol of the Hungarian national socialists from 1933 onwards.

expression. In the decision from 2013, the red star was erased from the list of symbols.[196] However, Parliament re-enacted it with a narrower scope: instead of just using or showing these symbols, the prohibition applies to disseminating, using in public or showing in public in a manner which is capable of disturbing public peace, especially in a manner which is capable of injuring the dignity of victims of dictatorships.[197]

196. 4/2013. (II. 21) Constitutional Court decision.
197. §335 Criminal Code, inserted by amending Act XLVIII of 2013.

Chapter 5. Possible Restrictive Measures That May Be Applied by Courts and Cases Where They May Apply

209. Since the COVID-19 pandemic, some meaningful restrictions have been introduced that curtail the freedom of speech or FOI. In September 2020, the government announced the emergency situation that allowed regulation by governmental decrees (paragraphs 125, 293 and 306). The emergency situation was lengthened numerous times, later due to the war against Ukraine. In particular, the crime of distributing false rumours (scaremongering) was extended during the COVID-19 crisis (*see* below, §202, Criminal Code §337). The amendment was criticized for being unnecessary because the existing rule would have sufficiently served the purpose. However, the Constitutional Court found the provision to be in harmony with the Constitution (*See* paragraph 195).

210. A new Civil Code was passed in 2013, with some changes to the rights attached to the person and their remedies. The Civil Code allows the person whose personal rights were violated to demand the following: (a) to have the fact of violation declared by court; (b) to have the violator stop the violating behaviour and be prohibited from continuing it; (c) to have the violator provide gratification either by a declaration or otherwise, and to give it publicity on the costs of the violator; (d) to have the perpetrator to terminate the detrimental situation and to restore of the original situation; and (e) that the economic gain achieved by way of the infringement of rights shall be transferred to him or her.[198] This latter point was inserted into the new Civil Code in 2013. If the infringement of personal right also violates public interest, the public prosecutor – with the approval of the entitled person – may file a suit and enforce all legal consequences except for compensation. In this case, the economic gain achieved through the violation of rights shall be transferred to public purposes. Compensation for damages may also be required based on the general rules of liability.[199] Besides, compensation for the offence can be demanded for the non-pecuniary damages. Under the new code, no damages shall be proven beyond the fact of the offence.[200]

211. In case anyone seriously insults a community or does so with unjustly hurtful expressions, any member of the community whose personality's important feature is to belong to the Hungarian nation or any other national, ethnic, racial or religious community is entitled to enforce personal rights within thirty days from the injury.[201]

212. Infotv., allows for protest against treatment of personal data (§21) as well as enforcement by court (§22) and compensation (§23).

198. §2:51(1) Civil Code.
199. §2:53 Civil Code.
200. §2:52 Civil Code.
201. §2:54(5) Civil Code.

213. Act XLVIII of 2008 on commercial advertising (§§5–22) can be enforced in administrative procedures either by the State Supervision of Financial Institutions, the Consumer Protection Office, or the Competition Office.

214. Act II of 2012 on offences, offence procedures, and the registry system of offences: §180: Insult. The possible sanctions include a fine between Forint (HUF) 5,000–150,000, confinement, or public labour.

215. The Criminal Code contains the following provisions and sanctions:

- §219: Misuse of personal data: one, two or three years of imprisonment.
- §220: Misuse of public data (to conceal, falsify or publish false public data). Imprisonment up to two or three years.
- §223–224: Injury to private secret or mail secret: up to one year/up to three years in qualified cases.
- §225: To humiliate a helpless person and to record or publish such record. Up to two or three years.
- §§226–227, 228: Defamation: the possible sanction may be imprisonment of up to one year or up to two years, depending on the circumstances.
- §226/A–B: Recording and publishing a defaming, falsified picture or video: one, two or three years of imprisonment.
- §265: Misuse of qualified data (State secrets) custody, or up to one year, three years, five years or eight years of imprisonment, depending on the circumstances.
- §331: Incitement for war: at least one, at most five years of imprisonment.
- §332: Incitement to hatred: the possible sanction may be imprisonment for up to three years.
- §333: Public denial of the sins of national socialistic or communistic regimes: up to three years of imprisonment.
- §334: Insulting a national symbol: the possible sanction may be imprisonment for up to one year.
- §335: Using symbols of dictatorships: the possible sanction may be a fine.
- §336: Incitement against law or ordinance: the possible sanction may be imprisonment for up to three years.
- §337: Distributing false rumours (disturbing the public peace): In 2020, an amendment was made. A second subsection was added, and the first subsection was narrowed to cases when the action is made in relation to public danger:
  (1) Whoever makes false allegations or spreads rumours or distorted facts, either on the scene of public danger or publicly in relation to the public danger, in a way that is capably to incite confusion or unrest among a larger group of people, is sanctionable up to three years imprisonment.
  (2) Whoever, during times of emergency, makes false allegations or spreads rumours or distorted facts publicly in a way that is capable to hinder or frustrate defence, shall be punished form one to five years of imprisonment.

- §338: Threatening the public with danger: the possible sanction may be imprisonment for up to two years or five years, depending on the circumstances.
- §384–388: Violating intellectual property rights: the possible sanction may be imprisonment for up to ten years, depending on several circumstances.

216. Act CLV of 2009 on the Protection of Qualified Data (State Secrets) – sanctions in the Criminal Code.

217. Act LXXVI of 1999 on Intellectual Property Law – violations of intellectual property rights may entail a civil procedure, or a criminal procedure, or even a procedure by the National Taxation and Customs Authority.

218. Court decisions are not precedents in the Hungarian legal system. The High Court of Justice (*Kúria*) may issue decisions on legal unification (*jogegységi határozat)* which are, however, compulsory in lower courts.

Part II. Regulation of Print Media

219. The new Act on Media Services and Mass Communication (Mttv.) handles print media and online journals under the same set of rules and calls them 'press products' (*sajtótermék*). The Act on Freedom of Expression and the Fundamental Rules of Media Content (Smtv.) also extends to print media and online journals beyond audiovisual media and radio. The Constitutional Court decision and the following amendment of the law by Parliament somewhat narrowed the scope of content restrictions.[202] The amendment passed in May 2012 maintained the effect of Smtv. on press products but introduced several exceptions. Currently, the obligation to provide balanced information and respect human dignity and sponsorship rules do not apply to press products. The obligation to respect privacy was abolished completely. But content that may be harmful to minors may be published in press products only in a way which ensures that minors do not have access to it, or, if this is not possible, with a notification.[203]

220. Mttv.'s effect on press products was not examined by the Constitutional Court. Therefore, the Media Council of the Media and Telecommunication Authority has the power to impose sanctions on press products if the content rules or the rules on registration are violated.

221. The new Criminal Code introduced a new sanction: making electronic data irrevocably inaccessible.[204] This can be applied in the following cases: if the data realizes a crime, if they were used as tools for a crime, or if they were created through crime. If such a sanction can be foreseen, already in the stage of investigation, it is possible to make information temporarily inaccessible, either by ordering the hosting provider to make the information inaccessible[205] or by ordering the service provider to block access to the information.[206] Both can be ordered only by a judge and only in criminal procedure, only in cases that are prosecutable through public prosecution (unlike, for example, defamation or insult). They work as an

202. 1746/B/2010 Constitutional Court decision.
203. §16 of Act LXVI of 2012, adding s. (1a) to §2 of Smtv., excluding §§13, 14(1), 19(1–2)(4) and 20(8–9) from being effective on press products, effective from 19 Jun. 2012.
204. §77 Act C 2012 on Criminal Code.
205. §336 Act XC of 2017 on Criminal Procedure.
206. §337 Act XC of 2017 on Criminal Procedure.

injunction: immediately enforceable without regard to an appeal. They are registered and administered by the Authority.[207] More on the sanctioning right of the Authority can be read in Part V below, in paragraphs 539–564.

222. The definition of 'press product' – which refers to printed press and online journals – is as follows:[208]

> §1. 6. Smtv.
> Press products are the issues of daily or other newspapers, printed or online journals, which are provided as a business service, for which a natural or legal person assumes editorial responsibility, and the primary purpose of which is to disseminate content, consisting of text or pictures to the public, in order to inform, entertain or educate. Editorial responsibility means the responsibility for the actual control of selecting and constructing media content, and does not necessarily entail legal liability in case of press products. An economic service is a service that is independent, business-like, profit-oriented, pursued systematically, and under economic risk-taking. Blogs can also qualify as online journals if they fulfil these criteria.

223. However, the law does not use the expression 'press product provider', only 'press product's publisher' – and 'publisher' is not defined in the law. Still, the Mttv. lays responsibility on the press product's publisher.[209] Traditionally, it was the editorial board which took responsibility for the content of the press and not the publisher – hence the expression 'responsible editor' (*felelős szerkesztő*).[210] 'Editor' is not defined by the law either, although the expression 'editorial responsibility' is used (not defined either).

224. Launching a printed or online press product needs registration.[211] The previous Press Law required notification, where no response had to be received from the Ministry, and publication could be started immediately. After a long fight, the Mttv. was amended to this effect, too, in 2011. The substantial difference lies in the possibility under the Mttv. to impose a sanction (*see* paragraph 195). Nevertheless, these rules were found constitutional by the Constitutional Court in its decision. Registration shall be requested from the Media and Telecommunication Authority

207. §337 (3–4) Act XC of 2017 on Criminal Procedure. In cases the service provider would not abide within the one-day deadline, the court may levy a fine.
208. Media content includes press products and media services. The definition for media services is 'media service provider' (*médiaszolgáltató*), which means the provider of audiovisual services, literally – 'the natural or legal person, or company without legal personality, which or who has editorial responsibility for the choice of the content of media services and determines its construction, but not necessarily legal liability.' §1(2) of Smtv. The section follows the definition of the AVMS Directive's definition of 'media service provider', which says: 'the natural or legal person who has editorial responsibility for the choice of the audiovisual content of the audiovisual media service and determines the manner in which it is organised'. (Article 1d) AVMS Directive).
209. §3 Mttv.
210. *See*: §18(2) a of the previous Press Law (Act II of 1986, effective until 31 Dec. 2010).
211. §5 Smtv., §46 Mttv.

within sixty days after starting the activity.[212] The Authority shall register the press product within fifteen days and may withdraw registration or erase the press product from the register only in certain well-defined cases, mainly related to the title's similarity to another outlet's title or if publication of the journal was not started for two years after registration, or otherwise it was not published for five years, as well as some other cases.[213] In 2012, a new cause for deletion from the register was inserted: it is prohibited to include in the title of a press product (or media service) the name of a person who had a leading role in twentieth-century dictatorships (funding, building or maintaining it), or the name of an organization or an expression which can directly relate to a twentieth-century dictatorship. This condition shall be examined, and if necessary, the opinion of the Hungarian Academy of Sciences shall be acquired.[214]

225. However, under the Mttv., violation of the rules on registration may be sanctioned with a fine of HUF 1 million.[215] As the rules on administrative matters are quite strict, it is not unlikely that fines will be levied for this reason in the future. For example, all the data of the press product must be reported to the Authority within fifteen days after any change (name, domicile, email or telephone number, name of contact person, company or other registration number of the publisher, title).[216] The law allowed six months for online press products to register after stepping into effect. In practice, the Office of the Authority was not able to process the many applications for registration until months after the legal deadline.[217]

212. §42(2) Mttv.
213. Other cases are: the founder or the publisher of the press product falls under the rules of incompatibility – he or she is the National Media and Telecommunication Authority's president, vice president, director, vice director; or the Public Service Fund's Board of Trustees' or Public Service Body's chairperson or member; director of the Fund, chairperson or vice chairperson of the National Telecommunication and Informatics Council; or member of the Media Council. Scientific or academic journals are an exception. (§46(3) Mttv.).
214. §41/A Mttv., inserted by Act CLXVII of 2012.
215. §46(8a) Mttv. The sanction was inserted after negotiations with the European Commission. Upon request of the Commission, the law allowed that publishing is started before registration, but a sanction was inserted in case the rules are not respected. Smtv. still allows that a law passed by Parliament in future may order registration as a condition of starting publication of press products (§5 Smtv.).
216. §46(7) Mttv.
217. §46(4) Mttv.

Chapter 1. The Journalistic Profession

226. Anybody can work as a journalist in Hungary; no education is required, and there are no special rules or conditions either. The 2010 law on *press freedom and fundamental rules of media content* does not give a definition of the word 'journalist';[218] in fact, it does not even use this word. Instead, it uses the expression – 'media content provider' (*médiatartalomszolgáltató)* which includes providers of printed and online journals, as well as of linear and on-demand audiovisual media and radio. Where the laws refer to journalists, they use the expression – 'the media content provider, its employee, or person in other employment-like-relationship' (*a médiatartalom-szolgáltató, annak munkavállalója vagy a médiatartalom-szolgáltatóval munkavégzésre irányuló egyéb jogviszonyban álló személy*).[219] Instead of this long definition, I will use the word 'journalist' in this monograph.

218. The previous Press Law, Act II of 1986 defined journalists as: persons pursuing information providing as their profession (*a sajtónál hivatásszerűen tájékoztatási tevékenységet végző személy*).
219. For example in §§6, 7, 21 of Smtv.

Chapter 2. Journalists' Rights

§1. Role of Journalists as Watchdogs of Society

227. The 2010 media law ensures protection for journalists from prosecution in case they breached the law in order to acquire public interest information, on some conditions as follows: (1) the information could not have been acquired in any other manner or only with disproportionate difficulty; (2) the violation of law did not cause a disproportionate or grave injury; (3) the breach was not against the law on State secrets. The exemption does not grant immunity against tort lawsuits.[220]

228. This rule was motivated by cases in which journalists of news programmes on commercial television provoked or participated in illegal actions so as to be able to record the action on camera. On one occasion, a reporter arranged to acquire an illegal parking card from the local authorities and recorded the process on a secret camera (2008). Police suspected him of falsifying official documents. In another case, reporters violated privacy when recording someone's illegal action with a secret camera and broadcasting the report.

229. Besides the general rules on access to public information,[221] media content providers are specifically entitled to receive the necessary information to fulfil their jobs.[222] However, in practice, journalist's work is still often hindered by civil servants' reluctance to give information.

§2. Journalists' Independence

230. The new Smtv. ensures journalists' protection against pressure from the media content provider's owner, sponsor or advertiser. The labour law obligation to perform instructions that would breach editorial or journalistic freedom shall not apply to journalists.[223] In practice, many journalists are employed by way of a 'mandate' contract rather than an employment contract. This deprives journalists of the protection provided by the Labour Code to all employees, such as paid holidays, sick leave, childcare leave, notice periods and others.[224]

231. Press products' founders and publishers shall be independent of the Authority and the public service media. This is ensured by rules on incompatibility. Founders or publishers of press products cannot be the National Media and Telecommunication Authority's president, vice president, director, or vice director; or the Public Service Fund's Board of Trustees' or Public Service Body's chairperson

220. §8 Smtv.
221. Act CXII of 2011 on informational self-determination and freedom of information.
222. §9 Smtv.
223. §7 Smtv.
224. *See* more in: Tóth Borbála, *Labor Relations and Media – Analyzing the Patterns of Labor Relations in the Media of SEENPM-Member Countries.* Hungary, https://www.mirovni-institut.si/data/tinymce/Novice/Labor%20Relations%20and%20Media_SEENPM.pdf, 2007.

or member; director of the MTVA, chairperson or vice chairperson of the National Telecommunication and Informatics Council; or member of the Media Council. Scientific or academic journals form an exception.[225]

§3. Protection of Journalistic Sources

232. This has been among the most controversial parts of the 2010 law, which was widely criticized by both international and domestic organizations and experts (*see* paragraph 122) and extensively examined by the Constitutional Court. The Constitutional Court vetted the law using Article 10(2) and the practice of the ECtHR. The court declared that the restrictions shall be defined clearly in law, with procedural guarantees that protect journalists even against illegitimate interference by investigative authorities, typically before a judicial review is possible. It found that the protective measures' function is primarily to protect the confidential relationship between the journalist and his source. It declared that the press' function is to serve the public and not to help the work of the authorities and that journalistic sources should only be subsidiary compared to other tools of evidence, and the regulation should reflect this. It also declared that prioritizing State secrets over journalistic secrets without respect for the individual circumstances of the case is a disproportional restriction of press freedom. It called attention to the fact that if documents and hard drives of the journalist may be seized by the authority, then the protection of sources remains merely declarative. The court also ordered that §155 of the Mttv. had to be amended so as to protect journalists from the unlimited investigative powers of the Authority. It declared that the rules on journalistic sources will be constitutional only if the journalist is able to deny revealing his confidential sources, and the procedural laws set out clear provisions on the exceptional cases when, under judicial supervision, the journalist might be obliged to cooperate with the authorities.

233. The requirements set by the Constitutional Court were fulfilled by Parliament on 24 May 2012. The amendment created a complex set of regulations through amendments to the Acts on Criminal Procedures, Civil Procedures, Administrative Procedures, and Offences, which effectively exempt journalists from giving testimonies about confidential issues, with narrow exceptions.[226]

234. In civil cases, journalists are allowed to deny testimony if their testimony would disclose the identity of a person who passed on information to them in relation to their journalistic activity. The denial applies only to those questions that are related to the identity of such a person.[227] In administrative cases, journalists are allowed to withhold an object that would otherwise be confiscated, to withhold data,

225. §46(3) Mttv.
226. New §170(1)(f), (6) and §396/A of Pp.; New §82(1)(d), (6), §83(4), §152(5), §207(2), §215(5a), §293(4), §601 of Act XIX of 1998 on Criminal Procedures; New §50/A(2), (2a), (5), §51(4), (4a), (4b), §53(4), (8), §57/A(7), §172o).
227. §170(1)(f) of Pp.

to deny testimony, or to not present an object of proof. Although the authorities may oblige the journalists to do so, journalists may appeal against the resolution.[228] In criminal cases, journalists are allowed to deny giving testimony if, with the testimony, they would disclose the identity of a person who gave information to them in relation to their journalistic activity; the denial again applies only to questions relating to the identity of the person. Court may oblige journalists to disclose the identity of the person, if it is inevitable to reveal a crime which can be punished with imprisonment of three years or longer, and if this proof is not substitutable.[229] The journalist may appeal this resolution.[230] During investigation of offences, journalists are allowed to deny giving testimony or to present an object of proof.[231]

235. The Smtv. declares that journalists are entitled to keep the identity of their sources confidential and to deny the transfer of any document, object or data storage device which is suitable to identify the source of information. In order to investigate a crime, in exceptionally justified cases defined by law, courts may oblige the journalist to disclose the source of information and to pass a document, object or data storage device which may be suitable to identify the source of information.[232] The legal amendments eliminated the right of authorities to disclose confidential sources, the lack of protection relating to official or State secrets and the public interest needed to justify the publication of the information.

236. In addition, the investigative rights of the Media Council were limited in the interest of protecting confidential journalistic sources in the amendment of May 2012. The Media Council may not oblige journalists to present information or a document which would disclose the identity of his or her confidential sources.[233]

237. In July 2011, police heard an investigative journalist as a witness and demanded that he reveal his confidential sources which he denied. The police seized his hard drive. The witness made a complaint at the Constitutional Court. Interestingly, the journalist's constitutional complaint was rejected, but the court found the lack of procedural guarantees for journalists relating to source protection in the whole legal system generally unconstitutional.

---

228. 50/A(2), §51(4) (c), §53(4)c, §57/A(7) of Ket.
229. §82(6) of Act XIX of 1998 on Criminal Procedures.
230. §215(5a) and §293(4) of Act XIX of 1998 on Criminal Procedures.
231. §29(2)d, 60c, 60/A, 70(2a), 76(1a) Act II of 2012 on Offences (the original act effective from 15 Apr. 2012).
232. §6 Smtv. effective from 3 Jul. 2012.
233. §155(5)b Mttv., effective from 18 Jun. 2012.

Chapter 3. Journalists' Liability

§1. General Information on the Liability System

238. As shown in Part I, several laws apply to journalists, and several restrictions appear at more than one point in the legal system. For example, protection of reputation appears in the Civil Code which may entail compensation for damages,[234] in the Smtv.[235] which may entail a rectification or a procedure by the Media Council[236] and also in the Criminal Code which may result in a fine or even imprisonment.[237]

239. After the 2010 law stepped into effect, there was a small confusion as regards the liable parties. In court practice, generally, the author of the piece and the editor had been sued jointly. The publisher usually had not been held liable (the previous Press Act held the publisher liable only for 'his or her obligations').[238] However, the 2010 laws define as liable parties the 'content provider' (who is not clearly identified and was non-existent in court practice) and the publisher (who was not previously held liable) but do not mention the journalist (or employee of the content provider) or the editorial board among the liable parties. In August 2011, an amendment inserted into the Code on Civil Procedural Order added the possibility to sue editorial boards as well (which are neither natural nor legal persons; they are not mentioned by the Smtv.).[239]

240. The Smtv. and the Mttv. define the liable parties as follows:

- Media content providers are liable for respecting the Smtv.[240] (courts, after some hesitation, not only identified content providers as the publishers of the press product but also accepted the suing of editorial boards as well, to conform with the previous practice).
- Publishers of a press product shall be liable to respect the Mttv.[241]
- Executive officers of a press product or a media service provider can be made liable for hindering the supervisory procedure of the Authority or for not disclosing the required data or not disclosing it in due time. The fine is HUF 3 million and it is compulsory to impose it in case of repeated infringement of the law.[242]
- Executive officers of a press product or a media service provider may be fined up to HUF 2 million in case of repeated violation of the law.[243]

---

234. §2:53 and Part Four, Title XXVI. Civil Code (Act V of 2013).
235. §12, 14, 16 Smtv.
236. Theoretically so, but actually there has been a co-regulatory agreement concluded between the Media Council and associations of the press and media.
237. §226–227 of Act C of 2012 on the Criminal Code.
238. §18(1) Act II of 1986 on Press (effective until 31 Dec. 2010).
239. §342–343 of Pp.
240. §21(1) Smtv.
241. §3 Mttv.
242. §156(3) Mttv.
243. §187(1) Mttv.

– Pp. orders that media service providers, editorial boards of press products and news agencies may be sued for not providing a right of reply.[244]
– Programme distributors and ISPs can be obliged by the Media Council to suspend or terminate distribution of a media service or to suspend an online press product, and they can also be sanctioned if they do not comply.[245]

241. New elements in the media regulation are the liability of the executive officers of media content providers[246] and the liability of ISPs and distributors for suspension/termination of the distribution of a media service or a press product.[247]

§2. Defamation and Libel

242. Defamation and libel are not differentiated from each other in the Hungarian language; therefore, I will refer to both as 'defamation'. Rather, the legal system differentiates between 'defamation' and 'insult'; the first is committed by statement of untrue facts, while the latter can be committed by opinions as well. Defamation is regulated at several points of the legal system – in the Civil Code (protection of reputation),[248] the Criminal Code,[249] and the Code of Offences.[250]

I. Civil Defamation

243. The new Civil Code made small but important changes to the regulation of civil defamation. First, it introduced insult into civil law: expressing an unjustly insulting opinion can be a violation of law: §2:45 Civil Code (Protection of honour and reputation, *A becsülethez és jóhírnévhez való jog*):

1. Violation of honour shall be especially an opinion which is suitable to negatively influence a person's social reputation, expressed in an unjustly hurtful manner.

The old rule of civil defamation remained intact:

– Violation of reputation shall be especially when someone states or distributes an untrue, offensive fact about another person, or makes true facts appear in false light.

244. *See* more in Hungarian at *Ismét módosultak a sajtó-helyreigazítás szabályai*, http://batki.info/index.php/ismet-modosultak-a-sajto-helyreigazitas-szabalyai, 2 Sep. 2011.
245. §188 Mttv.
246. §156(3) Mttv., §169(4) Mttv., §187(1) Mttv.
247. §188, §187(3) bh Mttv.
248. §2:45 Civil Code.
249. §226–227. Criminal Code.
250. §138 Act II of 2012 on Offences, effective from 15 Apr. 2012.

Second, it codified the already existing court practice when public personalities' personal rights are treated differently from the perspective of defamation:

> §2:44: Exercising fundamental rights that ensure free discussion of public matters may limit the personal rights of public personalities in a necessary and relative manner, without hurting human dignity.

This paragraph was tailored by the Constitutional Court because it originally contained also the conditions 'for respectable public interest' (*méltányolható közérdekből*).[251] The court held that discussing public matters is already in the public interest, and there is no need to further examine if there is any other, specific, 'respectable' public interest beyond that.

244. A compensation for damages and right of reply may also be claimed in such a case. *See* in more detail above, paragraph 182.

245. A decision of the Supreme Court declares that the limits of speech are wider in the case of public figures, by principle (BH2004.104, BDT 2010.2215.I). Whether a person is regarded as a public figure depends not on the person's position, status or his or her notoriety. It is the legal aspect of the situation in question which is relevant (BDT 2011.2420.I). Especially during election campaigns, the aspirants must withstand being criticized and being shown in a disadvantageous light by their political opponents (BDT 2011. 2592. I). This principle was applied by several court cases ([sic] 3.P.20460/2008/4; 2. Pf.20839/2008/5; Pf.I 20350/2007/5). The Constitutional Court formulated similar principles in relation to criminal defamation (36/1994. (VI. 24) CC decision), which is often referred to by ordinary courts also in civil procedures (Pfv.IV.20708/2007/5; 2. Pf.20839/2008/5; Pf.I.20350/2007/5; 2. Pf.20839/2008/5; Pf.I.20459/2009/9).

246. Several court cases refer to the hate speech decision of the Constitutional Court in order to support the protection of opinions, which also declared that opinions are protected without regard to their value or truth (30/1992. (V. 26) CC decision, referring to decisions largely the same as shown above: Pfv.IV.20708/2007/5; 2.Pf.20839/2008/5 – the latter also refers to the practice of the ECtHR).

247. True facts cannot establish violation of reputation under civil law (Pf.I.20350/2007/5).[252] The court also reiterated that public figures must tolerate even exaggerated opinions and strongly emotional value judgments. The same principles were declared in Pf.I.20145/2005/3.

248. Similarly, opinions enjoy more protection than untrue facts. Value judgments do not violate reputation; even if their content is contrary to the views of others, they are protected by freedom of expression (Pf.I.20376/2007/3).

---

251. 7/2014. (III. 7) Constitutional Court decision.
252. This is an important difference with criminal defamation where true facts can also result in a violation under certain circumstances (*see* paras 230–231).

II. Criminal Defamation

249.

§226. Criminal Code (Defamation, *rágalmazás*)
Anyone who alleges or rumours a fact that is capable of injuring the honour of another person or uses an expression directly referring to such fact commits an offence (*vétség*) and shall be punished with imprisonment up to one year, public work or a fine. If the defamation is committed ignominiously, or with great publicity, or causing a significant injury to interests, the punishment shall be imprisonment for up to two years.
§226/A. Criminal Code (Making defamatory false audio or video record)
Anyone who, in order to harm the reputation of another person, makes a false, falsified audio or video record or one with untrue content – if no other crime is committed – shall be punishable for up to one year imprisonment.
§226/B. Criminal Code (Publishing defamatory false audio or video record)
Anyone who, in order to harm another person's reputation, makes a false, falsified audio or video record or one with untrue content accessible shall be punishable for up to two years imprisonment. If the crime is committed with great publicity or causes significant harm, the punishment may go up to three years.
§227. Criminal Code (Insult, *becsületsértés*)
Anyone who – beyond the scope of §179 – uses an expression capable of injuring the honour of another person, either in connection with that person's fulfilment of employment or public commission, or public interest activity, or does so publicly, shall be punished with imprisonment up to one year, public interest work, or a fine. The injury can be realized by action as well (assault).
§228. Criminal Code (Insult of the dead, *kegyeletsértés*)
Anyone who defames a dead person or its memory in a way defined in §§226–227 shall be punished in the same manner as defined there.

250. Criminal defamation and insult may be persecuted only upon a private motion,[253] and both may be initiated also besides a civil procedure. Both criminal defamation and insult may be committed by stating true facts if the statement of the facts is not justified by public interest. In the wording of the law – proving the truth may be an excuse. But applying this proof is allowed by law only if the allegation was reasoned by public interest or by someone's legal interest.[254] Insults can also be committed by statements of opinion if they are capable of injuring one's honour. Although the law threatens both crimes with imprisonment, typically only 'reprehension' or a fine are applied as sanctions.

251. The making and publishing of defamatory false audio or video records were inserted in 2013 as new crimes. The trigger was a false video that was used in a political campaign in local elections in September 2013 in the town of Baja to give

253. §231 Criminal Code.
254. §229 Criminal Code.

evidence of election fraud. The video later proved to be falsified. Critics have said that the category of defamation was enough to deal with the case, and there was no need to add two new categories to the Criminal Code.[255]

252. Imprisonment was applied in only one case since the collapse of communism. The Court of Second Instance suspended the imprisonment of ten months for a two-year probationary period. The editor and the journalist of a journal accused an MP of being responsible for the execution of several of his fellows after the revolution in 1956, alleging that when he was in arrest, being an accused himself, he had disclosed others' activity to the authorities in his testimony, who were then hanged as a result. The court found that these were statements of untrue facts rather than opinions or value judgments. The court found that although the defamed person was a public figure, according to the principles defined by the 36/1994 Constitutional Court decision, the journalists were guilty of defamation. The mentioned principles hold that freedom of expression can be limited in such cases only if a person intentionally states untrue facts or, because of his or her professional duty, if he or she should have known that the facts were untrue. The court found that this was the situation in said case. In a third instance supervisory procedure (*felülvizsgálati eljárás*), the Supreme Court found that the lower courts mistakenly held that the defamation caused a serious injury of interests and therefore mitigated the sanction to fines (EBH2005.1193).[256]

253. Criminal defamation was the subject of a case which ended up in Strasbourg: a journalist was convicted for stating that a special Hungarian wine product was 'shit' (20. Bf.7368/2009/6). ECHR established violation of Article 10; *see also* above in paragraph 160.

254. Intentionally stating an untrue statement about a public figure does not justify applying a criminal sanction for defamation, especially if the statement is not capable of injuring one's reputation (Bhar.I.131/2008/4). This judgment also referred to the Constitutional Court decision which set the limits of speech wider in the case of public personalities. However, allegations which – in case they are true – may serve as a basis for criminal procedure against a public figure are beyond the limits of freedom of expression. Proving the truth shall be ordered in such case (BH2011.186).

255. Value judgments that were formulated through true statements that were albeit capable of injuring one's reputation but were not abusive did not establish defamation, as it would have resulted in a disproportionate restriction of the freedom of expression (Bhar.III. 356/2008/6).

255. http://mertek.hvg.hu/2013/10/29/harom-csapas-a-videobunozokre/.
256. About the decision, *see*, Judit Bayer, *'Hol a határ?'* in *Élet és Irodalom*, Vol. XLVIII, 7, (2004) 13 February.

256. A musician known for his provocative lyrics wrote injurious lyrics about – among others – a certain public figure. The court referred to both mentioned Constitutional Court decisions (30/1992. and 36/1994) and found that the expressions were not as injurious which should not be tolerated by a public figure, they were not obscene and they did not insult the reputation of the subject person (5.Bhar.200/2008/5).

257. Lower courts found it injurious that a representative of a local government called his fellow representative illiterate and partly educated (*félművelt*). However, the High Court declared that freedom of expression can be limited by the tools of criminal law only in very exceptional cases. It referred to Decision 36/1994 of the Constitutional Court (Bfv.II.699/2009/4).

258. An emblematic public figure of the radical right accused a blogger who insulted him. Although the Court of First Instance convicted the blogger, the second instance court and then the High Court acquitted him and referred to the said Constitutional Court decision (20.B.MV.35024/2008/12; 20.Bf.6953/2009/6; 3.Bhar.292/2009/10).

259. The court found that although the statements were capable of injuring the public figure's reputation, the action was not dangerous for society – which would be a constitutive element of any crime[257] (2.Bf.69/2009/4). The court referred to both mentioned Constitutional Court decisions.

260. A journalist accused a mayor and the local representative body of irresponsible management, misappropriation and malpractice. The court found this to be within the limits of freedom of expression, referring to the 36/1994 Constitutional Court decision (Bhar.37/2008/5). The courts also found in favour of the accused – and freedom of expression – in cases 1.Bf.106/2010/2; or in 2.Bf.408/2006/4; 2.Bf.156/2007/4.

261. However, in other cases, the court established the crimes of insult or defamation:

- A person against whom a policeman took measurements expressed his doubt regarding the policeman's mental capabilities and his capability to perform his job while also using obscene expressions. The court found that he committed insult (9.B.267/2009/23; 1.Bf.525/2010/3).
- Suggesting through the press that the mayor abused his powers and caused damage to the citizens of his town constituted criminal defamation according to the court in case 3.Bf.218/2008/4.

---

257. §4 Criminal Code. According to (2) of §10, an action is dangerous to society if it injures or endangers the order of Hungary or the rights of its citizens. '*társadalomra veszélyes cselekmény az a tevékenység vagy mulasztás, amely Magyarország állami, társadalmi vagy gazdasági rendjét, az állampolgárok személyét vagy jogait sérti vagy veszélyezteti*'.

– The court found using a certain idiom capable of constituting insult, even if used against a public figure (you do not shit at the place where you eat) B.278/2007/7; 4.Bf.961/2008/11.

III. Insult as Offence

262. See also in paragraph 185:

> §180: Act II. of 2012 on offences, offence procedures, and the registry system of offences; Insult.
>
> Anyone, who uses an expression capable to injure the honour of another person, or performs other similar action, commits an insult. Only upon private motion shall an offence procedure be started.

IV. Press Law

263. Even after the Constitutional Court review, a rule that prohibits showing persons in a humiliating, exposed situation, when it is for its own sake and derogatory, remained in the Press Law, applying also to printed press and online journals. The rule may be enforced by the Media and Telecommunications Authority.[258]

264. In May 2012, a further rule was inserted, supposedly to protect the talk show participants. According to this, a contract between a participant in media content and the media content provider may not limit the participant's right to enforce his or her rights to reputation, honour or privacy. If there is such a provision in the contract, it shall be deemed null and void.[259]

§3. Hate Speech

265. The new Civil Code in 2014 introduced a new provision which makes it possible for the victims of hate speech to sue under the civil law:

> §2:54.(5) 'In case anyone insults a community seriously or with unjustly hurtful expressions; any member of the community whose personality's important feature is to belong to the Hungarian nation, or other national, ethnic, racial or religious community, is entitled to enforce personal rights within 30 days from the injury'.[260]

258. §14(2) Smtv., §132a), 182c) Mttv.
259. §15(4) Smtv., effective from 19 Jun. 2012. The Media Council is not entitled to monitor compliance with this rule.
260. §2:54(5) Civil Code.

All legal consequences may be enforced within thirty days by the person harmed or by the public prosecutor.[261] In case a financial gain was achieved through the unlawful action, its revenue shall be transferred to public purposes.

266. The Criminal Code also regulates the following actions:

- incitement to hatred against communities;
- infringement of national symbol;
- use of symbols of dictatorships;
- public denial of the crimes of national socialist and communist regimes.

267. In a landmark decision in 1992 – discussed in detail in paragraph 172 above – the Constitutional Court set a high threshold for hate speech crimes. Consequently, although public discourse became more and more radical, courts never (except in one case below) found anyone guilty of incitement to hatred. Racist speech became gradually accepted in public speech and recently found its way even in Parliament.[262] Court declared that the danger must be imminent and the perpetrator shall recognize this danger and wish the occurrence of the violent consequence in order to declare him or her guilty. Going beyond the content of the Constitutional Court decision, courts even declared that someone who incites hatred, calls upon performing violent actions, and the occurrence of the violent actions shall be realistic and directly threatening.[263] Before the Civil Code amendment became effective, the government amended the Basic Law's rules on freedom of expression in order to prepare room for the civil law form of hate speech regulation, which was previously annulled by the Constitutional Court.[264]

268. In the first and the last court decisions, when someone was found guilty of incitement of hatred, direct intention was not required to establish this crime; someone who was aware that his expressions were objectively suitable to incite hatred was held to have committed this crime (BH1998.521). A year later, the Supreme Court approved the decision, but at the same time issued a decision of principle (*Elvi Bírósági Határozat*, EBH1999.5), which held that the perpetrator shall grasp the possibility that the hatred incited may grow into intolerant, excluding, depriving, even violent behaviour.

269. Using the symbols of dictatorships has a wider scope of application. Two such cases ended up in Strasbourg at the ECtHR (*see* the cases above in paragraph 160). These cases were predominantly occupied with the usage of the red star.

270. Hate speech provisions in the Smtv. create a lower threshold of liability for media content providers. The Constitutional Court examined the law but found this

261. §2:54(4) Civil Code.
262. *See* for example the minutes of Parliament on 3 Apr. 2012. The minutes of the Parliament are no longer accessible, only the minutes of a committee meeting that investigated the incident. https://www.parlament.hu/documents/static/biz39/bizjkv39/EMB/1204111.pdf.
263. BH2005.46.
264. Article IX, (4–5) Basic Law (part of the notorious Fourth Amendment of the Basic Law).

specific piece of regulation in accordance with the Constitution (*see also* paragraph 171). Smtv. provides a prohibition to incite hatred against or to exclude any nation, community, national, ethnic, linguistic or other minority, or any majority, or any church or religious group.[265] The rule may be enforced by the Media and Telecommunications Authority.[266]

§4. Privacy

271. Privacy, in its literal sense (*magánélet védelme*), does not have a long history in the Hungarian legal system. Instead, the law uses the formula 'protection of personal data' (*személyes adatok védelme*) which provides somewhat different protection, albeit for the same purpose.

272. Protection of personal data is regulated by the Civil Code and by the Law CXII. of 2011 on informational self-determination and freedom of information which is effective from 1 January 2012 (and which replaced the Act LXIII of 1992). The Regulation (EU) 2016/679 of the European Parliament and of the Council of 27 April 2016 on the protection of natural persons with regard to the processing of personal data and on the free movement of such data, and repealing Directive 95/46/EC (General Data Protection Regulation (GDPR)) and the Directive 2002/58/EC concerning the processing of personal data and the protection of privacy in the electronic communications sector (Directive on privacy and electronic communications) also apply.

273. The Civil Code provides a general protection of personal rights, among them the protection of someone's image and voice records. Recording or publishing of any of these needs the consent of the affected person, with the exception of the public appearance in the public interest (*nyilvános közszereplés*). This means that the criterion is not whether the person is a public figure but whether, on a specific occasion, he or she intentionally appeared in public. A person performing his job in a public space is not a public figure (BDT 1999. 4).

274. Protection of business secrets and private secrets is also part of the Civil Code.[267]

275. For violation of privacy rights, the different legal remedies found in the Civil Code may be demanded, which were discussed in detail in paragraph 182. The most frequently applied remedies are compensation for damages and symbolic gratification.[268]

265. §17 Smtv.
266. §132(a) Mttv.
267. §2:46–47 Civil Code.
268. Part Four, Title XXVI. Civil Code.

276. The new law on *personal data protection* and FOI abolished the position of the ombudsman for protection of personal data and access to public information[269] (*See* §281 for further details). Instead of this institution, the new law established the National Authority for Data Protection and Freedom of Information.[270] Beyond the powers similar to the ombudsman, the new institution will also have the right to impose a fine, in the sum from HUF 100,000 up to HUF 10,000,000, in case the rules on personal data are violated so that it affects a large number of persons or sensitive data, or may cause grave injury of interests, or threatens with damages.[271]

277. The rules on personal data allow a very limited use of personal information (these rules have not been changed by the Orbán Government). The GDPR, effective from 25 May 2018, is directly applicable also in Hungary, like in all Member States of the EU. As the Hungarian rules on data protection have been relatively strictly protecting personal data already since 1992, the GDPR rules did not bring a dramatic change in the perspective. The Infotv (*see* §297) has remained in effect to complete the rules of GDPR. Under domestic law, personal data may be collected only if the person gave his or her consent or if law orders so (law may define a scope in which local ordinances may also order so). Sensitive data may be handled only if the person gave his or her written consent or law orders so for public purposes (in cases of data relating to health, pathological addiction or crime), or (in cases of data relating to racial, national, ethnic origin, political opinion or party membership, religious or other conviction, trade union membership, sexual life) if it is necessary to apply an international treaty, to enforce fundamental rights contained in the Basic Law, or ordered by law in the interest of national security, the prevention or prosecution of crimes, or defence purposes.[272] In practice, these rules mean that the press can publish very little personal information, including pictures.

---

269. §23–27 of Act LXIII of 1992, effective until 31 Dec. 2011. The person for this position was elected by two-thirds majority of the Parliament for five years, from persons who have a university master degree, clean slate, outstanding theoretical knowledge or at least ten years of professional practice, and have meaningful experiences in procedures relating to the protection of personal data. The ombudsman had rights to receive complaints and investigate them, summon or notify those private or public organizations that violated the rules on data protection or access to public information, start a court procedure and a procedure of the Constitutional Court, recommend amendments to the laws, make recommendation and a report – but it did not have sanctioning rights. Instead, he applied the power of publicity, and the influence of his personal reputation. Some of the ombudsmen were often critical of practices of governmental institutions.
270. §40(1) Infotv. The president of this Authority is recommended by the Prime Minister, and appointed by the President of the Republic for nine years, from among persons who have a law degree, have the right to be elected in parliamentary elections, are Hungarian citizens, and have at least five years of experience in supervising procedures affecting data protection or FOI, or acquired a doctoral degree in any of these fields.
271. §60(4), 61(3) of Infotv.
272. §5 of Infotv. In addition, the new law adds several exceptions from the consent principle. Many of these are motivated by the need to make debt collection easier, and lowered the legal age to give consent to 16 years (§6).

278. The new Civil Code made even taking a picture or a voice record of someone conditional upon the person's approval. Exceptions are records or photos of a mass of people and public figures who attend a public event (in their capacity as public figures).[273]

279. For example, abuse of portrait was established when a picture taken of a minor with consent of the parent is used – without further consent – for advertising purposes (10.P. 20619/2006/23; Pf.I. 20329/2007/3).

280. Policemen's faces shall not be shown in pictures or television programmes when they carry out their official activity in a public place. The court referred to Constitutional Court decision 54/2000. (XII. 18) which declared it constitutional that members of the police are identifiable through a name shield or signs on their uniform.

281. The Smtv. brought a detailed provision for the protection of interviewees, which may have been motivated by events in talk shows or reality shows. It was further completed in May 2012 by another section which explicitly protects the privacy of the participants (This is also discussed above in paragraph 230). The original rules provide that the agreement to have someone's statement published or shown in media content may be retracted, unless it was made by a person performing public duties or political figure in connection with his or her public duties, or it is related to an event that is of importance for the citizens of Hungary or members of the Hungarian nation, or if it was made in relation to an event of the local, national or European public life. The new rule inserted in May 2012 provided that it is legally impossible to resign the right to enforce one's right to privacy, reputation or honour.[274]

282. The rules on sensitive data entail that once a person has been suspected of a crime, his or her personal data qualify as sensitive data and cannot be used without written consent. Therefore, press products refer to these persons by the initial letters of their names. However, before an official suspicion is raised, papers often publish the names of those people who are involved in a crime that attracts public interest. After a certain person is officially suspected, they can publish only the acronym. But, in case the whole name was published previously, this does not always ensure the incognito of the suspect any more. A ministerial decree governs what information police may disclose to the press in the investigative phase of a criminal procedure.[275]

283. All personal data that has been disclosed to the Media and Telecommunications Authority in the course of its procedure shall be kept confidential, and all employees of the Authority are obliged by law to keep these secrets.[276] If anyone

273. §2:48(1–2) Civil Code.
274. §15(4) Smtv., effective from 19 Jun. 2012.
275. 26/2003. (VI. 26) BM-IM joint decree (*együttes rendelet*).
276. §147 Mttv.

makes an announcement at the Media and Telecommunication Commissioner, he or she may ask that his or her identity is kept confidential.[277]

§5. Protection of Minors and Advertising Restrictions in Press Law

284. Smtv. also imposes certain restrictions for the protection of children:

> §19 (3) Smtv.
> Any media content that may seriously impair the intellectual, psychological, moral or physical development of minors especially by containing pornography or extreme, unjustified violence, may be published only together with a technical or other solution that ensures that minors cannot get access to it. In case a technical solution is impossible, then a notification shall be published about the possible threat to minors.[278]

285. In addition, the new amendment of May 2012 added a new section relevant to press products as well: 'It is prohibited to show a minor in any media content in a way that greatly endangers his or her moral or physical development, according to his or her age.'[279]

286. The Smtv. also sets detailed rules on advertising, which also apply to press products. Beyond the general rules that are laid down in the Act on Advertising (Act XLVIII of 2008), the Smtv. prohibits the advertising of drugs and healing procedures. It also orders that advertising be easily recognizable and prohibits covert advertising, advertising which insults religious or similar feelings, and advertising which spurs unhealthy, unsafe behaviour or behaviour that harms the environment.[280]

---

277. §141 Mttv.
278. The Media Council, using its right provided by §10(6) and §11(3) Mttv., issued a recommendation on the technical solutions recommended for linear and on-demand media services, but the question of press products have been left intact. In practice, online journals give a pop-up warning and require ticking 'I am over 18' for content considered not appropriate for minors.
279. §19(4a) Smtv.
280. §20 Smtv., the Mttv. contains more detailed rules on advertising, but those apply only to audiovisual media and radio.

Chapter 4. Right to Reply

287. The right to reply or rectification (*sajtóhelyreigazítás*) used to be regulated in the Civil Code,[281] but the new media regulation has transferred it to §12. Smtv. The rules were inserted into Smtv. practically without any changes:

§12. Smtv.

1. Anyone, about whom in any media content an untrue fact is stated, rumoured, or true facts are shown in false light, may demand the publication of a rectification, which shows which statements were untrue or unfunded, or which facts were shown in false lights and what are the true facts.
2. The rectification shall be published within five days after the reception of such a claim in a manner and extent similar to the objectionable part of the publication by daily papers, online press products and news agencies; in the case of on-demand media services within eight days after the reception of the claim, in a manner and extent similar to the objectionable part of the publication; in the case of other papers within eight days after the reception of the claim in the next issue, in a manner and extent similar to the objectionable part of the publication; and in the case of linear media services within eight days, in similar manner and the same part of the day, as the objectionable/objected part of the publication.

288. Rectification can be demanded by the person affected within thirty days after publication from either the media service provider, the press product's editorial board, or the news agency. Publication of the rectification may be denied only if the truthfulness of the reasoning in the claim can be rebutted immediately.[282] In case the media content provider or the news agency does not fulfil the request for rectification, the affected person may start a civil procedure against them within fifteen days after the last day of the publication obligation. The burden of proof is on the publisher. Only proof that is readily available on the trial and that is capable of confuting the claim's allegations immediately or proving the truthfulness of the publication may be applied. The rectification is an objective sanction – if the statements were untrue, it applies regardless of whether the media content provider knew or should have known that they were untrue.

289. In the draft of the Smtv., a right of reply would have been extended to any content that infringed somebody's honour or human dignity.[283] In 2001, there was a similar legislative attempt to extend the right to reply to opinions as well (*lex Répássy*), but the law was nullified by the Constitutional Court.[284]

281. §79(Old) Civil Code, effective until 31 Dec. 2010.
282. §342 of Pp.
283. Original version of §12(2) in Bill T363, amended by amendment T363/21. Accessible at: http://www.parlament.hu/irom39/00363/00363-0021.pdf.
284. 57/2001. (XII. 5) ABh. The act was sent to the Constitutional Court by the President of the Republic before promulgation, using his right of constitutional veto – thus it never stepped into effect.

290. Compulsory legal unification resolutions were issued by the court in the matter of rectification. These formulated the following principles:

- The statement shall be examined as a whole rather than isolated parts of it.
- The real content of the statements shall be considered, with special regard to the context and the social concepts.
- Unimportant details and mistakes do not form a basis for rectification.
- Statement of opinions, value judgments, critiques and debates of social, political, scientific and artistic nature cannot form a basis for rectification.[285]
- Only persons who are unambiguously identified in the statement – either by name or any other method – may ask for rectification.[286]
- The affected person may ask for the publication of his reply letter. In case it is not published, the court may oblige the press to do so, defining the text of rectification itself.
- The rectification must contain which statements of facts are untrue, which are shown in false light and what are the true facts. The text shall not be formulated so that it loses its rectifying nature.[287]
- Truth shall be proven by the press outlet, even if it published another person's or press outlet's statement.
- Informing the audience about a criminal procedure in progress or a criminal judgment not yet legally final shall not form a basis for rectification. However, if the criminal procedure does not lead to conviction, the press outlet is obliged to give information about that upon request of the affected person.[288]

291. Untrue facts shall form a basis of rectification even for public figures; however, other expressions of critical opinion fall in the realm of freedom of expression (5.P. 21702/2005/6). Rectification may be awarded even if the untrue facts are not injurious to reputation (Pfv.IV.21.982/2011/4.szám).

292. A police officer's mental and professional capabilities were belittled in an article by making allegations about his or her educational background and professional experience. Although the allegations were partly untrue, the court found that the article as a whole constituted an expression of opinion and was therefore not subject to rectification, the same applied with regard to the public office that the policeman fulfilled. A reference to his or her past as being an agent of the national secret service III/III department was, however, unproven statement of facts; therefore, rectification was awarded in that respect (Pfv.IV.22.014/2010/5.szám).

285. PK 12.
286. PK 13.
287. PK 15.
288. PK 14.

Chapter 5. Access to Public Information

§1. Legal Background

293. Since 1992, protection of personal data and access to public information have been treated under the same law in Hungary. This law has been replaced by the Act CXII of 2011 effective from 1 January 2012 (Infotv.), but the structure has been retained. In 2020, a governmental decree restricted access to public information during an emergency situation. This decree (*see* below under §1), along with 106 other decrees, remains in effect due to the lengthened emergency situation, now because of the war.[289] Further laws governing the area are:

- Act XC of 2005 on electronic freedom of information.
- Act XXXVIII of 1992 on public finances (§15/A-18).
- Act CLV of 2009 on qualified data (State secrets).

294. In 2013, an important amendment stirred debate around the Infotv. The first version of the amendment was passed by Parliament only two days after the submission of the bill. The President of the Republic sent the law back to Parliament for reconsideration, and the watchdog organizations expressed their deep concern regarding the vague restrictions that the bill formulated. The amended version somewhat softened the criticized parts. One of the controversial amendments is the new §30(7) which orders that a separate law – which would require a simple majority of the votes, unlike Infotv. – shall govern those data requests which target the whole economic activity of a Public Service Body in an itemized manner or based on its books and accounts. If a data request is denied because of this, the requesting person may initiate an examination at the Information Authority. The amendment clearly hinders the activity of NGOs to inquire documentation about the use of public money (The original version of the amendment prohibited 'abusive data requests' and did not provide any possibility to review. Compared to that, this is a narrower restriction).

295. Another important amendment was necessary because a new Civil Code stepped into effect on 15 March 2014. The new Civil Code omitted a provision which the old Civil Code contained on how information on economic activity financed from the public budget or EU funds forms an exception to business secrets. The new §27(3), (3a) and (3b) of Infotv. says that any information connected to the use, possession, handling, utilizing, disposing or encumbering of State or local government property, central or local budget, EU fund, public budget allocation or allowance, or acquiring any right relating to such shall be public information and form an exception to business secrets. Publication, however, shall not result in a disproportionate injury to business interests unless access to the information is not possible otherwise.[290] A new provision is added to further oblige any person who gets

289. *See* Act XLII of 2022 on the prevention and management of the consequences in Hungary of an armed conflict or humanitarian disaster in a neighbouring country.
290. §27(3) Infotv.

into business or financial relationship with the State budget (even indirectly) to give information about the legal relationship on any public information defined above.[291] If the information is denied, the requesting person may turn to the body which exercises legal supervision of the person holding the information.[292]

296. The position and office of the Data Protection Commissioner (ombudsman) were terminated on 1 January 2012, and a new authority was created instead: the National Authority for Data Protection and Public Information. The Authority belongs to the government, and its head is appointed by the president upon recommendation of the Prime Minister, while the commissioner was elected by the Parliament with a two-thirds majority and was truly independent of the government.[293] Academic analysis found that the reorganization was not based on legitimate policy goals.[294] The Data Protection Commissioner, who was elected in 2008 for six years, was thus removed from his office three years ahead of his legal termination of office. The ECJ found that early removal of the commissioner breached the requirement of independence incorporated in the Directive on Personal Data.[295] After the ECJ ruling, the Minister of Justice apologised to the commissioner and wished him success in his further professional activity.[296] Besides, a compensation was paid to him from the central budget.[297]

297. Even before the amendment, while the legal background could be called satisfactory, Hungarian authorities were often reluctant to publish public information. This tendency is now clearly strengthened by making it even more difficult for civil society to get access to public information. A new civil organization emerged in 2011 which dedicated its activity solely to FOI (*Átlátszó*, meaning: Transparent). The Hungarian Civil Liberties Union (TASZ) also has a long history of fighting for this freedom, and it has initiated several court proceedings.[298] Several of these cases were won by HCLU, but in several other cases, the court approved the denial of access to the information, which was a sign that the practice of the Hungarian law is more restrictive than its wording.[299]

298. The Constitutional Court annulled the decision of the Supreme Court which approved previous court and administrative decisions that denied access to public information. The Constitutional Court annulled the decisions and declared that they violated the fundamental right to public information.[300]

---

291. §27(3a) Infotv.
292. §27(3b) Infotv.
293. www.naih.hu.
294. http://real.mtak.hu/135192/2/jogelmeletiszemleforgacs.pdf.
295. Case C-288/12, *see also* http://europa.eu/rapid/press-release_MEMO-14-267_en.htm.
296. http://os.mti.hu/hirek/98715/az_igazsagugyi_miniszterium_kozlemenye.
297. http://nol.hu/belfold/bocsanatkeres-es-69-millio-errol-szolt-a-megallapodas-1473191. The case is similar to the case where the leader of the Highest Court, András Baka, was illegally removed from his office. After the Court of Strasbourg established the violation of his freedom of expression (*see* §165 above), he was given compensation, but no reinstatement into his position.
298. For example: 2.Pf.20.520/2010/4.
299. For example: Pfv.IV.20.276/2008/10.szám, Pfv.IV.20.871/2008/9.szám.
300. 5/2014. (II. 14) Constitutional Court decision.

299. Public contracts between the Media Council and the media service providers were not published. The public contracts of both national commercial radios and the two national television channels were renegotiated after the legislative reform in 2011. The Media Council did not allow access to information about the new media service fees[301] because Mttv. allows media service providers to define which information shall be treated as secrets.[302] Átlátszó managed to acquire these contracts in 2013 which proved that the frequency fees were indeed lowered in 2011 (while the irrationally high fees promised in the tender were keys to both radio's successes in 2009). The contracts of the two national commercial television channels were acquired by the TASZ in a court procedure in 2013.

300. The TASZ filed a lawsuit for the publication of plans for the extension of *Paks* Nuclear Plant.[303] The court decided in favour of the applicant. This was preceded by a similarly successful court case in the same subject matter.[304]

301. TASZ filed a lawsuit against the National Security Office (*Nemzetbiztonsági Hivatal*) for data whose qualification has lapsed. At first instance, the court rejected the application, and at the second, it accepted it. In the third turn, the Supreme Court annulled the final decision and maintained the effect of the first instance judgment. TASZ submitted a complaint to the Constitutional Court (19.P. 20069/2007/4; 8.Pf. 20524/2007/6; Pfv.IV. 20871/2008/9).

302. An investigative journalist filed a lawsuit to get access to the documents of an investment (motor-centre) financed by public money. During the trial, the defendant gave partial access to the documents. The court obliged it to give full access (with two exceptions) (22.P. 20941/2010/9).

303. State-owned companies were obliged to give access to the data on salaries, bonus payments and severance payments of their senior executives. The motion was filed by a journalist and the courts in all three instances ordered publication of the requested data (19.P.23385/2008; 2.Pf.20001/2009/3; Pfv.IV.21148/2009/6). Public duty is not narrowed to official duty. All bodies using State property perform public duty and thus are under the effect of the law on FOI (BDT 2005.1216.I). A private company performed selective garbage collection upon a contract concluded with the local government. The contract was requested and the request was rejected by the

301. 1987/2011. (XII. 20); András Pethő, Elsumákolt díjjal hömpölyög tovább a rádióbotrány, http://www.origo.hu/itthon/20120328-mediatanacs-az-advenio-es-az-fm1-mediaszolgaltatasi-dija.html, origo, 29 Mar. 2012; Krisztina Nagy, Egy szűkszavú közlemény titkai, in Mérték Médiaelemző Műhely, http://mertek.postr.hu/egy-szukszavu-kozlemeny-titkai, 19 Dec. 2011; Gábor Polyák, Titkok és hazugságok – az országos médiaszolgáltatók szerződései, in Mérték Médiaelemző Műhely, http://mertek.postr.hu/adatigenyles, 22 Mar. 2012.

302. §153(2) Mttv.

303. *Példás gyorsasággal – atomerőmű v. nyilvánosság.* http://tasz.hu/informacioszabadsag/peldas-gyorsasaggal-atomeromu-v-nyilvanossag, 18 Jan. 2012.

304. Szekszárdi Városi Bíróság, 13.Gf. 40.024/2011/4.szám. https://tasz.hu/cikkek/peldas-gyorsasaggal-atomeromu-v-nyilvanossag/.

company, arguing that their activity falls outside public services. Court ordered giving access to the data ([sic] 24.P.86199/2009/5; 47.Pf.635861/2009/1).

304. The Supervisory Authority of Financial Institutions denied access to documents and minutes born in the course of preparing a certain resolution. In the court procedure, the court examined whether the applicant defined the requested documents with the necessary preciseness and whether fulfilment of the request during the trial shall be deemed as a lawful fulfilment of the FOI request. The authority could not give ample justification for denying access to the requested documents, so the court obliged it to reveal those (38.P. 21849/2009/5; 2.Pf. 21425/2009/4).

305. A civil association sought access to management data of a parking company (which collects parking fees). The company rejected fulfilment of the request because of alleged non-existence of the information and because the request was not precise enough. Court obliged the company to reveal its income but not to reveal how it were spent and how much was distributed to the local municipalities (1.P.86732/2008/8, 47.Pf.638836/2008/4, Pfv.IV.20962/2009/4).

I. Emergency Situation

306. In 2020, the government announced the emergency situation, which has been lengthened since then up until today, when closing this manuscript. Among other measures, it also issued a decree on derogations from certain provisions on requests for data during an emergency.[305] This included restrictive measures on public information requests. Among others, the time to fulfil or reject such requests was raised to forty-five days (lengthened once with another forty-five days).

307. The government did not publish local and regional epidemic data, unlike all other EU Member States,[306] 'in order to avoid panic'.[307] No death rates of hospitalised patients were published, which was assessed as above 80% at the peak of the pandemic.[308] The governmental information presented the Russian Sputnik and the Chinese Sinopharm vaccinations as the most effective, which data was put into doubt by Katalin Karikó biochemist[309] who criticized the lack of age and other data in the statistics (*See* §345 for censorship on public television). The published official data were not corrected later. At the same time, the official information on the victim, although anonymised, could be promptly re-identified based on their age,

305. Government Decree 521/2020. (XI. 25.) on derogations from certain provisions on requests for data during an emergency.
306. https://444.hu/2020/03/17/az-osszes europai-orszag-kozol-teruleti-adatokat-a-koronavirusos-betegekrol-kiveve-magyarorszagot.
307. https://infostart.hu/belfold/2020/03/19/kormanyinfo-tiz-tizenotszoros-a-lappangas-szazezres-lehet-a-megbetegedes.
308. https://who.maps.arcgis.com/apps/dashboards/ead3c6475654481ca51c248d52ab9c61%20, https:/coronavirus.jhu.edu/map.html.
309. Katalin Karikó is Hungarian-American biochemist who specializes in RNA-mediated mechanisms, ex vice president of BioNTech.

gender and other (sensitive) data, in one specific case revealing a stigmatizing illness of the British vice-ambassador.[310] According to the position of the Data Protection Authority, the published data were not personal data because they were anonymised – re-identification was not examined.

II. Public Documents and Meetings

308. The Act on Electronic Freedom of Information discusses the publicity of all official public institutions. The Parliament publishes on its website the bills and all documents relating to them, like amending proposals, commission recommendations, the minutes of the parliamentary discussions, statistics of votes, and the minutes of the committees where the bill was handled. If either the committee meeting or the parliamentary session gets restricted from the public, then the minutes are not public either.

309. All laws and regulations are published in the official journal *Magyar Közlöny*, which is now accessible online, too: (http://www.magyarkozlony.hu/). Other legal instruments to be published in the journal are:

- Court decisions that are meant to provide a legal unification (*jogegységi határozat*) and decisions of the National Election Committee (*Országos Választási Bizottság*).
- All non-normative actions of the Parliament, the President of the Republic, the Prime Minister or the National Election Committee (with some exceptions) and certain non-normative actions of the ministers are also published in the official journal.
- The Constitutional Court has the right to order certain decisions to be published in the official journal.

310. The current, daily updated versions of laws are publicly accessible in the National Collection of Laws (Nemzeti Jogszabálytár, https://njt.hu/) and the former text versions of laws are also accessible. Other private databases exist, but search and track-changes functions are limited, full functions are available only for subscribers, with fees tailored for law firms.

§2. Court Hearings

311. Court hearings are generally public. This principle is declared in Article XXVIII(1) of the Basic Law.[311] The Constitutional Court discussed this question in

310. https://jog.tk.hu/blog/2022/07/informacioszabadsag-es-covid-magyarorszagon.
311. The formulation is very similar to the equivalent sections of the previous Constitution (§57).

its Decision 58/1995. (IX. 15) ABh on limiting publicity in the interest of the privacy of the accused, and in 20/2005. (V. 26) ABh on limiting publicity in the interest of a more rapid and simple procedure. There is not one general regulation on the publicity of court hearings and documents, but it is governed by several fields of law, primarily procedural acts.

312. Pp. allows the court to exclude the public from part or the whole of the trial, if it is absolutely necessary in order to protect State secrets, official secrets, business secrets or other secrets defined by law in the interest of public morals or upon the request of the party, if it is justified in the interest to protect his or her personal rights. In addition, the public may be excluded from the hearing of witnesses in order to protect the life or bodily integrity of the witness or his or her relatives.[312]

313. The Act on Criminal Procedures allows the court to restrict publicity on the trial or part of it upon the initiative of the prosecutor, the accused, the defence lawyer, the victim or the witness, for reasons of public morals, or in the interest of a minor, or for the protection of a witness, of State secret or official secret.[313]

314. The *OIT* passed its Decision 100/1999. (XII. 1) on the publicity of procedures and Regulation No. 7 of 1999 on the press contact person who shall release official information to the press, be available for interviews and make official statements and a press plan.

315. Even if the public is excluded from trial, the judgment must be announced publicly in civil cases without exception.[314] In criminal cases, parts of the judgment may be announced by restricted publicity if the information is to be kept confidential.[315]

316. In criminal procedure, voice and image recording may be done with the permission of the judge (the chairperson of the judge council). In civil procedure, no permission is needed, but the court may define the manner of the recording. Recording may be prohibited if it disturbs the trial. Parties and other civil participants of the trial may be recorded only with their consent, but the judge, prosecutor, defence attorney and the keeper of the minutes may be recorded without consent.

317. The data protection ombudsman criticized the lack of a unified legal regulation and reported that representatives of the press are often required to pre-register in order to attend a court trial, and what is worse – the list of attendees is limited and discriminative. In his report, the ombudsman found that publicity of court trials is not appropriately ensured, thereby violating the freedom of expression, the right to get information, and the rule of law.[316]

312. §5(2) Pp.
313. §237(3) Act on Criminal Procedures.
314. §5(3) Pp.
315. §239(2–3) Act on Criminal Procedures.
316. 1439/2009 OBH jelentés.

318. The law on judicial organization sets out detailed rules on the publicity of the trials, the right to access the court buildings and their safety conditions.[317]

§3. Court Documents

319. A court judgment database was established in 2007; however, it is inconsistent, and its search functions are unreliable. To give an example to its impracticality, the judgments bear a different name in the search database than their legal reference. All judgments appear in a downloadable Word document, and each of them bears the same name (anonim.rtf), which makes searching among several downloaded judgments even more embarrassing. Only court decisions after 1 July 2007 form part of the database; each is anonymized (the names of the parties erased from the decision) in the interest of protecting privacy, even those cases which gained public attention and where the parties are well-known public figures. This makes searching after the names of the parties impossible.

320. According to the law on *electronic freedom of information*, only decisions of the Supreme Court (*Kúria*) and those of the Tables of Judgments (*Ítélőtábla*) have to be published compulsorily. It is not obligatory to publish decisions on standing orders (warrants for payment, *fizetési meghagyás*), executive actions (*végrehajtási határozat*), decisions in company registry cases (*cégbírósági határozat*), in insolvency procedures *(csőd – és felszámolási),* other registration cases of courts (*bíróságon vezetett névjegyzékekkel kapcsolatos*) and all decisions of lower courts (lower court decisions are published only if they are reviewed in higher courts). In certain cases, like those relating to family matters, the judgments are not published if any of the parties request not to, while in cases relating to sexual criminal offences, the decisions are published only if the victim requests so.[318] Other decisions may be ordered to be published by the chairperson of the court.

321. The OIT (OIT, Regulation No. 2007. 3) brought an implementation regulation on publishing and anonymizing court decisions. According to this, the decisions that are published are only:[319]

- decisions in merit of the Supreme Court (*Kúria*);
- decisions in merit of the Table of Judgments (*Ítélőtábla*);
- judgments that review administrative decisions, in case the procedure was one-staged and no appeal is possible: such are the court decisions that review the Radio and Television Board (ORTT) and the NMHH;
- preceding decisions of a published decision in the same case;

317. §13, §167–171 Bszitv.
318. §17(7–8) Act XC of 2005 on electronic freedom of information.
319. §16–17 Act XC of 2005 on electronic freedom of information.

– legal instruments issued by the courts: decisions for the unification of law (*jogegységi határozat*), court decisions on principles (*elvi bírósági határozat*); collegium opinions (*kollégiumi vélemény*), principle decisions (*elvi döntés*) and collegium positions (*kollégiumi állásfoglalás*).[320]

322. The lack of lower court decisions makes the database unreliable, especially as it does not provide information on whether a decision does not exist or is not published. The public policy think tank *Eötvös Károly Intézet* (EKINT) prepared a detailed report on the database. According to EKINT's report,[321] the database's operation does not fulfil the requirements of Act XC of 2005 on electronic freedom of information because lay persons are unable to find court decisions easily and because the scope of published decisions is unjustly limited.[322]

323. The TASZ requested access to the complaints submitted to the Constitutional Court, which was denied. The civil organization demanded the public data in court, but it was unsuccessful. Finally, HCLU turned to the ECtHR, which established the violation of Article 10 for not disclosing the complaint of a parliamentarian pending before the Constitutional Court.[323]

§4. Meetings of the Parliament

324. Audience can sit at the place appointed by the Speaker of the House.[324] Their number is defined by the Speaker of the House.[325] The public sessions are recorded, edited and distributed by a single company specifically designated and commissioned by the Parliament. The videos are distributed on a closed video system to the media service providers, who may join the system at their own cost. The signals shall be transformed into a real-time video programme which will be published on the online homepage of the Parliament.[326] According to the speaker's ordinance, the press may not record videos in the session and the corridor next to it, only in the place specifically designated to them.[327]

---

320. §17(4) of Act XC of 2005 on electronic freedom of information.
321. Eötvös Károly Intézet, a think tank for public policy matters, www.ekint.org.
322. *Az igazságszolgáltatás nyilvánossága, különös tekintettel a bírói határozatok nyilvánosságára*, https://ekint.org/lib/documents/1479484404-a_targyalasok_nyilvanossaga.pdf, EKINT 2009.
323. *Társaság a Szabadságjogokért v. Hungary* ([2009] ECHR 37374/05).
324. §55. of Act XXXVI of 2012 on the Parliament.
325. §58. of Act XXXVI of 2012 on the Parliament.
326. §59. of Act XXXVI of 2012 on the Parliament.
327. §8 of 9/2013 Speaker's Ordinance about Detailed Rules of Entering to and Staying at the House, the Office of Parliament, and other buildings relating to the Parliament as well as the relating duties of the Parliamentary Guard.

Chapter 6. Press Council

325. There is no 'press council' or other similar organization in Hungary. The Media Council is part of the Media and Telecommunication Authority, which has the right to supervise all media outlets, including press products. It is liable for registering printed and online press products and may impose a sanction in case the rules were violated. The official power of the Media Council had not been affected either by the Constitutional Court decision or by the amendment. The Media Council may lead investigation at any press product publisher, editorial board or journalist[328] and may impose sanctions in case the relevant rules in Smtv. are violated.[329]

326. A number of journalist organizations exist, each with its own political and religious views. The ex-monopolistic MUOSZ is still by far the biggest organization with its 5,800 members. All other organizations were established after 1989. The biggest ones are – MÚK (Community of Hungarian Journalists), MAKUSZ (Association of Hungarian Catholic Journalists), and the Press Trade Union (*Sajtószakszervezet*). All organizations have their own ethical codes, and they have one common ethical code as well.[330] There is one further organization which, although it did not play an important public role earlier, is now the co-regulatory partner of the Media Council – MLE.[331]

327. Mttv. makes co-regulation possible under limited conditions. Competences of the self-regulatory organizations are defined in contracts concluded between the organizations and the Media Council. According to the law, the co-regulatory organizations may oversee whether sections 14–20 of Smtv. are followed. These include content rules on the protection of the constitutional order of Hungary, minors, minorities, majorities, rights of interviewees and those who appear in media content, and the basic rules on advertising. These competences are exercised only 'prior' to the authority's procedure.[332]

328. The limits of co-regulation are clearly understandable from the section below:

> §191. (1) the Mttv.
> Under the public administrative agreement defined in Article 195 (hereinafter: public administrative agreement), the Media Council shall have the right to authorize the self-regulatory body to perform self-management tasks beyond the scope of administrative powers in relation to its registered members and

---

328. §155 Mttv.
329. §182(c) Mttv.
330. Available in Hungarian at: http://sajtoszakszervezet.hu/index.php?option=com_content&view=article&id=49:a-magyar-ujsagiro-szervezetek-kozos-etikai-alapelvei&catid=30:etikai-allasfoglalasok&Itemid=44.
331. www.mle.org.hu.
332. §191(1) Mttv.

media service providers, broadcasters, intermediary service providers or publishers of media products agreed to be bound by the terms of the Code of Conduct as defined in Article 194 (hereinafter jointly referred to as: undertakings under the scope of the Code) in official cases specifically defined in Article 192 (2) within the powers vested with it under the agreement, prior to specific exercise of powers of the competent authority.

329. The co-regulatory procedure does not prevent the Media Council from proceeding against the media content provider.[333] The Authority concludes a contract on co-regulation with an appropriate organization.[334] The contract authorizes the organizations to enforce the content rules of the media laws.[335] Co-regulation may extend to printed and online press products and to on-demand audiovisual media. The scope of competence extends to sections 14–20 of the Smtv. and content rules of the Mttv. regarding on-demand audiovisual services.[336]

330. Four self-regulatory bodies concluded a contract with the Media Council in order to perform co-regulation in July 2011: (i) MTE; (ii) the Self-Regulatory Body of Advertisers; (iii) MLE; and (iv) the Association of the Hungarian Electronic Media Service Providers (MEME). MTE has eleven members, among them the most popular online news portals (*origo.hu and index.hu*), two news portals specialized in economy (*napi.hu*, *portfolio.hu*), a leading media company with mixed portfolio (sanomamedi*a.hu*) but also a children's site (*egyszervolt.hu*), the Hungarian incumbent telecom service provider (*Magyar Telekom Nyrt*) and a popular online game site (Honfoglalo.hu).[337] MLE has fifty-six member organizations, overwhelmingly printed press publishers.[338] MEME had in 2011 more than fifty television channels among its members – including the public service media conglomerate – and four big radio channels[339] (*see* links to the contracts in footnote 89).

331. The Media Council supervises the activity of the self-regulatory bodies and may overrule their decisions.[340] The bodies shall provide a detailed report to the Media Council yearly, which is evaluated by the council both individually and as a whole:

> §201 (2) the Mttv.
> (…) the Media Council shall assess the decisions of the self-regulatory body – in terms of their compliance with the provisions of the public administration agreement and the Code of Conduct constituting an integral part thereof on an individual and aggregate basis.

333. §191(3) Mttv.
334. §190–191 Mttv.
335. §192(1) Mttv.
336. §192(2) Mttv.
337. www.mte.hu.
338. www.mle.org.hu.
339. www.memeinfo.hu.
340. §199(2) Mttv.

332. The Media Council may give notice to quit the contract with immediate effect if the self-regulatory body repeatedly or gravely violates the contract, does not fulfil its duties, or proceeds not according to the code of conduct.[341] Three of the four co-regulatory contracts are almost equal, with literally identical Codes of Ethics (the one which is different from the others is the contract of the Self-Regulatory Body of Advertisers, which is bound to differ because of its different subject matter). The provisions of the codes are almost identical to the text of the law but somewhat more detailed. The topics included embracing those provisions of Smtv. that regulate content (§§14–20, *see* paragraph 288 above).

333. The co-regulation has been criticized by both domestic intellectuals and international organizations for creating an undue compromise with the Media Council. An international partnership mission led by Aidan White and comprised of leading press freedom and media development organizations[342] said: 'The forms of co-regulation that have been developed in response to the legislation are not substitutes for self-regulation and are effectively outsourcing censorship with the co-operation of national and international media owners alike.'[343]

334. Although the co-regulation scheme does not provide the industry with the required independence, it is necessary under the new regulation because in its absence, the Media Council could levy fatal fines on media outlets – a fine of up to HUF 200 million (for on-demand media service providers with SIP, *see* paragraphs 469–470 and 474–475), or HUF 25 million for national daily papers, or even erase a media service provider (not press products) from the registry.[344]

341. §196(1) Mttv.
342. Article 19, Freedom House, Index on Censorship, Independent Journalism Centre Moldova, International Press Institute, International Media Support, European Federation of Journalists, Media Diversity Institute, Open Society Media Programme, the Network for Reporting on Eastern Europe, South East Europe Media Organization and South East European Network for Professionalization of Media.
343. Hungarian Media Law: International Mission Condemns Chilling Effect and Calls for Change, Budapest 16 Nov. 2011, http://www.cij.hu/en/hungarian-media-law-international-mission-condemns-chilling-effect-and-calls-for-change-2.
344. §187(3) ba, bc Mttv.

Part III. Regulation of Audiovisual Media (Broadcasting)

335. Mttv. and Smtv. aimed to instal a platform-neutral regulation; therefore, they use new names for the media outlets. 'Media content' includes any type of media; 'media services' include audiovisual media and radio, whether broadcast or online; and 'press products' include printed press and text-based online content.[345] The laws do not use the word 'broadcasting' (*műsorszolgáltatás*) instead the word 'media services' (*médiaszolgáltatás*) is used.

336. In 2019, an amendment aiming to manage emergency situations, established an obligation applying to all media service providers. In the event of a state of exception, state of emergency, preventive defence situation, terrorist threat, unexpected attack or emergency, the Parliament, the Defence Council, the President of the Republic and the Government, as well as persons and bodies defined by law, may, to the extent necessary and in accordance with the situation, oblige media service providers to publish public interest announcements related to the situation free of charge in the form and at the time they determine, and may prohibit the publication of certain announcements and programmes. The MTVA (hereinafter referred to as the 'Fund') shall be responsible for ensuring the conditions for publication. When publishing, the client must be clearly identified.[346]

345. §203. 1, 40–43, 60. Mttv.
346. §15 Mttv., effective as of 1 Jan. 2020.

Chapter 1. Public Service Broadcasting

337. Public service broadcasting was reorganized in 2010 in Hungary in the course of the media reform. There had been three public service media companies – the Hungarian Television (with its two channels), the Hungarian Radio (with its three national channels and some more regional) and the 'Hungaria' Television, with its channel 'Duna'. The National News Agency was a separate institution as well. All listed institutions had Boards of Trustees whose members were selected by Parliament upon appointment of the party factions. The two televisions' and the radio's three boards were completed with civil society representatives: members appointed by civil organizations and selected by a lottery. Although the Rttv. prescribed a subscription fee, this was lifted by Parliament in 2002, and all institutions were funded from the central budget.

§1. The Concept and Mission of Public Service Broadcasting

I. Independence Challenges of the Hungarian Public Service Broadcasting

338. Public service media in Hungary, as in some other post-communist countries, has never really transformed from state media into an independent, community-serving media. Its financing was subject to the political climate and partly, later, fully originated from the central budget. Its leaders were also often selected on a political basis and rarely as a result of a political agreement between parties. In the first half of the nineties, Hungarian Television and Hungarian Radio made constant attempts to increase their independence from the government, but there were constant counterstrikes from the ruling governments – this process was named the first media war.[347] The so-called second media war was fought for dominance of the public service media through their Boards of Trustees. The Parliament did not elect oppositional members into the Board of the Hungarian Television from 1998 until 2002.[348]

339. After the media law reform in 2010, public service media was subjected to profound transformation: more than a thousand employees were fired, and several programmes ceased while new ones started or restarted after a long pause. However, serious professional mistakes have signalled that the public service media is not able

347. Judit Bayer, *Magyar Médiatörténet a késő-Kádár kortól az ezredfordulóig* 159–198 (Péter Bajomi-Lázár ed., Akadémiai Kiadó 2005); Péter Bajomi-Lázár, *A magyarországi médiaháború* (Új Mandátum 2001). *See also*: 'Médiaháború' in Magyar Virtuális Enciklopédia, http://www.enc.hu/1enciklopedia/mindennapi/mediahaboru.htm; *see also*: Elemér Hankiss, *Rights of Access to the Media* 243–258 (András Sajó & Monroe Price eds, Kluwer L. Intl. 1996); Ildikó Kováts & Gordon Whiting, *Glasnost and After. Media and Change in Central and Eastern Europe* 97–127 (David Paletz, Karol Jakubowicz & Pavao Novosel eds, Hampton Press 1995); Miklós Sükösd, *Democracy and the Media. A Comparative Perspective* 122–164 (Richard Gunther & Anthony Mugham eds, Cambridge U. Press 2000).

348. Archívum, http://sajtoszabadsag.mediakutato.hu/archivum/1999_01.html, *Sajtószabadság Központ. See also*: 22/1999. (VI. 30) ABh.

to fulfil its role: a falsified reportage about Cohn-Bendit's press conference,[349] a blurred head of a public figure who was considered as 'persona non grata' on screen,[350] a more than partial interview with President Schmitt before his resignation,[351] and a biased reportage on the Roma minority by Pesty Fekete Doboz.[352]

340. The viewership rate of Hungarian Television is around 7%–8% and has been constantly low since the appearance of commercial television channels in 1997.[353] Taking the principle of Patrik Donges, which says that public service television should hold equal distance from politics, economy and society, we may say that Hungarian Television is too close to politics and too far both from economy and society.[354] Hungarian Television never seemed to care about its low viewership rates, while not serving the interests of the political ruling class caused occasional battles around the directors' positions or withdrawal of funding in the pre-Orbán era.[355] Although Hungarian Television broadcasts advertisements, its rates per minute are significantly lower than average market prices (only approximately 10% of its income stems from advertising revenues).[356]

341. During the third term of the Orbán Government (2014–2018), the public service media service was extended with four new television and four new radio channels.

342. The public service media is openly supportive of the government, even propagandistic.[357] Leaked documents and voice records revealed from 2020 to 2022 how political censorship was applied in the newsrooms of MTVA since 2019.[358]

349. *See* more in paras 565, 586. The journalist who falsified the reportage was promoted within the public service television.
350. Index: *kitakarták Lomnici arcát a köztévé híradójában*, http://hvg.hu/itthon/20111206_lomnici_kitakart_arca_hirado, Index, 6 Dec. 2011. This event launched a long hunger-strike and demonstration by several employees and ex-employees of public service television.
351. HVG, 'Tragikomikus' – a Schmitt-interjú miatt akadt ki a MÚOSZ. https://hvg.hu/itthon/20120405_obersovszky_schmitt (5 Apr. 2012).
352. *See* more in para. 586.
353. Késik az MTV feltámadása – nézettség, http://www.origo.hu/teve/20111024-kesik-az-mtv-feltamadasa-nezettseg.html, origo 24 Oct. 2011.
354. Die Zukunft des öffentlichen Rundfunks – Internationale Beitraege aus Wissenschaft und Praxis 59–61 (P. Donges ed., 2003); *see* more in: Bayer et al., *Közszolgálatisági média és az európai versenyjog* (L'Harmattan, 2010).
355. *See* news from 2005: A Magyar Televízió a legrosszabbul finanszírozott tévé Európában (MTV is the worst financed television in Europe), http://www.tvarchivum.hu/?id=70187 (24 Oct. 2005, no longer available); and from 2010: MTV: távozik a cégvezető (Executive officer resigns), http://www.mfor.hu/cikkek/MTV__tavozik_a_cegvezeto.html (16 Feb. 2010).
356. Péter Bajomi-Lázár, Václav Stetka & Miklós Sükösd, *Közszolgálati televíziózás az Európai Unióban in Médiakutató* 4 (2010). Also accessible at http://www.mediakutato.hu/cikk/2010_04_tel/01_kozszolgalati_televizio_unio.
357. Polyák, G. (ed.), *State Media – Propaganda Without Limits, in Soft Censorship in Hungary 2016.* By Mérték Média Monitor. pp. 39–45. http://mertek.eu/wp-content/uploads/2017/06/Mertek_Booklets_12.pdf.
358. Wirth, Zs.: 'Please don't report about this at all! Thanks!' How the Hungarian state news agency censors politically unpleasant news, 7 Mar. 2022, https://www.direkt36.hu/en/ne-ird-meg-semmilyen-formaban-koszi-igy-hallgatja-el-a-kormanynak-kinos-hireket-az-allami-hirugynokseg/.

According to the revelations, it was prohibited to broadcast information about the low efficiency of Chinese and Russian vaccines, about the Russian credit provided for the nuclear power plant being built in Hungary (Paks-2); report on foreign publications that were critical with the Hungarian government, especially the deficiency in press freedom, human rights organizations; it was prohibited to acknowledge that Donald Trump lost the presidential elections for several weeks;[359] and topics like migration, the rule of law, the 'child protection act' (*see* paragraph 135) and churches needed prior approval with the top leadership. Other leakages revealed that it was compulsory to represent the danger of migration several times each day and that regular directions on positions and content were communicated from 'above' in an intransparent way. Among others, using the word 'refugee' was banned; even persons with official refugee status needed to be addressed as 'migrants'. Refugees had to be depicted as violent and threatening people who flooded Europe, but Hungarian police stopped them.[360] Leaked voice recording of the head of foreign policy informed about a closed meeting where instructions were given regarding the coming European Parliamentary elections. The journalists were ordered to actively campaign for the government or file their resignation.[361] The public service Board of Trustees was divided along political lines and dismissed the submitted claim that requested to examine this case (Three oppositional members submitted their request for examination, and the five governmental members rejected the request and warned the oppositional member to avoid political topics in future).[362] The Media Council remained passive in the case, even though its head is the employer of MTVA's director.[363]

II. Legal Background

343. The mission of public service television is declared in the Smtv. and in more detail in the Mttv. Smtv. provides that there shall be public service media in Hungary, with the aim to preserve and reinforce national identity, European identity, national, family, ethnic, and religious communities, to care and enrich Hungarian and minority languages and fulfil the cultural and informational needs of citizens.[364] The Mttv. declares among its principles that public service media is an 'inevitable condition of the appropriate operation of a democratic social order' and that its interest shall be taken with special emphasis when applying the law.[365] In its

359. https://www.szabadeuropa.hu/a/a-maffiaban-lehet-hasonlo-gondolom-ilyen-a-kozteve-belulrol-mtva-m1/30938814.html.
360. https://www.szabadeuropa.hu/a/szerkesztoi-utasitas-a-koztevenel-ebben-az-intezmenyben-nem-az-ellenzeki-osszefogast-tamogatjak-mtva-fidesz/30940923.html, *see also*: https://www.szabadeuropa.hu/a/a-maffiaban-lehet-hasonlo-gondolom-ilyen-a-kozteve-belulrol-mtva-m1/30938814.html.
361. https://www.szabadeuropa.hu/a/szerkesztoi-utasitas-a-koztevenel-ebben-az-intezmenyben-nem-az-ellenzeki-osszefogast-tamogatjak-mtva-fidesz/30940923.html.
362. https://media1.hu/2020/11/26/kozmedia-kiszivargo-hangfelvetel-kozszolgalati-kozalapitvany-napirend-elutasitas/.
363. https://www.szabadeuropa.hu/a/vizsgalat-mtva-hangfelvetel-mediatanacs-rendorseg-feljelentes-bende-balazs/30991807.html.
364. §11 Smtv.
365. §6 Mttv.

part about public service media, a list from (a) to (p) details the goals of public service media. As it follows from the wording of the law, providing online content is an implied obligation of public service media (*see* above in paragraph 296). Among the usual and internationally common goals, the act adds elements that are new in Hungary, such as:

- respecting the institution of marriage and of family;
- teaching and supporting constitutional rights, basic values of constitutional order and the rules of the democratic social order;
- introducing Hungary and the Hungarian culture, as well as the culture of the national and ethnic minorities of Hungary, to Europe and the world;[366]
- the renewed definition of public service media explicitly mentions audiovisual, radio, news agency services, and online services. The biggest change is that the National News Agency has become part of the public service media provider.[367]

More detailed rules are to be laid down in the Public Service Code,[368] which is drawn up by the Media Council and can be amended by the Public Service Body with the approval of the Board of Trustees.[369] (*See* more about these bodies below.)

§2. The Organization of Public Service Broadcasting

344. After the reorganization carried out by the new media regulation, now the Media Service Supporting and Property Management Fund (*Médiaszolgáltató és Vagyonkezelő Alap, MTVA* – hereinafter MTVA) is responsible for employing the staff of the public service media enterprise and managing their incomes and property. While the legal regulation retained a façade of independent companies, the public service media is, in fact, directed and managed by MTVA, which is closely supervised by the Media Council or the president of the Media Council.[370] The role and relevance of MTVA will be unfolded in more detail below.

345. The previously existing four public service foundations[371] that owned the four public service media provider companies (hereinafter: Ltds) had been consolidated into one, newly established Public Service Foundation (*Közszolgálati Közalapítvány,* hereinafter: 'Foundation'). The Foundation is managed by a Board of Trustees, half of whose members are recommended by the governing parties, while

366. §82 Mttv.
367. §203. 31. effective since 1 Jul. 2015.
368. The document is accessible in Hungarian at: http://www.mtva.hu/index.php?p=news&act=lst&cid=707&mid=62.
369. §95 Mttv.
370. §183(k) Mttv.
371. Hungarian Television Ltd. (Magyar Televízió Rt., MTV), Hungarian Radio Ltd. (Magyar Rádió Rt., MR), 'Hungária' Television Ltd. (Hungária Televízió Rt., or 'Duna'), and the Hungarian News Agency (Magyar Távirati Iroda, MTI).

the other half are by the other parties and then elected by Parliament by a two-thirds majority of the votes;[372] plus one more member and the chairperson are delegated by the Media Council. Under the previous law, the board had a representation of civil society, but its operation did not fulfil democratic expectations.[373] However, as the Foundation lacks real influence, the board also lost its relevance.[374] All four Ltds were owned by the Foundation, but their existence is formal because all their property and staff were transferred to MTVA.[375] In 2014, they were unified into one Ltd. (Duna Ltd).[376] The definition of public service broadcasting was changed accordingly.[377] The property of the public service broadcaster was appropriated by the State and ordered to be managed by MTVA.[378] This amendment did not mean a big change for the radio and television companies. However, it was a new situation for the Hungarian News Agency, MTI (*Magyar Távirati Iroda).* With this amendment, MTI also became embedded into the MTVA conglomerate and effectively subordinated to the governmentally captured MTVA. As MTI enjoys a monopolistic market presence in the Hungarian news market, this move has proved, in the long run, to be very decisive for the further deterioration of Hungarian media freedom and pluralism. Findings of investigative journalists have revealed that MTI operates as a private news factory of the Orbán Government. Orbán's speaker and the Governmental Communication Office have regularly given exact instructions on what to write. Repeated instructions emphasized that governmental communications have to be published literally, including the titles. The same applied to the company Opus Global, owned by Lőrinc Mészáros, the proxy ownership holder of Orbán or the government.[379]

346. MTVA is entitled to manage all property which is allocated for the purposes of public service broadcasting.[380] MTVA is responsible for preparing and sponsoring the programmes, supporting the organizational transformation of the community media services and of the public broadcaster, and sponsoring other

---

372. All rules of Mttv. applying to the two-thirds majority election of officials, are transferred to Act XXXVI of 2012, on the National Assembly (Parliament).
373. Kristóf, Kádár András, Furatórium, Avagy miért nem működik az MTV Közalapítvány kuratóriuma? in Beszélő, October (2001). Also accessible at http://beszelo.c3.hu/01/10/06kadar.html.
374. Managing directors of the Ltds are elected by the Board of Trustees, upon recommendation of the president of the Media Council. The president shall name two persons, who shall be accepted by the Media Council, and the Board of Trustees has the right to select one of them with two-thirds majority. If the selection is unsuccessful, the president shall name other two persons – who shall be accepted again by the Media Council and one of them selected by the board, however, in this second round a simple majority is enough. In the selection procedures of 2010, the managing directors could be selected in the second round only. Content of the contract may also be defined partly by the Media Council. The contract may be concluded for unlimited period only.
375. §86 Mttv.
376. Amended by Act CVII of 2014, effective since 1 Jul. 2015.
377. §203. 32. Mttv.
378. §215/B. Mttv. inserted by Act CVII of 2014, effective since 1 Jul. 2015.
379. https://telex.hu/direkt36/2022/03/04/kiszivargott-iratok-mutatjak-hogyan-diktalnak-orbanek-mti-hirugynokseg.
380. §137/A. Mttv. inserted by Act CVII of 2014, effective since 1 Jan. 2015.

activities, such as movies and music pieces.[381] It has a wide range of entitlements without the limitations that generally apply to the protection of State-owned property.[382] For example, there is no need to apply the public procurement procedure if the limit is under the European minimum.[383] Generally, a tender is required for acquisitions, but it can be a closed tender in several cases, and no tender is needed in seventeen cases.[384] MTVA is also entitled to transfer property without consideration, with the approval of the Media Council and of the minister responsible for State-owned properties.[385]

347. MTVA is managed by the Media Council.[386] Its director, vice directors and supervisory board members are appointed and employed by the Media Council's president[387] (their salaries and other allowances are defined by him; vice directors are recommended by the director to the president).[388] The detailed rules on MTVA's financial management are also defined by the Media Council.[389] MTVA provides funding for the public service broadcaster. It consists of the various fees received by MTVA (unfolded in more detail below in §3.).

348. The budget is now defined by MTVA after an amendment in 2014 diminished the role of the Public Service Budget Council. The latter's role is limited to expressing opinions on MTVA's budget plan, which may or may not be respected by MTVA.[390] The Public Service Budget Council's three members are: the managing director of the Ltds, the director of MTVA, and one member delegated by the Head of the SAO on an ad hoc basis.[391]

349. A further public service organization is the Public Service Body, which is supposed to represent various parts of civil society. Its members are delegated by organizations listed in the act so that each individually named organization or each category of organization may delegate one member for three years. The individually named organizations are – the Hungarian Academy of Sciences, the Hungarian Catholic Church, the Hungarian Reformist Church, the Hungarian Evangelic Church, the Association of Jewish Churches, the Hungarian Olympic Commission, the Hungarian Rector's Conference, and the Hungarian Chamber of Commerce and Industry. Further categories are defined, in which the organizations belonging to that

381. §108(1) Mttv.
382. *See* the law on State-owned property, Act CVI of 2007.
383. Inserting an exception as §120. p) into the Act CVIII of 2011, on public procurements.
384. §136/A.(3), (5)a–h, (6)a–f inserted by Act CVII of 2014, effective since 1 Jan. 2015.
385. §137/D. Mttv. inserted by Act CVII of 2014, effective since 1 Jan. 2015.
386. §136(6) Mttv.
387. This person is appointed by the Prime Minister for nine years to be the president of the Authority, and is automatically the president of the Media Council. Although the president of the Media Council needs to be elected by two-thirds majority, until election, or if the election is unsuccessful, the president of the Authority may exercise all rights as president in the Media Council, except for voting.
388. §136(11–12) Mttv.
389. §136(16) Mttv.
390. §108. (2, 4–5). Mttv. as amended by Act CVII of 2014, effective since 1 Jul. 2015.
391. §108 Mttv.

category may delegate one member altogether (if they cannot agree on the person, it is decided by lottery). The categories are: associations of local self-governments; national self-governments of ethnic minorities; Hungarian cultural organizations registered in the neighbouring countries, provided that they have more than 100 members; national organizations protecting the interests of families; national organizations protecting interests of disabled persons; national organizations in the field of literature, theatre, movie, performance, music, dance, fine arts and applied arts.[392]

350. The Public Service Body's responsibility is to amend the Public Service Code with the approval of the Board of Trustees and supervise the realization of the code.[393] Initially, the code is issued by the Media Council, with the agreement of the Board of Trustees and consulting with the directors of the Ltds.[394]

351. The Public Service Body shall ensure civil control of the public service broadcaster. The managing directors shall make a report yearly to the body which votes about acceptance of the report (with simple majority).[395] If the report is rejected, the body may initiate the termination of the managing director's employment (with a two-thirds majority). The final decision is made by the Board of Trustees, with simple majority.[396]

352. Detailed provisions of incompatibility apply to the members and presidents of the Board of Trustees, Public Service Body, Public Service Budget Council, and the director and senior employee of the public service media providers, excluding positions in public authorities and other official bodies and in companies related to the media or telecommunication field. The incompatibility provisions are the same as those applying to members and president, vice president, director and vice directors of the Media Council.[397]

353. The Media Council is entitled to review the public media service system and to decide whether to maintain or change it. Before the decision, the Council shall consult with the director of MTVA (who is, however, his employee) and shall pay respect to the goals of economic effectiveness, the budget plans of the following year and the public service mission as defined in §83.[398] Since 1 July 2015, the Media Council is also entitled to review the system of public media services and decide on whether to maintain the existing media services or to amend their system.[399] Practically, this meant adding new services to the existing public service television channels, namely four new television and four new radio channels. One

392. §97 Mttv., Appendix I. Mttv.
393. §95(3, 5), §97(6–7) Mttv.
394. §95(2) Mttv.
395. §97(8) Mttv.
396. §97(9–10), (12–13) Mttv.
397. §43(1), 88(1), 97(5), 104(1), 108(3)c Mttv.
398. §98(8) Mttv.
399. §98(8) Mttv. as amended by Act CVII of 2014.

of the television channels was turned into a twenty-four-hour news thematic channel, and one of the new channels was a sports thematic channel.

354. It is also up to the Media Council to decide about the various technological possibilities that are applied by the public media service providers to provide their services, including media services directed abroad. Before making the decision, the council shall consult with the director of the fund and respect technical and economic aspects and the goals of media policy.[400]

355. The public service media provider is obliged to create a strategic plan not later than 31 May each year. Part of the strategic plan should be the measurement of the public service value, the detailed rules of which should be regulated jointly by the affected organizations, with the coordination of the public service media provider.[401]

§3. The Financing of Public Service Broadcasting

356. Public service broadcasting is financed both from the State budget and advertising revenues. The State's public service contribution is based on the number of households using television sets, and its sum is defined in the appendix of the law. The contribution shall be paid on the third day of each month by the State to MTVA, in twelve equal instalments, in advance, but the minister may conclude a contract for seven years about payment of this contribution.[402] Mttv. defines both the estimated number of households (4 million), the amount of the fee (HUF 1,350) and the result: HUF 64.8 billion. This shall be corrected yearly by the *consumer price index* of the previous year.[403] MTVA is entitled to cede its income from this contribution.[404]

357. Further incomes of MTVA are the media service fee (paid by linear media services that may provide service after registration), tendering fee, penalty and compensation arising from breach of media service contracts, fines, the part of the frequency licence fees that are not used up by the Authority, subsidies that must be paid by SIP linear media service providers (*see* paragraphs 469–470 and 474–475), targeted subsidies from the central budget, incomes from entrepreneurial activity, property management, interests and private donations (*önkéntes befizetések*).[405]

358. Subsidization policy, business plan and the annual account of MTVA shall be approved by the Media Council. Beyond a value limit defined by the Media

400. §98(7) Mttv.
401. §100/A. 100/B. inserted by amending Act CVII of 2014, effective since the 1 of Jan. 2015.
402. §136(5) Mttv.
403. Appendix 4. Mttv.
404. §136(4) Mttv.
405. §136(3) Mttv.

Council, prior approval of the Media Council is needed to make payments.[406] Allocation of money other than defined in the business plan and the subsidization policy also needs prior approval from the Media Council.[407] This gives full control of the public service media's monetary management to the Media Council. On organizational influence, *see* above in paragraph 302. The yearly budget of MTVA is approved by Parliament.

359. The law does not mention whether MTVA may form a reserve – therefore, it is probably up to the Media Council's approval of the business plan (The Authority, however, may form a reserve of up to 25% of its income of that year).

360. The public service media provider may exercise entrepreneurial activity but may use its profit only for providing public media services or the development of such. It may cede its right to develop entrepreneurial activities to MTVA without consideration (with respect to MTVA's activity performed in the interest of supporting the public service media). MTVA may also apply its income from this activity to pursue the goals of the public service media providers.[408] This regulation was inserted into the law as a new amendment in 2011 and practically deprives the individual public service companies of their economic self-determination – whatever their entrepreneurial income is, it must flow into the central public service budget.

361. The public service media provider may hold no share in other media service providers or foundations.[409]

362. Public service media may not broadcast more than eight minutes of advertisement per clock hour (it used to be six minutes under the previous law; twelve minutes are allowed in commercial media). Advertisement also includes 'picture journal that includes commercial communication'. Advertising may be broadcast only before or after programmes, except if the programme has natural pauses (like sports events) or consists of more parts. Split screen and virtual advertisements may be broadcast only related to sports events.[410]

406. §136(10) Mttv.
407. §136(10) Mttv.
408. §108(8) Mttv.
409. §108(9) Mttv.
410. §36 Mttv.

Chapter 2. Private Broadcasting

§1. Different Categories of Private Broadcasters

I. Linear and Non-linear Services

363. The law distinguishes between linear and non-linear media services and also between audiovisual and radio services (In addition, it also regulates press products, among them online press products, but these are text-based services that do not feature audiovisual or radio content as their main service).

364. The law follows the AVMS Directive[411] in its main features of regulation but adds more rules for on-demand services than the Directive. For example, it also prescribes quotas for on-demand services – more than 10% of the programmes published in a calendar year shall be Hungarian works, besides more than 30% of European works.[412]

365. On-demand services shall also be registered with the Authority, and a report shall be made within fifteen days if any change in the data has occurred. Violation of the rules on registration may be punished with a fine of up to HUF 1 million.

366. On-demand services shall protect minors by categorizing and restricting content for minors under eighteen by applying a technological method to prevent minors from accessing content that is categorized as V and VI (The rest of the six categories do not apply for on-demand services).[413]

367. On-demand services that are settled outside of Hungary but in another Member State of the EU may be obliged to follow the Media Council's decisions in certain cases, as explained in more detail below in paragraphs 546–551.[414]

368. To implement the AVMS Directive's 2018 amendment, video-sharing platforms' have been regulated in the E-Commerce Act.[415] Beyond what is required by

411. Directive 2010/13/EU of the European Parliament and of the Council, OJ L95/15.
412. §20(2) Mttv. §203 37 defines what 'Hungarian works' are. It opened the definition impractically wide, which was narrowed in May 2012 and further narrowed in June 2012, *see* in more detail in para. 356 below.
413. These are: 'Content which is suitable to harmfully influence the physical, mental or moral development of minors, especially by featuring violence as its dominant element, or by directly and naturally depicting sexuality shall belong into category V.' (§9(6) Mttv.). 'Content that is suitable to seriously harm the physical, mental or moral development of minors, especially by containing pornography or extreme, as well as unjustified violence, shall belong into category VI.' (§9(7) Mttv.). In addition, §19(2) of Smtv. also provides that pornography and content with extreme or unjustified violence is restricted in on-demand services by a technical method which ensures that minors do not have access to it under normal circumstances.
414. §177(1) Mttv.
415. Act CVIII of 2001. on certain aspects of electronic commerce services and information society services.

the Directive, the E-Commerce Act also requires that video-sharing platforms register at the Authority, similar to press products and media services.[416] Further, detailed rules discuss co-regulation with the Authority. However, effectiveness of any rule is diminished by the narrow scope: only video-sharing providers that are settled in Hungary are subject to the scope of the act.[417]

369. To transpose its anti-LGBT policy, the government pushed through a comprehensive legislative package, labelled 'law for the protection of minors'. One element of this legislative package amended the Media Act, by extending category 'V.', which is content that is deemed unsuitable for minors. The new text includes content that includes 'the promotion and depiction of gender identity deviation, gender reassignment and homosexuality'.[418] One particular concern is that it includes the mere 'depiction' of even 'homosexuality'. It effectively also prohibits any discussion in media about gender dysphoria or any deviation from the sex assigned at birth. It is also found particularly injurious to the dignity of sexual minorities that the said content is in the same bucket as content where violence is the defining element or the naturalistic representation of sexuality. The amendments met with wide protests in and outside of Hungary.[419]

II. National, Local, Regional Broadcasting

370. The law differentiates between national, local and regional (*körzeti*) broadcasting. Local media service is one that reaches no more than 100,000 people per year or a town with a population of no more than 500,000.[420] A regional media service is one which reaches more than the local population but less than half of the population of the country.[421] A national media service is one that reaches at least half of the population of the country.[422] The public service broadcaster has the right to provide local and regional services as well.[423]

371. The smallest types of broadcasters are broadcasters of small communities – these are local linear radio community services that cover an area not bigger than a circle of 1 km from the broadcasting transmission station (*adóállomás*).[424]

416. §15/C. of the Act CVIII of 2001 on certain aspects of electronic commerce services and information society services.
417. §1(1a–1d) of the Act CVIII. of 2001. on certain aspects of electronic commerce services and information society services.
418. §9(6) Mttv.
419. AP, 2021, Hungary: Lawmakers pass law barring LGBT content for minors, https://apnews.com/article/government-and-politics-europe-hungary-laws-business-d093db541d1ad00bd4b28bb3a22cdb1b; Dunai Márton, 2021, Hungarians protest against PM Orban's LGBTQ rights crackdown, https://www.reuters.com/world/europe/hungarians-protest-against-pm-orbans-lgbtq-rights-crackdown-2021-06-14/.
420. §203 15. Mttv.
421. §203 25. Mttv.
422. §203 52. Mttv.
423. §98(6) Mttv.
424. §203 24.

III. Community Broadcasting

372. The 2010 law has introduced community broadcasting, melting the previously existing two categories of non-profit and 'public broadcasting' (but not 'public service', *közműsor-szolgáltató*).[425] The status is granted by the Media Council to certain local or regional media service providers upon request, and the conditions are reviewed at least every second year.[426] Community broadcasters are exempted from paying the licence fee but are subject to stricter rules on advertising, similar to public service broadcasters.[427]

373. Linear community broadcasters should either serve a certain social, national or ethnic minority, a cultural or religious group, or the special needs for information or cultural programmes of a certain settlement, a region, or a reception area (*vételkörzet*) or should provide public service programmes in the overwhelming majority of their programming time. They should have a broadcasting code (*médiaszolgáltatási szabályzat*). They should provide information on the given social or local community and provide news and cultural programmes, strive to take into account those with hearing impairment (in case of audiovisual media), follow the Hungarian and European programming quotes, have at least four hours of programming time a day, and provide a programme that is self-made, edited and original (not repeated) at least four hours weekly. They are obliged to provide public service programmes in at least two-thirds of their weekly programming time, including the news for the given community, political information programmes, cultural programmes, and other content not primarily for the given community. In case of radio service, at least 50% of its weekly programming time shall be devoted to providing Hungarian music programmes.[428]

374. The transition from being a non-profit broadcaster under the previous law to being a community broadcaster under the new law is subject to the decision of the Media Council. The broadcasters had to apply for recognition by the Media Council until 30 June 2011. Several broadcasters failed to do so and lost their community status even if it was to remain valid for several years longer, even until 2017. These broadcasters are allowed to continue operations as commercial broadcasters[429] [*1785/2011. (XII. 7); 1782/2011. (XII. 7); 1779/2011. (XII. 7); 1780/2011. (XII. 7); 1783/2011. (XII. 7); 1784/2011. (XII. 7); 1785/2011. (XII. 7); 1786/2011. (XII. 7); 1787/2011. (XII. 7); 1788/2011. (XII. 7); 1791/2011. (XII. 7)*]. In one case, the Media Council denied registration because of previous violations of the community obligations [*1804/2011. (XII. 7)*]. Applications after the deadline were also not accepted *[141/2012. (I. 25)]*.[430]

---

425. §66 Mttv.
426. §66(5–6) Mttv.
427. §44(9) Mttv. and §36 Mttv.
428. §66(4) Mttv.
429. §209(2) Mttv.
430. The decisions are accessible in Hungarian at: http://www.mediatanacs.hu/hirek.php?hir_id=803.

375. The amendment of May 2012 declared that community statuses may be awarded only after winning licensing procedures initiated by the Media Council under the 2010 law or upon the decision of the Media Council. This excludes a media service provider which has a frequency originally won in a licensing procedure carried out by ORTT and could operate as a community media service provider. Surprisingly, Klubrádió is such a media service provider, although the frequency licence in question is under court review at the time of writing.

376. The details of the tender are also defined by the Media Council, as is the amount of subsidies. Until September 2011, approximately HUF 100 million less was allocated for community broadcasters, and the decisions were passed later in the year than usual, which caused difficulties in the management of the community broadcasters.[431] This – together with the other changes[432] – puts smaller community broadcasters into a difficult situation.

§2. Licensing Requirements

377. Linear services may be provided after being registered at the Authority. On-demand media services may be provided freely, but they also shall register at the Authority within sixty days after starting the services.[433] Originally, the act also contained the obligation of prior registration in this case, but that was amended after negotiations with the European Commission in February 2011.[434]

378. Instead of prior registration, a fine was introduced, which may be applied in case any rule on notification is violated.[435] And still, Smtv. allows that a law may order registration as a condition of starting publication of press products.[436] Analogue linear media services shall apply for a licence in open tenders that are published by the Media Council. In the field of radio licences, dynamic changes were taking place during 2011 (*see* more above in paragraphs 84–89). There are no more television tenders because of the digital switch-off (31 October 2013). The frequency licences of the two currently existing nationwide terrestrial television stations lapsed on 9 July 2012. While a day before, it was still not known whether they

431. Gergely Gosztonyi A közösségi médiaszolgáltatók a hatályos magyar jogi szabályozásban, in Médiakutató 4 (2011).
432. For example, in the practice of the previous Authority (ORTT), the smaller the media provider was, the less resources they had to own in order to get the subsidies. The new Authority did not follow this practice (as of September 2011). (Gosztonyi, 2011).
433. §41(2) Mttv.
434. Commission Vice-President Kroes Welcomes Amendments to Hungarian Media Law, http://europa.eu/rapid/pressReleasesAction.do?reference=MEMO/11/89, 16 Feb. 2011; Neelie Kroes: Letter to Tibor Navracsics, Deputy Prime Minister of Hungary, https://2010-2014.kormany.hu/download/8/01/10000/kroes.pdf.
435. Residues of the previous version can be observed in §45(1)c, which provides that the 'planned date of starting the media services' shall be submitted to the Authority when notifying about the service.
436. §5(1) Smtv.

will receive an extension from the Media Council, they concluded a public contract on the last day of the deadline, but its conditions were not officially disclosed until closing this manuscript.[437]

I. Registration of Linear Media Service Providers

379. The application for registration must include a range of data, among them the name, domicile and contact data of the future distributor, the planned time for news services, the planned programme structure, the planned number of subscribers, the signal or emblem of the media services, and so forth. Changes to any of these data shall be reported to the Office of the Authority within fifteen days, and failure or delay of this may entail a fine of up to HUF 200 million [sic] (for SIP media service providers, *see* paragraphs 503–509) or 50 million (for other media service providers).[438] In principle, linear media services may be started only *after* registration, but in case the Authority fails to act in time, the service may be started anyway. The Office of the Authority shall pass a decision about registration (and set the media service fee) within forty-five days, but if the Authority does not decide within this deadline, the service provider may start its media service. In this case, the Authority shall inform the media service provider within fifteen days about the fact of registration and the amount of the fee.[439, 440]

380. All linear media service providers shall pay a fee to the Authority, even those that do not use scarce resources because they pursue their activity through cable, satellite, digital terrestrial broadcasting, or IP technology. Only public service and community service providers are exempted from paying the fee.[441] The Constitutional Court found in 2008 that the fee was legitimate because of its purpose which was to support public and community services.[442] But the same Constitutional Court decision found it unconstitutional that the law did not list aspects for establishing the fee.[443] The 2010 law prescribes the aspects of consideration for the Authority to define the media service fee – the extent of reception area, the spending potential of the population, and the market share of the media service provider.[444] The fee is to be paid quarterly in advance, and a delay in payment qualifies as a serious violation of the law.[445] In case the service provider gets delayed with

---

437. Diószegi József: Elsötétül a TV2 és az RTL Klub? – Hétfőn lejár a frekvenciaengedély, Napi.hu, 6 Jul. 2012. http://www.napi.hu/magyar_gazdasag/elsotetul_a_tv2_es_az_rtl_klub_hetfon_lejar_a_frekvenciaengedely.524634.html.
438. §42(9–10) and §187(3)ba–bb. Mttv.
439. §42(3) Mttv.
440. §42(4) Mttv.
441. §44(9) Mttv.
442. András Koltay, András Lapsánszky & György Andrássy, *A médiaszabályozás kommentárja* 125 (CompLex 2011).
443. 37/2008. (IV. 8) AB decision.
444. §44(6–7) Mttv.
445. §44(4) Mttv.

the payment, the Media Council is entitled to terminate the contract with a fifteen-day deadline.[446] In cases where there is no contract, non-payment is a cause for erasure from the registry.[447]

381. The Authority may deny registration if the media service provider is a person or organization affected by the rules on incompatibility,[448] if the provider or any of its owners have a debt arising from previously providing media services, if providing the service would violate the rules on ownership concentration (*see* below in Part IV.), if the notification does not contain the necessary data even after a call for completion of documents, or if the name of the media server is identical or misleadingly similar to a previously registered and existing linear media service, or if the provider did not pay the administrative fee.[449]

382. The Authority shall erase the linear media service from the registry in the following cases: if denial of registration would be necessary; if the service provider requested so; if the service provider did not pay its debt to the Authority after being summoned in writing; if the service provider does not start its service within six months, or suspends it for more than six months, except if it gives justification for it; if court prohibited trademark abuse because of its name; and if the Media Council ordered so because of repeated and serious violation of the law.[450] The same applies to linear media service provided through a satellite of which the government has no disposal.[451]

383. On-demand media services and ancillary media services[452] also need to notify the Authority. It requires somewhat less data than linear media services' registration; for example, the signal, emblem or structure are not needed, but the planned date of starting the services is required in their case, too. Fewer rules of

446. §44(3) Mttv.
447. §42(7)c Mttv.
448. §43 and §118 Mttv.: People excluded from providing media services are: president of the Republic, Prime Minister, members of the government, State secretary, administrative State secretary, vice State secretary, mayor of Budapest, vice mayor of Budapest, other mayors and vice mayors, chairperson and vice chairperson of the county meeting, MP, member of the European Parliament, chairperson and member of the Board of Trustees of the Public Service Foundation and of the Public Service Body, managing director and vice managing director of MTVA, chairperson, vice chairperson or member of the National Telecommunication and Informatics Council, members of the Media Council, president of the Media Council or persons in employment (or similar) relationship with the mentioned organizations; local or county government representatives, public servants of the government (*kormánytisztviselő*), officials of a political party's national or regional organization or person in employment (or similar) relationship with a political party, telecommunication or media service providers, programme distributors, advertising agencies, publishers of press product, chief executive officer of publisher company or members of its executive board or supervisory board. (§118(1)a–c).
449. §42(6) Mttv.
450. §42(7) Mttv.
451. §42(8) Mttv.
452. Ancillary media services are services that include content, but are neither media services nor telecommunication services, for example EPG. (§203 23. Mttv.).

incompatibility apply.[453] They also must report any change in their data to the Authority. Registration shall be withdrawn by the Authority if incompatibility arises or if the namc is equal or misleadingly similar to another previously registered and still existing on-demand media service. The Authority shall erase an on-demand media service from the registry if withdrawal would be necessary, if the service provider requested so, if the service has not been started for one year after registration or suspended for more than one year, or if court-ordered prohibition of trademark abuse because of the media provider's name. If any rules on registration are violated, the Office of the Authority may levy a fine of HUF 1 million. This is much less than the fine for linear service providers, but it may be applied for the violation of *any* rule on registration – which are mainly administrative rules.[454]

384. Online press products have to be registered similarly to on-demand services. This is discussed more extensively above in paragraphs 166, 206–207.

II. Licensing Rules

385. Analogue linear media services need to apply for a licence in a tender. An amendment passed in May 2012 added that analogue linear media services may be provided exclusively upon the basis of a public contract concluded with the Media Council.[455] This implies that a court decision does not substitute the Media Council's action to enter into a public contract. Nothing can force the Media Council to conclude a public contract if it denies to do so. A previous version of the amending bill even said that 'The Media Council is not obligated to conclude the contract.'[456] This was omitted in the process of finalizing the law.[457]

386. Announcing the tender, evaluating the applications and concluding the contract are the tasks of the Media Council. The Media Council also has the right to issue a licence without tender for a maximum of three years for the purpose of performing public duties.[458] Licences are valid for seven years for radios and ten years

453. Provider of on-demand media services may not be president, vice president and director, vice director of the National Media and Telecommunication Authority, chairperson or member of the Public Service Foundation's Board of Trustees and of the Public Service Body, managing director of MTVA, chairperson, vice chairperson or member of the National Telecommunication and Informatics Council, director of a public service media provider, chairperson or member of its supervisory board, member of the Media Council, or employee of any of these (§45(2) Mttv.).

454. §45(8) Mttv.

455. §207(1) Mttv. Public service media providers are an exception.

456. This sentence was meant to complete §63(3) Mttv.

457. Amending proposals Nos T/7022/18; T/7022/27; unified proposal No. T/7022/37. Erased before the final voting (by proposal No. T/7022/55). On the story of the amendments *see*, A médiatörvény módosítása miatt aggódni nem kell félnetek ..., http://mediajogfigyelo.blog.hu/2012/05/21/http_mediajogfigyelo_hu_11 (21 May 2012).

458. §48(4) Mttv. Such public duties are media services relating to emergency, natural or industrial disaster, or the special educational, cultural, informational needs of a community or relating to an event of that community. The first who applies should be awarded such licence – however, it is not regulated whether or how the Media Council should announce the possibility to apply for such a licence. The council has a right of discretion in granting such a licence.

for audiovisual media services. They may be renewed once for a maximum of five years or until the end of digital transition.[459]

387. The law defines compulsory and recommended elements of the calls for tender and declares that the principles of evaluation shall be transparent and non-discriminative as well as proportional. The principles and aspects of evaluation shall be defined in the call for tenders and cannot be changed afterwards.[460] However, the Media Council has the right to modify and withdraw the call for tender until fifteen days before the deadline.[461] Council also has the right to terminate the tendering procedure even after the applications have been submitted if – among others – according to the discretion of the Council, aspects of media policy, principles or goals defined in the law or in the call for tender cannot be realized or enforced.[462] This means practically that the Media Council may interrupt the tender if none of the applicants are favourable to her and announce a new call for tender. This may be repeated as many times as necessary until the 'media policy goals' of the Council can be achieved.

388. In the tendering procedure, the rules on administrative procedure are to be applied.[463] In theory, this ensures more transparent decision-making, but the law provides wider competence of discretion to the Media Council than to the previous authority. The Media Council is free to enforce its media policy goals without objective control.

389. The tender decision may be appealed against in court within fifteen days (not longer than thirty days in any case). The appeal can be based only on a violation of law (and not the subjective aspects applied by the Media Council). The court shall decide within thirty days, and neither an appeal nor supervisory claim or renewal of the trial (*perújítás*) is allowed against the court decision.

390. The licence fee shall be paid quarterly in advance, with the exception of the first instalment when half a year's fee shall be paid in advance. In case of delay, the Media Council may – or may not, upon her decision – notice the contract with a deadline of fifteen days.[464]

391. It is possible to grant a temporary licence for a maximum of thirty days without tender, upon request, for a local terrestrial frequency. The conditions are that a frequency plan was published by the Authority, but no contract is concluded until that date; or that a licence has been granted but the licensee would not start providing the service until sixty days after the termination of the temporary service;

459. §48(5) Mttv.
460. §60(3–4) Mttv.
461. §52–53 Mttv.
462. §61(1)c Mttv.
463. §48(2) Mttv.
464. §63(10) Mttv.

or that the Authority proves that the media service can be provided without disturbing others or without violating international provisions.[465] This possibility is open only once a year for each enterprise and only three times per area per year, leaving at least fifteen days between the contracts.[466]

465. §65(1) Mttv.
466. §65(5) Mttv.

Chapter 3. Programme Standards

§1. Impartiality

392. This has been one of the most debated areas of Hungarian media content regulation both in the past and during the media reform. The Hungarian law does not use the word 'impartiality' (*pártatlanság),* however. Instead, it uses the word: 'balanced' (*kiegyensúlyozott*). This obligation appears in §13 of Smtv. and in §12 of the Mttv. among a range of other words like 'balanced, precise, exhaustive, objective and responsible' (*kiegyensúlyozott, pontos, alapos, tárgyilagos és felelős*)[467] and applies to all media service providers. Upon pressure from the European Commission in February 2011, Mttv. released press products from the obligation to provide balanced coverage.

393. Smtv. and Mttv. have slightly different provisions regarding this point – Smtv. obliges those linear media service providers that perform 'informing activity' (*tájékoztatási tevékenységet végző*) to provide many-sided, factual, topical, objective and balanced information in their news and information programmes about the local, national and European events and discussed questions that are meaningful for the citizens of the Hungarian Republic and the members of the Hungarian nation. The detailed rules of this obligation are defined by (another) law, according to the requirements of proportionality and of ensuring democratic public opinion.[468]

394. However, Mttv.'s requirement to provide balanced information applies to all media service providers in general, that is, to on-demand service providers.[469] The law also sets out that the balanced quality of the information shall appear within each programme or within a series of programmes. By this, the law applies a pluralism criterion that is much stricter than the 'internal pluralism' set forth in German constitutional jurisprudence which first introduced this concept; the German Constitutional Court required that each channel is balanced as a whole[470] (While 'external pluralism' means that the whole media landscape represents a plurality of political opinions, which is realized in Hungary, as declared by the Hungarian Constitutional Court in 2007).[471] In the same decision, the Hungarian Constitutional Court declared that the requirement of providing balanced coverage is not in itself unconstitutionally abridging freedom of expression.[472]

395. Failure to provide balanced information may be objected to by any viewer or listener at the Authority, which carries out a special procedure that cannot entail a fine, only an obligation to publish the Authority's decision.[473] Initiating the procedure is rather complicated – the complainant is supposed to write to the media

467. §83(1)m Mttv. Mentioned in connection with public service obligations.
468. §13 Smtv.
469. §12(2) Mttv.
470. BVerfGE 57, 295.
471. 1/2007. (I. 18) AB decision at III. 3.2.
472. 1/2007. (I. 18) AB decision at V. 2.3.
473. §181 Mttv.

service provider first, within seventy-two hours after the objected programme. The media service provider shall respond within forty-eight hours, and the complainant – if the response is unsatisfactory – may turn to the Authority within another forty-eight hours or within ten days after the programme in case no response is given. Because of the narrowness of the deadlines and the subject of procedure, several of the complaints may be invalid because of procedural reasons.[474] *See* more on this topic below in paragraphs 561–569.

396. Balanced information and the procedure for its enforcement are not subjects of the co-regulatory agreements. This is the exclusive competence of the Media Council (in case of SIP media service providers, *see* paragraphs 503–509) and of the Office of the Authority (in case of other service providers).[475]

§2. Cultural Diversity

I. National Culture and Minority Culture

397. All recognized national and ethnic minorities of Hungary are entitled to cultivate their culture and language, as well as to receive regular information through public media service programmes.[476] This may be performed by subtitles or multi-language publication. The national self-governments (or national organizations) of minorities may autonomously define the principles of using the programming time that is available for them. These cannot affect the content and the editing of the programme, supposedly only the timing of the programmes.

398. The law on the *rights of minorities* devotes a chapter to the rights related to media content.[477] This reiterates the rules in the Mttv. and adds a few details. For example, it provides for the publication of minority public service programmes in such a time and manner that they are accessible to the majority of the affected community, and the service shall be accessible in all relevant regions where the given minority lives to secure the organizational and financial foundations of minority public service programming, its continuous development and such programmes' archivation, preservation and keeping them accessible.[478]

399. Among the goals of the public media service, cultivating and developing culture and language, including the national and ethnic minorities' culture and

474. The new regulation extended the right to complain to everyone, while the previous law required being personally affected by the report. Under the previous law, the complaints were dealt by the Complaints Commission. *See* criticism of the Complaints Commission's operation also in: Judit Bayer, *A panaszbizottság ügyei*, 3 Médiakutató 1–11 (2001).
475. §181(1) Mttv.
476. §99 Mttv.
477. §§44–49 of Act CLXXIX of 2011 on Minority Rights.
478. §45b) of Act CLXXIX of 2011 on Minority Rights.

language, is prioritized.[479] So is introducing the Hungarian culture and that of minorities to Europe and the world.

400. Preservation and development of culture (beyond other goals) shall also be considered by the Media Council when appointing the beneficiaries of must-carry obligations.[480] Must-carry obligations are justified in the law with the reason to protect culture (Hungarian, national, ethnic minorities' and European) and languages (national and ethnic minorities).[481]

401. Cultivating culture and language and showing the culture and life of minorities are potential parts of the Public Service Code.[482] Various cultural organizations listed in the law may delegate members to the Public Service Body (*see* details in Part II).[483]

II. Protection of Hungarian Works

402. Hungarian works are those that were created fully or partly in the Hungarian language[484] or in the language of a minority in Hungary if they are related to the life or culture of that minority; music pieces if they are performed in the Hungarian language (or in a language of a minority, as above), instrumental music pieces which form part of the Hungarian or a minority culture in Hungary. The definition of Hungarian works has been amended three times after passing the law, always narrowing the scope of the provision. The latest amendment narrowed the scope of music pieces so that music that is sung in a foreign language cannot qualify as Hungarian, even if the performers are Hungarians.[485]

403. All linear audiovisual media service providers must show European works in at least half and Hungarian works in at least one-third of its programming time; at least one-tenth of the time of the content of an on-demand media service provider must be Hungarian works, and 30% European works; more than half of the yearly programming time of a public service media service provider must be Hungarian works (while more than 60% European works).[486]

404. Linear radio service providers must devote at least 35% of their yearly programming time to providing Hungarian music works, but at least 25% of those shall be published not longer than five years ago.[487] Community radios shall provide at

479. §83(1)a–b Mttv.
480. §75(3) Mttv.
481. §73 Mttv.
482. §96d–e Mttv.
483. Appendix I Mttv.
484. In the latter case, if the Hungarian part is longer than any other part in another language.
485. This amendment was part of the amending package in June 2012 and is effective from 3 Jul. 2012.
486. §20(3) Mttv.
487. §21 Mttv.

least 50% Hungarian music.[488] This may seem disadvantageous to those radios which have a niche profile, such as 'Jazzy'.

III. Other Quotas

405. Linear audiovisual media service providers shall devote at least 10% of their yearly programming time to providing European works made by independent programmers or bought from independent producers not more than five years earlier and at least 8% to providing similar Hungarian works.[489]

406. Linear public service media providers shall devote more than one-quarter of their yearly programming time to provide works that are produced by independent programme producers or are bought from such producers not earlier than five years and more than 60% to European works; more than a quarter must be European works created by or bought from an independent producer, prepared not earlier than five years beforehand.[490]

407. All audiovisual media service providers must make efforts to gradually make their programmes accessible for people with hearing impairment. Public media service and a SIP media service provider (*see* paragraphs 503–509) are obliged to ensure that all news, political advertising and programmes about challenged persons or about equality, as well as movies, public service programmes and games, are available with subtitles or sign language interpretation (in its biggest media service). The full availability shall be achieved gradually: four hours in 2011, increased by two hours each year. Availability of news, political advertising and programmes about challenged persons or about equality shall reach ten hours per day until 2014, while movies, public service programmes and games shall be available full-time from 2015 with subtitles or sign language interpretation. This obligation should not apply to programmes which are transmitted in the original language (other than Hungarian), with the exception of those which target national minorities in Hungary.[491]

IV. Subsidizing Filmmaking

408. Linear audiovisual media service providers with SIP (*see* paragraphs 503–509) are obliged to use 2.5% of their yearly income from advertisements to subsidize new Hungarian filmmaking. This obligation may also be fulfilled by paying a sum to the MTVA or by subsidizing a new film defined in an agreement

488. §66(4) Mttv.
489. §20(1)b Mttv.
490. §20(3)a, c Mttv.
491. §39 Mttv. The last sentence inserted by amending Act CVII of 2014, effective since 1 Jan. 2015. Programmes for national minorities are regulated in §99 of Mttv.

between the media service provider and the fund. This sum may be deducted from the basis of company tax (*társasági adóalap*).[492]

409. MTVA also subsidizes a variety of activities in order to develop cultural life. Among others, it subsidizes public service programmes, community media service providers, movies, and music works through open tenders.[493]

§3. Protection of Minors (Indecency and Violence)

410. Mttv. orders that all programmes be put into one of the six categories depending on their supposed effect on children.[494] The law gives a detailed description of each category, suggesting why a certain programme should belong to one or the other, and defines in what way they may be restricted.[495] The Media Council may, upon request, decide officially about the categorization of a certain programme (for a fee).[496] The first category is for programmes that are appropriate for children – programmes in this category are not restricted in any way. Category II is for programmes that children under 6 years of age may not understand, may misunderstand or may induce fear in these children.[497] These programmes are not to be broadcast between programmes that are intended for children under 6 years of age; otherwise, they may be broadcast at any time, with the appropriate pictogram.[498] The third category is for programmes that children under 12 may not understand, may misunderstand or may induce fear in these children.[499] These programmes may not be broadcast between programmes that are intended for children under twelve; otherwise, they may be broadcast at any time, with the appropriate pictogram.[500] Category IV is for programmes that are capable of harmfully influencing the physical, mental or moral development of youths under 16, especially by referring to violence or sexuality or if their theme's main element is a conflict solved in a violent manner.[501] Such programmes may be broadcast only between 9 pm and 5 am, with the appropriate pictogram.[502] Category V is for programmes that are capable of harmfully influencing the physical, mental or moral development of minors, especially if their main theme's dominant element is violence or because of a direct and natural depiction of sexuality. These programmes are not appropriate for youths under eighteen.[503] Such programmes may be broadcast only between 10 pm and 5

492. §136(8) Mttv.
493. §137(1) Mttv.
494. §9(1) Mttv.
495. §9(2–7) Mttv.
496. §9(9) Mttv.
497. §9(3) Mttv.
498. §10(1)a Mttv.
499. §9(4) Mttv.
500. §10(1)b Mttv.
501. §9(5) Mttv.
502. §10(1)c Mttv.
503. §9(6) Mttv.

am and may not be displayed in on-demand services without a technical tool to prevent minors from having access to them under normal circumstances.[504] Category VI is for programmes that are capable of seriously harming the physical, mental or moral development of minors, especially by containing pornography or extreme or unjustified violence.[505] These programmes may not be broadcast at all, and in on-demand services, they may be provided only with technical tools that prevent minors from having access to them under normal circumstances.[506] The manners of restriction: showing a pictogram (a circle with the appropriate number which signals the age under which the programme is not recommended) throughout the programme on the screen for information to parents; not broadcasting it between children's programmes; not broadcasting it between 5 am and 9 pm or 10 pm; and full prohibition.[507] In audiovisual media, the categorization must be announced before all programmes and the sign of the respective category shall be displayed throughout the programmes.[508] In radio, the categorization does not need to be announced if category II–III is broadcast at night (between 9 pm and 5 am, or category IV–V is broadcast between 11 pm and 5 am).[509] In audiovisual media, the pictogram does not need to be shown continuously if the programmes are started later than what would be obligatory because of their category: category II–III programmes between 9 pm and 5 am; category IV programmes between 10 pm and 5 am; and category V programmes between 11 pm and 5 am.[510]

411. The prohibition of direct sexuality, violence or pornography – categories V and VI – apply to on-demand media as well: they must publish such programmes only with effective technical means to prevent children from accessing them under normal circumstances. The Media Council gave a recommendation on these technical means.[511] The recommendation suggests that all set-top boxes have filters and that only set-top boxes that are able to filter also certain programmes rather than whole channels are applied. Online services, if they provide category V or VI content, shall apply a rating and ask the user about the user's age, display an optical sign that gives information about the categorization and give advice to the user on using filter software to protect children in their environment. The recommendation extends to mobile content as well, setting forth that the service provider should provide content that is harmful to children only if they have child locks to filter out such content. It sets out the mentioned principles in detail. It also puts emphasis on raising awareness by media providers, schools, parents and adults in general. With an amendment in 2019, category VI, formerly prohibited programmes, will be allowed to be broadcast if coded and made available only for adult audiences.

---

504. §10(1)d and §11(2) Mttv.
505. §9(7) Mttv.
506. §10(1)e and §11(2) Mttv.
507. §10 Mttv.
508. §10(2)b; (4) Mttv.
509. §10(3) Mttv.
510. §10(5) Mttv.
511. Accessible at http://www.mediatanacs.hu/uploads/9/11/1308744432ajanlas_hatekony_muszaki_megoldasokra_2011_06_22.pdf.

412. In addition, a new provision was inserted in May 2012 which prohibits showing minors in media content (including printed and online journals and on-demand services) in a way which would greatly endanger their moral or physical development, according to their age.[512]

§4. HUMAN DIGNITY

413. After the amendments passed in May 2012, Smtv.'s provision prescribing respect for human dignity in content applies only to audiovisual and radio media services (both linear and non-linear). It is forbidden to show persons in a humiliating, defenceless (*kiszolgáltatott*) situation for its own sake (*öncélú*) and in an offensive manner.[513] Mttv. mentions human dignity only in respect of advertisements.[514] Smtv. also obliges all media content providers to respect the constitutional order of Hungary (but the amendment of May 2012 omitted the obligation not to violate human rights during their activity).[515] These provisions can be controlled and sanctioned by the Media Council.

414. The Media Council found that a reportage with a psychiatric patient's mother infringed on the patient's human dignity; thus, the media service provider violated the obligation to respect human dignity. The Court of First Instance found that the media service provider intended to objectively present an abuse of rights committed by the hospital. The Court of Second Instance approved the original decision of the Media Council, arguing that the programme in itself, objectively taken, violated human dignity. The Supreme Court found that the Media Council may only examine whether the programme's theme, character and viewpoint violates the basic values inherent in human rights. It also found that it was a question of civil law (and thus, not the competence of the Media Council) whether a person who appears in a programme gave approval to his or her representation or not (Kfv.III.37.554/2010/5).

415. A programme contained statements suitable to incite hatred against gay minorities. The Media Council's decision suspended the licence for ninety minutes and was approved by the court of both instances. Courts held that the media service provider was responsible if the moderator of the talk show did not only fail to moderate the expressions of the guests but also used expressions capable of inciting hatred (4.Kf.27.745/2010/7).

512. §19(4a) Smtv., effective from 19 Jun. 2012.
513. §14 Smtv.
514. §24(1)a Mttv.
515. §16 Smtv.

§5. Right of Reply

416. Right of reply used to be regulated by the Civil Code, but the media reform in 2010 transposed those regulations into the Press Law. The definition of the media outlets was changed so as to adapt it to the changed technological environment; in other parts the provision has remained the same.

417. If any media content published untrue facts about someone, either as a statement or as an allegation, or if true facts are put in false light in connection with someone, that person may demand the publication of a declaration which shows which statements of facts were untrue or unfunded, or which facts were shown in false light, and what are the true facts. The rectification shall be published in a manner and length similar to the original statement (the objected part of that) within five to eight days, depending on the nature of the media service – five days in case of daily printed press, online press product and news agency; eight days in case of on-demand media service and other printed press and linear media services.[516] The Act on Civil Procedures provides a special, faster procedure for right of reply cases.[517]

418. Court practice has developed certain principles in right of reply cases for the protection of freedom of expression. These are as follows:

- Even if the law does not contain that untrue fact should be injurious to reputation, this flows from the nature of the provision.
- The contended facts should refer to a concrete person, whether defined by name or otherwise. If not named, the person should be clearly identifiable, at least for those who live in his personal environment.
- Allegations and rumours equally establish the basis for rectification. The press can only escape from liability if untrue facts arise from an official source, such as a press conference of the police.[518] If the press describes a debate and gives room to both sides' arguments, then is the press not liable for the truthfulness of those arguments.
- Allegations and rumours equally establish the basis for rectification. The press can only escape from liability if untrue facts arise from an official source, such as a press conference of the police. If the press describes a debate and gives room to both sides' arguments, then is the press not liable for the truthfulness of those arguments.
- Opinions cannot form the basis of rectification.[519]
- Political, artistic, social or scientific debates or discussions cannot form the basis of rectification.[520]

---

516. §12 Smtv.
517. §342–346 Pp.
518. BH2002. 51.
519. PK. 12. (A position of the civil collegium of the court).
520. *Ibid.*

- The publication as a whole shall be considered; isolated parts alone cannot be construed as forming the bases for rectification. The objected parts shall be construed in their context.[521]
- Political public figures shall bear a wider scope of criticism than ordinary people.[522]
- Rectification shall be published in printed press on the same page or place, with equal font sizes, in the same part of the day in linear media, in the same type of programme.

419. The practice of various levels in the court system varies widely. Therefore, often, a case which is lost by the press at first instance is won at the second and lost again in the supervisory (extraordinary legal remedy) procedure.

420. The Hungarian Parliament had initiated several times that right of reply extends to opinions as well. Until today, this has never gone through either the Constitutional Court or the Parliament itself.[523]

521. *Ibid.*
522. BH2004. 104.
523. *See lex Répássy*, 57/2001. (XII. 5) ABh; and the original form of Bill T363 (on Press Freedom and the Basic Rules of Media Content) §12(1).

Chapter 4. Political Broadcasting

§1. Rules on Political Independence of Broadcasters

I. Incompatibility of Linear Media Ownership

421. The Media law lists a number of rules on incompatibility in connection not only with linear audiovisual media service providers but also on-demand services and even printed press. The law is somewhat casuistic here – it lists almost all State functions as incompatible with having a media licence or running a media outlet. Still, they did not prevent Andy Vajna who was a Government Commissioner for the film industry since 2011, from buying TV2 Group in 2015, the second biggest national commercial channel.[524] The acquisition was made possible by a state-owned bank.[525] Besides, he also acquired a popular radio station,[526] and, in 2017, made acquisitions in the newspaper market.[527]

422. The practical relevance of most of these provisions was low until 2010 when a person chose to sell his share in a media conglomerate in order to become a member of the government (minister for national development and responsible for Chinese–Hungarian economic relations). He also used to be CEO of the Hungarian incumbent telecommunication company, Matáv, between 1996 and 2000. The media company he sold in 2010 was the sole owner of one weekly political paper, a political radio and a minority owner of a music radio. However, the new owners of the media company are not less influential in the political sphere. Informal ties between political parties and media companies have been on the increase in the past few years. Several linear audiovisual or radio media service providers systematically represent one or the other political opinion or views of a certain political movement (Hír TV, Echo TV, ATV, Lánchíd Rádió, Info Rádió).

423. A person entitled to provide linear media services cannot be: the President of the Republic; the Prime Minister; member of the government; State secretary; public administration State secretary (*közigazgatási államtitkár*); vice State secretary (*helyettes államtitkár*); any mayor or vice mayor; chairperson and vice chairperson of a county meeting; MP of the European Parliament;[528] chairperson or

524. Urbán, Ágnes (Mérték Médiaelemző Műhely) (2015) Összeesküvők. https://mertek.eu/2015/10/16/osszeeskuvok-2/.
525. Index (2015) Vajna közel 7 milliárdot kap a TV2-re az államtól. https://index.hu/kultur/media/2015/12/15/vajna_kozel_7_milliardot_kap_a_tv2-re_az_allamtol/.
526. Mérték Médiaelemző Műhely (2016) Sok kicsi sokra megy, avagy Andy a rádiós piacon. https://mertek.eu/tag/radio-1/.
527. Bienvenu Helene, '*Newspaper Closes in Hungary, and Hungarians See Government's Hand*', The New York Times (11 Oct. 2016), Retrieved 28 Nov. 2018; Gábor Földi, '*Hivatalosan is Andy Vajnáé a Bors*' (in Hungarian). Retrieved 16 Nov. 2017.
528. §118(1)a Mttv. – referred to by §43(1) Mttv.

member of the Public Service Foundation's Board of Trustees and of the Public Service Body; director or vice director of the fund; president, vice president or member of the National Telecommunication and Informatics Council; director of public service media provider; chairperson or member of the supervisory committee; member or president of the Media Council, or an employee of any of these;[529] representative of a local government or county self-government; government official; an official of a political party's national or regional organization or employee of a political party;[530] a judge or a prosecutor;[531] CEO of any public administrative organ; CEO of the Hungarian National Bank, of the Competition Authority, of the Hungarian National Property Management Ltd.; president, vice president, chief secretary, CEO or auditor of the SAO; member of the Competition Council;[532] president, vice president, director, vice director or employee of the Media and Telecommunication Authority;[533] and the close relatives of several of these.[534]

424. An organization entitled to provide linear media services cannot be a political party or an enterprise established by a party, a State organ, a public administrative organ (except if the law provides otherwise in a state of emergency) or any enterprise in which the Hungarian State has an influential share.[535] In addition, the law also excludes any enterprise in which the listed persons have (direct or indirect) ownership or a right to influence decisions (acquired by contract or in any other manner).[536]

425. Local linear media services cannot be provided by an enterprise in which the local mayor, local vice mayor, the mayor or vice mayor of the capital or their close relatives are in the board of director's executive body or supervisory board or a foundations' Board of Trustees – provided that the reception area covers at least 20% of the municipality.[537] Similarly to the general rule above, any enterprise in which close relatives of the mayor, vice mayor, the mayor or vice mayor of the capital, the chairperson and vice chairperson of the county public meeting, and the representative of the local or county municipality have (either direct or indirect) influencing ownership, or a right to influence decision-making, cannot have entitlement to provide linear services, in cases the service in question covers at least 20% of the affected local government.[538]

529. §118(1)b Mttv. – referred to by §43(1) Mttv.
530. §118(1)c Mttv. – referred to by §43(1) The word 'employee' should include all in an employment-like relationship.
531. §43(2)a Mttv.
532. §43(2)b Mttv.
533. §43(2)c Mttv.
534. Precisely: the close relatives of those listed in §118(1)a–b and §43(2)b–c of Mttv.
535. §43(3)a–b–c Mttv.
536. §43(3) Mttv.
537. §43(4) Mttv.
538. §43(5) Mttv.

II. Incompatibility of On-Demand Media Ownership

426. On-demand services are subject to fewer rules: similarly to press products, they shall be independent of all sections of the Authority and of public service media. They may not be provided by the president and vice president, director and vice director of the National Media and Telecommunication Authority, chairperson or member of the Public Service Foundation's Board of Trustees or of the Public Service Body, the director of the fund, the president or vice president or member of the National Telecommunications and Informatics Council, director of public service media provider, chairperson or member of its supervisory board, member of the Media Council, or any person in employment relationship with any of these organizations. A person who registers an on-demand service shall make a declaration that no legal cause of incompatibility exists in relation to him or her, and it would not emerge through registration.[539]

III. Incompatibility of Public Service Media Provider's Director and CEO

427. The director of the public service media provider shall make a written declaration before signing his contract that no reasons for incompatibility exist in relation to him or her.[540] The rules are partly the same as those applying for linear media services in general. The director cannot be the President of the Republic, Prime Minister, member of the government, State secretary, public administration State secretary (*közigazgatási államtitkár*), vice State secretary (*helyettes államtitkár*), mayor of Budapest, vice mayor of Budapest, mayor and vice mayor, chairperson and vice chairperson of a county meeting, of the European Parliament;[541] chairperson or member of the Public Service Foundation's Board of Trustees and of the Public Service Body, director or vice director of the fund, president, vice president or member of the National Telecommunication and Informatics Council, director of a public service media provider, chairperson or member of the supervisory committee, member or president of the Media Council, or an employee of any of these;[542] and representative of a local government or county self-government, government official, official of a political party's national or regional organization, or employee of a political party.[543]

428. There are further rules for economic incompatibility – any person who has direct or indirect ownership in an enterprise that performs telecommunication or media services, programme-selling, programme distribution, publishing, advertising agency or printed press distribution cannot be president, vice president, managing director or vice managing director of the Authority;[544] they cannot pursue

539. §45(2) Mttv.
540. §104(4) Mttv.
541. §118(1)a Mttv. – referred to by §104(1) Mttv.
542. §118(1)b Mttv. – referred to by §104(1) Mttv.
543. §118(1)c Mttv. – referred to by §104(1) Mttv. The word 'employee' should include all in an employment-like relationship.
544. §118(1)f Mttv. – referred to by 104(1) Mttv.

political activity and cannot make a declaration in the name of any party.[545] Further, the director or CEO (or close relative of these) of the public service media provider cannot be related[546] to an enterprise that is in a business relationship with the public service media provider.[547] The director and CEO of the public service media cannot pursue any other activity than scientific, educational, literature, artistic, or other activity under copyright. He or she is not entitled to receive a fee even for these activities.[548]

§2. Fair Representation in Election Periods

I. General Rules on Election Campaigns

429. A new Act on Election Procedures was introduced in 2013, not without waves of controversies. First, the law was not signed by the President of the Republic but was sent to the Constitutional Court which annulled the law's regulation on political advertising. These rules would have prohibited political advertising in all media services except the public service media and movies.[549] In February 2013, the Fourth Amendment of the Basic Law was passed, which included into the Basic Law those rules which were just annulled by the Constitutional Court – obviously with the intention that they are untouchable even for the Constitutional Court (*see also* 151). In April 2013, the Act on Election Procedures was passed again by the Parliament, including those rules that were previously annulled by the Constitutional Court but which were now constitutional, thanks to the amendment of the Basic Law. This manner of regulation was also criticized by the Venice Commission and also by the Tavares Report of the European Parliament.[550] Reacting to the international and political pressure, the Parliament passed a fifth amendment to the Basic Law in September 2013, which removed the questionable changes of the fourth amendment and retained only the restriction that political advertising can be published in media services in campaign period only free of charge; adding that fundamental law shall define the detailed rules which must ensure equal treatment. In October 2013, the Act on Elections Procedure was also amended accordingly. The regulation on political advertising became very detailed; below, the main rules are described.

430. Commercial media is allowed to publish political advertisements during campaign period, but with several restrictions. First, publication is free of charge

545. §118(3) Mttv. – referred to by 104(1) Mttv.
546. Have ownership share, or be executive officer or member of the supervisory board.
547. §104(2) Mttv.
548. §104(3) Mttv.
549. 1/2013. (I. 7). Constitutional Court decision.
550. CDL-AD(2013)012-e Opinion on the Fourth Amendment to the Fundamental Law of Hungary Adopted by the Venice Commission at its 95th Plenary Session, Venice, 14–15 Jun. 2013; On the situation of fundamental rights: standards and practices in Hungary (pursuant to the European Parliament Resolution of 16 Feb. 2012) (2012/2130(INI)), http://www.europarl.europa.eu/sides/getDoc.do?pubRef=-//EP//TEXT+REPORT+A7-2013-0229+0+DOC+XML+V0//en.

(obviously making commercial media uninterested in publishing political advertisements). Second, prior notification is necessary: a national media service provider shall inform the National Elections Committee at least fifty days before the day of general election, whether it would like to ensure the possibility of political advertising, define the channel(s), and the number of minutes to be devoted to it.[551]

431. Public service media providers have an obligation to publish political advertisements. The total length and the time span of telecast are defined by law (470 minutes for party lists, 130 minutes for minorities' lists, and 300 minutes for European Parliament's elections and local elections), and the minutes shall be equally distributed between lists and public service media providers.[552] The National Elections Committee is entitled to calculate the final number of minutes per media service provider, also taking into account the number of minutes that commercial media plans to devote to political advertisements.[553]

432. Registered press products may publish political advertisements in election campaigns under the following conditions: the price list shall be submitted to the SAO within five days after setting the election date. Political advertisements may be published after the SAO has registered and published the price list, and the press product shall also publish its price list online. Deviation from the price list is prohibited. After the voting, within fifteen days, the press product shall inform the SAO which political candidates' political advertisements they published, for how many minutes, in which time slot, and for what price. This information is published by the SAO online.[554] The advertisements shall be readily recognizable as such. Publishing political advertisements is not restricted to press products (both online and offline) outside campaign period. There are no restrictions for political advertisements on billboards, movie theatres or other carriers, either.

433. Mttv. provides the specific framework rules which must be interpreted together with the Election Procedures Act. In media services – unlike in press products – no political advertising may be published outside election periods, unless in connection with an already called referendum[555] (election period is counted from when the day of elections is set until the beginning of the day of election.)[556] Media service providers are not responsible for the content of the political advertisement.[557] No opinions or evaluative explanations may be attached to political advertisements.[558]

434. In case media service providers or press products are suspected of having violated the rules on election campaigns, objections may be raised to the local,

551. §147/F(1) Act on Election Procedures.
552. §147/A(1–2), §147/B, §147/C. Act on Election Procedures.
553. §147/F(2) Act on Election Procedures.
554. §148.
555. §32(3) Mttv.
556. §40 Act C of 1997 on Election Procedure.
557. §32 Mttv.
558. §147(2) Act on Election Procedure.

regional or national election committee, depending on the coverage of the media content provider.[559] The election committee may oblige the editorial board of a printed press product, a media service provider or a news agency to publish its decision within three days or in the next issue.[560] The election committee may impose a fine, depending on all circumstances of the case, like the type of media service provider, its area of coverage, the features of the press product, the weight and repetition of the legal violation, and whether or not it happened intentionally. The highest fine is fifty times the minimum wage.[561]

II. Campaign Silence (*Kampánycsend*)

435. On the day of voting, no political advertisements may be published by media service providers (i.e., radio and television or on-demand services).[562] Thus, press products (including online press products) are not prohibited from publishing political advertisements.[563]

436. On the parliamentary election day of 2010, the voting process could not be finished by 7 pm because of a change in the procedural law. At some voting points, 500–700 (altogether several thousand) people were queuing at 7 pm, when some media outlets started to publish exit poll results. At 7:15 pm, the Election Commission announced extension of campaign silence, which was lifted only at 10:15 pm. However, the already published exit poll results spread through mobile phones, by word of mouth and the Internet.[564]

III. Internet Self-Regulation in Election Campaigns

437. On the Internet, the MTE gave a recommendation which provided an interpretation of the relevant laws in an online environment. Principally, during campaign silence, Internet content providers shall not publish new content that may influence citizens in their decisions on election. Further, they should make their previously published materials of this kind inaccessible on the first two hierarchical levels. In practice, all online journals 'covered' their opening site with a warning that notified the user about the campaign silence and allowed access to the content only through a click. A second click was necessary to see the political content. In addition, they recommend that the content providers not organize live interviews or

559. §151(1) Act on Election Procedure.
560. *Ibid.*
561. §152(2–3) Act on Election Procedure.
562. §147(4a) Act on Election Procedure.
563. The Act on Election Procedures uses two synonym, but different words to define political advertising in media services (*politikai reklám*) and political advertising in press products (*politikai hirdetés*).
564. *See* the story in Hungarian: *Három órával volt hosszabb a kampánycsend*, http://index.hu/belfold/2010/valasztas/kampanycsendhosszabbitas/ (11 Apr. 2010).

chat or forum talks with public personalities who might have an interest in the outcome of the elections. Opinion polls shall not be published later than the eighth day before the election day, and on election day, they shall be made inaccessible from the first two hierarchical levels. They should not publish self-made poll queries or voting applications or links to another site's voting application or statistics referring to previous results of such queries or applications. It provides further detailed recommendations on user-generated content and content of political organizations.[565]

438. Two online news portals violated campaign silence in 2010, on the day of local government elections, according to the resolution of the National Election Committee. They published MTI news lawfully but completed it with political opinions which violated rules on election.[566]

§3. News and Current Affairs Programmes

439. Presenters and reporters who appear in news and political information programmes[567] may not add any opinion or evaluative explanation to any political news (published in any media service provider).[568] If an opinion or evaluative explanation is given, it should be signalled as being such, separated from the news, and its author shall be identified.[569]

440. News programmes cannot be sponsored, and no product placement is allowed during these.[570]

441. Linear audiovisual media service providers with SIP (*see* paragraphs 535 cf.) are obliged to publish at least twenty minutes of news programmes between 6 and 9 pm. each day. An amendment in 2019 also set a maximum of 45 minutes, abolished the obligatory morning news section for television, and limited those of radio.[571] Linear radio service providers with SIP shall publish at least ten minutes and a maximum of 45 minutes of uninterrupted news on each working day between 6:30 and 8:30 am. News or reportage taken from another broadcaster, or ones that do not serve the purpose of informing democratic public opinion or ones of criminal theme, shall not take longer than 35% of the news programme on a yearly average.[572] The 2019 amendments appeared to serve the market dominance of public service broadcasters in the field of news programmes. The time limit of 45 minutes

565. Old Codes are available (in Hungarian) at: http://archiv.mte.hu/valasztasikodex.html. The latest Code is from 2010.
566. *See* the story in Hungarian at: Kampánycsendet sértett az atv.hu és a 168ora.hu, http://index.hu/belfold/2011/11/15/kampanycsendet_sertett_az_atv.hu_es_a_168ora.hu/ (15 Nov. 2011).
567. Political information programmes are defined as programmes that analyse or discuss Hungarian or international political or public events in at least 90% of their time but are not news programmes. (§203 56. Mttv.).
568. §13(3) Mttv.
569. §13(4) Mttv.
570. §28(1)a, 30(3)a Mttv.
571. Amendment effective since 1 Aug. 2019.
572. §38(1) Mttv.

was immediately evaded by adding two programmes with different titles after one another. Prominent expert and contributor Gábor Polyák noted with some sarcasm that the limitation of news programmes would mean, in the case of the propagandistic, government-captured channels, that they can devote less time to character-smearing and political propaganda.[573]

§4. Political Advertising

442. The media law restricts advertising and sponsoring activities of political parties and political movements. These may not sponsor any programmes in media services, nor can their name, logo or catchword appear in the name of the sponsor.[574] Product placement is also prohibited in news and political information programmes.[575] Also, news and political information programmes may not be supported in audiovisual media services, with the exception of thematic news channels.[576]

443. The person who orders a political advertisement or in whose interest it is published may not exercise influence on the editing of the media service.[577] All political advertisements must be immediately and clearly distinguishable from other media content. This shall be achieved by optical and acoustic means in audiovisual services and only acoustic means in radio services.[578] The one who orders an advertisement shall be clearly identified.[579]

444. Similar rules apply to public announcements and social advertisements – the Media Council decides upon request whether a programme qualifies as political advertising, social advertising or public announcement (in reality, several social advertisements have been published in order to propagate the government's goals or programmes). Political advertisements are not counted when calculating the time spent on commercial advertising.[580]

445. Presenters and reporters who appear in news and political information programmes of public service and community media services cannot appear in any commercial or political advertisement (with the exception of self-advertising of the public service media).[581]

573. https://media1.hu/2019/07/18/valtozik-az-rtl-hirado-es-a-tv2-tenyek-az-uj-mediatorveny-miatt/.
574. §27(1)a, 27(4) Mttv.
575. §30(3)a Mttv.
576. §28(1)a, 28(3) Mttv.
577. §32(1) Mttv.
578. §32(2)a–b Mttv.
579. §32(3) Mttv.
580. §35(2)b Mttv.
581. §36(4) Mttv.

446. The Media Council supervises whether the rules on political advertising are respected.[582]

447. The government's advertisements were examined by the Media Council and by the 'prosecution' upon the announcement by the NGO Mérték Media Analysis. However, both authorities found that the advertising clips saying 'The Hungarian reforms are successful' were not political advertisements but social purpose advertisements. The legal difference between the two is that political advertisements are limited to the election campaign period and are paid from the party budget. There are no such limitations regarding social purpose advertisements: they can be prepared and disseminated from the public budget and at any time of the year.[583]

448. A decree has also ordered that bank advertisements on government-aided mortgages show the governmental logo and text 'the Hungarian reforms are successful' in an exactly defined visual manner.[584]

§5. Outdoor Advertising

449. In 2017, the government intended to regulate outdoor advertising. The official purpose of the act was to diminish political corruption and intransparent spending. However, the political background was that a major owner of outdoor advertising posts, Lajos Simicska, had departed from the governing Fidesz party, and the government became interested in regulating his commercial activity, as well as limiting the appearance of harshly critical political posters. The law was a response to the 'poster war' which started in the spring when the oppositional Jobbik party published suggestive pictures about the Prime Minister and people close to him, who were critical of the supposed corruption matters.

450. The original recommendation held that no outdoor political advertising was allowed outside of the campaign period. This would have required a two-thirds majority of the MPs, which was not achieved. Some parts of the bill were passed with a simple majority, but the remainder was rejected by the President of the Republic. The new attempt was to amend the Act on Protection of Townscapes,[585] which required only a simple majority. The amendments are:

- Public organizations which receive more than half of their budget from the central budget can advertise through outdoor advertising posts only on the official price (*listaár*); no individual discounts are allowed.

582. §184(1) Mttv.
583. 1537/2015. (XI. 24.) NMHH decision, 160/2016. (II. 9.) NMHH decision, http://nmhh.hu/cikk/169753/A_Mediatanacs_1602016_II_9_szamu_dontese, http://nmhh.hu/cikk/169030/A_Mediatanacs_15372015_XI_24_szamu_dontese.
584. MK Decree 2/2016. (III. 5.) by the Head of the Prime Minister's Cabinet, about the detailed rules of advertising home mortgage benefits. (*a családi otthonteremtési kedvezményre, valamint az otthonteremtési kamattámogatásra vonatkozó reklámok és hirdetések részletes szabályairól*).
585. Act LVII of 2016 on the Protection of Townscapes.

- Official prices and contracts concluded shall be notified to the authority which publishes them.
- Non-compliance entails removal of the illegal advertisement within two days and a fine of EUR 5,000 (HUF 150,000).[586]

The law affects primarily political parties, but cultural institutions and theatres are also affected. It does not apply to NGOs, some of which pursue political activities.

451. In addition, a new governmental decree was published in April, effective from 28 May 2017, on the execution of the Act on the Protection of Townscapes regarding the publication of advertisements. This decree effectively bans new, low-budget political parties from glueing smaller paper posters as usual by:

- prohibiting the use of advertising pillars for advertising purposes, with the exception of public education purposes;
- prohibiting the fixing of advertisements by glueing;
- defining the obligatory size of advertisements between 2 and 9 square metres and 11 square metres for giant posters.[587]

452. The 'poster war' continued in August and September, when new posters were posted by anonymous 'private persons' with very similar content to the previous 'Jobbik' posters. The governmental authorities ordered removal of the posters with the reasoning that 'they are very similar to the Jobbik posters', and therefore they 'should be regarded as the advertisements of an organization managed from public budget allocations, therefore they fall within the scope of the poster act'.[588] This event points out the theoretical complexity of the advertisements of political opinions.

453. The Poster Act's scope extends to the persons who ordered the advertisement rather than those in whose interest the advertisement was published. Even in the latter case, it would not always be crystal clear whose interest is served by posters which call attention to government corruption: it could be any political party other than the government or even the whole society. However, the governmental party's political advertisements, which popularize the government's policy measurements and plans, are called 'public interest advertisements' and are not regarded as having to respect the limits on political advertising. They are not financed from the party budget but the central public budget. *See,* for example, the AB decisions 19/2016. (X. 28) and 20/2016. (X. 28) in which the Constitutional Court declared that advertisements by the government in relation to the popular vote were not political advertisements. (*see* paragraphs 189–191)

---

586. Article 11.G. of Act.
587. Articles 3–4. MK 2017/63. (IV. 28.).
588. Reasoning of the decision, according to the information of HVG, a weekly quality newspaper. http://hvg.hu/itthon/20170926_Erobol_nyomja_le_a_kormany_a_plakattorvenyt_kijatszokat_leszedetik_a_nevtelen_hirdeteseket.

454. Jobbik, which is the primary target of the law, initiated a complaint procedure at the Constitutional Court (14 July 2017). The reasons, among others, were that the law would have required a qualified majority because it affects political party finances[589] and that government authorities became empowered to supervise party financing rather than the SAO, which is contrary to the Basic Law. The Act on Political Parties[590] prohibits the supervision of party finances by State administrative organs. The Constitutional Court dismissed the complaint.[591]

589. Dull Szabolcs, *Elképesztő húzással, erőből átnyomta a Fidesz a plakáttörvényt* (2017). https://index.hu/belfold/2017/06/23/rendkivuli_parlamenti_ulesen_szavaznak_a_plaktattorvenyrol/.
590. Act XXXIII of 1989, on the operation and finances of political parties.
591. 3001/2019. (I. 7.) AB határozat, http://public.mkab.hu/dev/dontesek.nsf/0/292E4C815F938587C1258162002ED24A?OpenDocument.

Chapter 5. Advertising Rules

§1. Various Forms of Commercial Communication

455. The definitions of commercial communication, advertising, product placement, teleshopping and sponsoring very closely resemble the wording of the European AVMS Directive. Commercial communication includes all kinds of advertising, including advertising, sponsorship, teleshopping, and product placement, among others:[592]

> §203 20.
> Commercial communication is media content the purpose of which is the direct or indirect promotion of goods, services or image of a natural or legal person, or company without legal personality that pursues economic activity. These contents appear in media content or next to it, for payment or other consideration, or for self-promotion. Among commercial activities are advertising, the representation of the sponsor's name, trademark, image or product, teleshopping and product placement.

456. Advertising is defined as any communication, information or representation which qualifies as a programme and aims to facilitate the sale or other use of marketable tangible properties – including money, securities, financial instruments and natural resources that can be utilized in the same way as things –, or services, real properties or property rights, or – in connection with the above purpose – aims to promote the name, the brand or the activities of an undertaking, or to increase awareness of goods or trademarks.[593]

457. Social advertising is a public-purpose message or notice that does not qualify as a political advertisement, is either published for consideration or for free, does not serve advertising purposes, and aims to influence the viewer or the listener of the media service in order to achieve a goal of public interest.[594] Social advertising messages are mostly subsidized by the government and sometimes by civil organizations.

458. Teleshopping means an advertisement which contains direct offers for the sale, purchase or other utilization of goods, services, rights and obligations for payment or consideration by way of establishing contact with the distributor or the service provider, including phone-ins operated as business undertakings transmitted in the media service.[595] Teleshopping window means a teleshopping facility, the uninterrupted duration of which is at least fifteen minutes.[596]

592. §203 20. Mttv.
593. §203 59. Mttv.
594. §203 64. Mttv.
595. §203 65. Mttv.
596. §203 66. Mttv.

459. The law defines sponsorship as any contribution provided by an undertaking in order to finance a media service provider or a programme with the purpose of promoting its name, trademark, image, activities or products.[597] Split screen advertisement means an advertisement in audiovisual media service which covers a certain part of the screen and is published during a programme which does not qualify as commercial communication.[598] Public service announcement means 'any information which is published without consideration, originates from an organization or a natural person fulfilling State or local governmental responsibilities, which provides specific information of public interest for the purpose of attracting the attention of the viewers or the audience and does not qualify as political advertisement'.[599] Virtual advertisement is an advertisement that is inserted subsequently into the programme signal or into the programme digitally or by any other method.[600]

460. Covert commercial communication is one which may mislead the audience about its nature, even if it was published not for consideration.[601] Under the previous law, this category was mainly applied to sanction product placement, which was not regulated in the law then. Surreptitious advertising – while it was regulated in the old law – is not prohibited by the Mttv. but by the law on advertising.[602] Product placement is defined as any form of commercial communication which contains products, services, the trademark of the above, or any reference to them appearing in a programme for payment or similar consideration. The definition literally follows the AVMS Directive. *See* detailed rules below in paragraphs 484–486.[603]

Advertising Tax: The Law and Its Supervision by the European Commission

461. In 2014, an advertising tax was introduced. All companies which publish commercial communication were to pay a tax based on the income produced by publishing the commercial communication. In the case of self-advertising, the costs of the advertisement shall form the basis of the tax. The progressively growing tax, with levels between 0% and 50%, was found in violation of European law by the European Commission.[604] Approximately 80% of all the tax income was paid by RTL Hungary because of the specific details of the rules.[605] The law was amended after the procedure at the European Commission was announced, and the rate was lowered to 5.3% maximum, but kept the complicated set of exceptions, among them that of companies with a lower tax base (advertising income) than HUF 100 million (approx. EUR 325,000). The point in the procedure by the European Commission was that meaningful exceptions would grant a selective advantage to certain companies while unduly favouring companies that did not make a profit in the previous

597. §203 63. Mttv.
598. §203 53. Mttv.
599. §203 27. Mttv.
600. §203 72. Mttv.
601. §203 4. Mttv.
602. §3q. of Act XLVIII of 2008 on economic advertising.
603. §203 68. Mttv.
604. European Commission C(2016) 6929 final, 4. Nov, 2016.
605. Act XXII of 2014 on advertising, effective from 18 July, the tax is payable from 15 Aug. 2014.

year. This realized a selective treatment of the business enterprises to be counted as State aid, which is incompatible with the common market.[606]

462. Consequently, the law was amended in the summer of 2017,[607] setting the rate at a maximum of 7.5% but retaining the exemption for companies with a tax base lower than HUF 100,000 (approx. EUR 325,000); however, this can count as '*de minimis*' aid under the European rules,[608] as pointed out as a possibility by the European Commission.[609]

§2. Restrictions on Advertising Content

463. Hungarian law follows the European Directive on Audiovisual Media and adds a few further restrictions.[610] Similarly to the AVMS Directive, the Mttv. prohibits commercial communication that violates human dignity, contains or supports discrimination based on gender, racial or ethnic origin, nationality, religion or philosophical conviction, physical or mental disability, age or sexual orientation.[611] In addition, the same article prohibits inviting minors to purchase or hire certain products or to use a service, that it directly calls on minors to persuade their parents or others to purchase the advertised goods or to use the advertised services, that it exploits the special trust of minors placed in their parents, teachers or other persons or their inexperience and credulity; and that it unreasonably shows minors in dangerous situations.[612]

464. Mttv. also prohibits commercial advertising that expresses religious, conscientious or philosophical convictions – but thematic media services that feature religious topics form an exception (the previous media law, the Rttv., did not contain such an exception).[613] Another new provision is that commercial communication may not injure the dignity of a national symbol or a religious conviction.[614] This is particularly interesting for being on the edge of an undue restriction of freedom of expression with its first half, while its second half reiterates the prohibition already set out in a previous subsection.

465. The content restrictions of those commercial communications that advertise alcoholic beverages also contain the EU rules and several other details. Such advertisements may not be aimed specifically at minors and may not encourage immoderate consumption of alcoholic beverages;[615] further, they may not show

606. European Commission C(2016) 6929 final at 65, 74, and 77.
607. With Act XLVII 2017, effective since 1 Jul. 2017.
608. §5 of the Act XXII of 2014, on Advertising Tax.
609. European Commission C(2016) 6929 final at 100.
610. §24 Mttv.
611. §24(1)a–b Mttv.
612. §24(1)c–f Mttv.
613. §24(1)g Mttv.
614. §24(1)h Mttv.
615. §24(2)a,c Mttv.

minors consuming alcohol, depict excessive alcohol consumption in a positive light and refraining from alcohol consumption in a negative light; show exceptional physical performance or driving vehicle as a result of the consumption of alcoholic beverages; or create the impression that the consumption of alcoholic beverages contributes to social or sexual success; or claim that the consumption of alcoholic beverages has stimulating, sedative or any other positive health effects or that they are a means of resolving personal conflicts; or create the impression that excessive alcohol consumption may be avoided by consuming beverages with low alcohol content or that high alcohol content is a positive attribute of the beverage.[616] All of these provisions were included in the previous media law (Rttv.) as well.

466. The law also contains the EU rule that the person who orders the publication of the commercial communication, or the one who has an interest in such publication, may not exert editorial influence over the media service except for the time and date of publication.[617]

§3. Time and Frequency Restrictions

467. Again, following the AVMS Directive, the Mttv. provides that the duration of advertisements in linear media (both audiovisual and radio) shall not exceed twelve minutes within the clock hour. This includes split screen advertisements, virtual advertisements, teletext with advertisements and the promotion of the programmes of other media services, except trailers of the own programmes or trailers of another media service provider in which the media service provider in question or its owner has influential participation.[618] Further exceptions apply to teleshopping windows, political advertisements, public service announcements, social advertisements, sponsorship announcements, product placements, teletext of a local media service, and virtual advertisements which appear in programmes other than those produced or ordered by the media service provider,[619] media service providers that broadcast exclusively advertisements and teleshopping, linear audiovisual media services that advertise the media service provider or its other media services exclusively; announcements that serve the sole purpose to advertise the media service itself or the products complementing the programmes broadcast in the media service.[620]

468. Teleshopping windows may not exceed three hours each calendar day, with the exception of a thematic media service that broadcasts primarily teleshopping or teleshopping windows.[621]

616. §24(2)b,d–h Mttv.
617. §25 Mttv.
618. §35(1), (2)e Mttv.
619. (Or another media service provider in which the media service provider in question or its owner has an influential participation).
620. §35(2) Mttv.
621. §35(3) Mttv.

469. In sports programmes and other programmes which have natural breaks, advertisements may only be broadcast during the breaks in linear media. Split screen advertisements and virtual advertisements form an exception, though.[622]

470. A cinematographic work, news or political information programme which exceeds thirty minutes – with the exception of television series or documentaries – may only be interrupted with advertisements or teleshopping once every thirty minutes in linear audiovisual media service. But, the thirty minutes shall include the duration of advertisements and trailers.[623]

471. Stricter rules apply to public service media, although the rules have become lighter compared to the previous regulation. In both radio and television, advertisement and teleshopping may not exceed eight minutes within the clock hour. For community media, however, the law has retained the previous rule (which had applied to public media as well) – six minutes is the maximum duration.[624] Teletext that contains advertisements shall also count here.[625]

472. The main difference, however, is that public and community media services may not broadcast advertisements during programmes, only between them, with the exception of 'composite' programmes which consist of more than one part, sports programmes and other programmes which have natural breaks.[626]

473. Split screen advertisements and virtual advertisements in public and community media services may only be broadcasted in relation to sports programmes.[627]

474. The public media service provider must reserve two minutes per two hours for public service announcements in its media service which has the highest audience share.[628] If a programme is longer than two hours and it is impossible to interrupt it by its nature, then this obligation shall not apply.[629] However, information from the official disaster management organ must be published even by interruption of programmes, if it gives information about the expectation of events that endanger or harm human life or property, or the mitigation of damages of such an event, or tasks that are to be done, it is justified according to the disaster management organ and if the media service provider was informed of this fact in due time. This obligation applies not only to public service but also to community broadcasters and to commercial SIP media service providers (*see* paragraphs 503–509). But the latter

622. §34(1) Mttv.
623. §34(2) Mttv.
624. §36(1) Mttv.
625. §36(2) Mttv.
626. §36(3) Mttv.
627. §36(5) Mttv.
628. §36(6) Mttv., first sentence.
629. §36(6) Mttv., second sentence.

may publish such an announcement in the manner defined by them – which probably means that they are not obliged to interrupt programmes. In absence of a request for the broadcast of a public service announcement, the reserved period may also be used for other programmes.[630]

§4. SPONSORSHIP

475. The Smtv. and Mttv. both provide rules on sponsorship. Smtv. provides that sponsors shall be identified at the time of the publication or directly preceding it. No audiovisual media service or its programme may be sponsored by an enterprise that prepares other audiovisual media services or movies.[631] Sponsored media content may not encourage or call for the purchase of the sponsor's product or that of a third person defined by the sponsor, nor for the consumption of their service or for refraining from any of these.[632] Propagation of the product (besides naming the sponsor) qualifies as covert advertising and is hence prohibited (KGD2006. 140). Appearance of the sponsor may not have an advertising effect (KGD2005. 108).

476. The sponsor may not influence the media content or its publication in a manner that relates to the liability or editorial freedom of the media content provider.[633] These provisions incorporate subsection 1 of Article 10 of the AVMS Directive into Hungarian law.[634] The rest of the EU provisions on sponsorship are implemented through Mttv. Both laws allow that naming the sponsor may take place at the same time as the programme or immediately before or after the programme.[635] Identification may happen not only by the name of the sponsor but also by name or trademark of either the sponsor or another undertaking designated by it, or by using a sign, or a reference to either the sponsor or another undertaking designated by it, or their product, activity or service; or their distinctive sign or logo.[636]

477. Political parties and movements, as well as companies producing tobacco products, may not sponsor programmes or media services.[637] Not even the name, slogan or emblem of a party or a political movement may appear in the name or the displayed name of the sponsor.[638]

478. In addition, companies which primarily produce products that cannot be advertised or provide services in relation to such products cannot sponsor media services or programmes by featuring or promoting this product or this service (which

630. §36(6) Mttv., third sentence.
631. §20(8) Smtv.
632. §20(9) Smtv.
633. §20(10) Smtv.
634. §29 Mttv.
635. §20(8) Smtv. and §26(3) Mttv.
636. §26(2) Mttv.
637. §27(1) Mttv.
638. §27(4) Mttv.

does not exclude that they sponsor programmes or media services by featuring or promoting another of their products or services).[639]

479. Implementing subsection 3 of Article 10 of the AVMS Directive, the law says the following:

> §27 (3)Mttv.
> The prohibition laid down in § 20 (7) of Smtv. shall not apply to the sponsorship tied to the publication of the name and trademark of an undertaking in connection with a medicine or a medicinal procedures, or sponsorship tied to the promotion of medicines, medicinal products or procedures, which may be used without a medical prescription. Programmes sponsored by an undertaking engaged in the manufacture or distribution of medicines, medicinal products or the supply of medicinal procedures may not promote medicines, medicinal products or medicinal procedures accessible upon medical prescriptions only.

480. In order to make it possible for live coverage of shows or events that are sponsored (in real life) to be broadcasted, the law allows sponsors of the event or its participants to appear on screen with their names or logos, products or services. These shall qualify neither as sponsorship nor as surreptitious commercial communication on the condition that the media service provider has no material interest in this and the manner of transmission does not give the sponsor an unjustified emphasis.[640] Interviews made at the event, or in connection with the event before or after it, or during its interval are also included.

481. If a logo or symbol of a product or service appears in a programme belonging to a person or company which sponsors another person or company that appears in a programme of the audiovisual service provider, the rules on sponsorship shall apply with the exception of naming the sponsors.[641]

482. News and political information programmes may not be sponsored by audiovisual media services – this is an EU obligation.[642] However, thematic media services that provide news or political information programmes are an exception.[643] This exception may be questionable from a competition law perspective and from the perspective of independence of news services; however, it applies to the sponsorship of the media service provider and not the programmes themselves. The AVMS Directive does not include such exemption in favour of thematic media services.[644]

639. §27(2) Mttv.
640. §27(5) Mttv.
641. §27(6) Mttv.
642. §28(1) Mttv., Art. 10. AVMS Directive.
643. §28(3) Mttv.
644. 'News and current affairs programmes shall not be sponsored', Art. 10(4) AVMS Directive.

483. However, programmes that give reportage of official events of national holidays may not be sponsored either, which is beyond the Directive's recommendation ('Member States may choose to prohibit the showing of a sponsorship logo during children's programmes, documentaries and religious programmes', subsection 4 Article 10) as national holidays are not religious.[645] The latter (programmes reporting on the official events of national holidays) may not be sponsored on the radio either.[646]

§5. Product Placement

484. In the regulation of product placement, the law follows the European Directive on Audiovisual Media Services, with a few additional restrictions. The law similarly declares that product placement shall be prohibited, with the exception of cinematographic works intended for showing in movies, films and series made for audiovisual media services, sports programmes and light entertainment programmes, and if the manufacturer or distributor of the product (or the provider of the service) provides the goods or services for free of charge and does not provide any further financial contribution.[647] It is prohibited to place products in news programmes and political information programmes, in programmes reporting on the official events of national holidays, and in programmes with religious or ecclesiastic content.[648] It is also prohibited to place products in children's programmes (which are defined as programmes intended for minors under fourteen) with the exception of the free contribution of products mentioned above (also mentioned in Article 2 of the Audiovisual Directive and in subsection (2)b) of the Mttv.).

485. Beyond tobacco and medicinal products that are prohibited objects of product placement in the Directive and in Mttv. as well, Mttv. also prohibits the placement of products that may not be advertised, according to Mttv. or other legislation.[649] In fact, Mttv. does not define more prohibited goods, but Smtv. and the Advertising Act do. These are (beyond medicines and tobacco products) – weapons, ammunition, and explosives.[650] The Advertising Act[651] further prohibits (beyond those already mentioned) other goods and services: tools that are especially dangerous to public safety; dangerous dogs (as defined in a special act) and animal fights; human tissue and organs; abortion, institution that performs abortion, or means or procedure suitable to perform abortion.[652]

645. There are three official national holidays in Hungary, all celebrating political events: 15 March, 20 August and 23 October.
646. §28(2) Mttv.
647. §30(1) Mttv.
648. §30(3)(a), (c), (d) Mttv.
649. §30(4)(b) Mttv.
650. §20(7) Smtv.
651. Act XLVIII of 2008 on basic conditions and certain restrictions of commercial advertising (Advertising Act).
652. §§14–17 Advertising Act.

486. Similar to the Directive, neither content nor scheduling of programmes may be influenced in a way which would affect editorial independence and responsibility. In addition, a product placement shall not directly encourage the purchase or rental of goods or services or give undue prominence to the product in question.[653] Viewers and listeners shall be clearly informed of the fact of product placement, with optical or acoustic signs at the beginning and end of the programme and after advertisements, except if the programme was not prepared or ordered by the media service provider itself or a company influenced by it.[654] The Media Council is entitled to issue recommendations concerning compliance with these rules.[655]

§6. Restrictions by the Anti-LGBT Legislation on Advertisements

487. In 2021, the law on stricter measures against paedophile criminals has been passed. However, the law, beyond legitimate restrictions in the criminal law, banned the representation of homosexuality and transsexualism, among others, in advertisements (*See also* paragraphs 135–137 and 369.) The respective prohibitions were incorporated into the advertising law and the media law. In the advertising law, it is prohibited to make accessible to persons below eighteen any advertisement that depicts sexuality as an end in itself or promotes deviations from the identity of the sex assigned at birth, gender reassignment and homosexuality.[656]

488. Content that is capable of unfavourably influencing children's appropriate physical, mental and moral development, especially by promoting or depicting sexuality as an end in itself, pornography, deviations from the identity of the sex assigned at birth, gender reassignment and homosexuality should not qualify as a social purpose advertisement or as a public communication. *See* the changes related to the media law under paragraph 369.

653. §31(1) Mttv.
654. §31(2–3) Mttv.
655. §31(4) Mttv.
656. §8(1a) of the Advertising Act. Effective as of 8 Jul. 2021.

Chapter 6. Right to Information

§1. Access to Major Events

489. The regulation of access to events that have major importance for the population of Hungary or of other Member States of the EU is greatly similar to the rules of the AVMS Directive. The law implements all sections of Articles 14 and 15 of the AVMS Directive and adds some practical rules mainly relating to the competences of the Media Council. This part of the regulation applies only to audiovisual media services and not to radios – although the Hungarian Act treats radios in most aspects equally to audiovisual media services.

490. Similar to the Directive, the law provides that audiovisual media service providers may not exercise their exclusive right to transmit events in a way that would deprive a significant portion of the domestic audience (and of the audience in other Member States, respectively) from following the event without paying a subscription fee, either in real-time or through a delayed transmission.[657] Exercising exclusive transmission rights acquired after the stepping into effect of the Protocol attached to the Council of Europe Convention on Transfrontier Television may not violate the provisions on transmitting events of high interest in the States signatories to the Protocol.[658]

491. If a media service provider acquired the right of exclusive transmission but exercising its right would exclude at least 20% of the domestic audience from following the event through audiovisual media services, the audiovisual media service provider is obliged to make an offer to another audiovisual media service provider that seeks such an offer – provided that it is accessible for at least 80% of the citizens of Hungary without paying a subscription fee. The offer must be fair and reasonable, with appropriate consideration according to the market conditions. The service provider, who holds the exclusive transmission right, cannot argue in this case that it is not entitled to transfer the right.[659] The same applies to events highly important for the audience of any other State accepting the Protocol, or EU Member State, in relation to media service providers under the jurisdiction of that signatory State or Member State.[660] The parties are obliged to conclude the contract (both parties are obligated by the Mttv.), and if they cannot agree within fifteen days, both are entitled (though not obliged) to ask the Media Council to carry out a 'legal dispute procedure' (defined in §172–174 Mttv., *see* in paragraphs 544–545).[661]

657. §§16(1), 17(1) Mttv.
658. §17(2) Mttv.
659. §18(1) Mttv.
660. §18(2–3) Mttv.
661. §18(5) Mttv.

492. The list of events of major importance for the society is defined by the Media Council after a public hearing (*nyilvános meghallgatás*).[662] The Media Council held a public hearing on 14 September 2011, on which it presented a draft list of events of major importance for society.[663] It published the summary of opinions and comments in a document online, in which it reacted to the suggestions.[664] The Media Council did not accept any of the suggestions expressed at the public hearing. In February 2012, it published a list of important events.[665] The list contains fourteen different sports events, the same that were mentioned in its draft list. The critical voices raised were that several in the list of sports events attract relatively little public attention. Some of them objected that certain sports clubs may suffer a decline in revenue if they cannot sell the right of transmission to private broadcasters; others criticized spending public money on broadcasts that were otherwise transmitted on private channels and, generally, the interference in the market of sport-financing.[666]

493. The Media Council also defined whether these events shall be transmitted live or deferred in time.[667] The list should contain events that raise interest in a wide range of viewers, that are of world or European or national interest, and that are transmitted in a significant part of the European countries (except for those events that are of exclusively national interest).[668]

§2. Short News Reporting

494. All linear audiovisual media service providers settled in the territory of the EU are entitled to get access in a fair, reasonable and non-discriminative manner to the transmission of events that are listed in the decision of the Media Council (or defined as having high importance by any other Member State), and transmitted exclusively by an audiovisual media service provider settled in Hungary. Access may mean either access to the transmission signs, recording at the venue of the event, or transition of the record about the event.[669] If another media service provider settled in the same Member State holds exclusive rights of transmitting the event, access shall be requested from that broadcaster. The parties are obliged to conclude the contract, which must be concluded with rational conditions. The consideration may not exceed the justified costs of granting access. If the contract is not concluded within fifteen days, any of the parties are entitled to initiate a 'legal dispute procedure' at the Media Council.[670]

662. §16(2) Mttv., first sentence.
663. http://www.mediatanacs.hu/hirek.php?hir_id=749.
664. http://www.mediatanacs.hu/uploads/9/11/1318586224kiemelt_esemenyek_eszrevetelek_fin.pdf.
665. http://www.mediatanacs.hu/uploads/9/12/1329210150osszesitett_lista_20120213.pdf.
666. Ágnes Urbán, Hajrá, Mtv! in Mérték Médiaelemző Műhely. http://mertek.postr.hu/hajra-mtv, (29 Feb. 2012).
667. §16(2) Mttv., second sentence.
668. §16(2) Mttv.
669. §19 Mttv.
670. §19(3) Mttv.

495. The audiovisual media service provider that has acquired access may choose the extracts freely from the programme, but the total time of short extracts may not exceed 10% of the programme concerned, or fifty seconds at most, except if a longer time is agreed in the contract.[671] The short extracts may not be published individually, only as parts of general news and information programmes. If the linear audiovisual media service provider wants to publish the short extracts through on-demand services, then the programmes must be identical in both the linear and on-demand services.[672] The audiovisual media service provider which presents the short extracts shall indicate the one which holds the exclusive transmission right.[673]

671. §19(4–5) Mttv.
672. §19(7) Mttv.
673. §19(6) Mttv.

Chapter 7. Access to Networks

Judit Bayer & Gábor Polyák

§1. Must-Carry Rules

496. The Universal Service Directive of the EU provides that Member States may impose reasonable must-carry obligations where a significant number of end-users of such networks use them as their principal means to receive radio and television broadcasts, provided that the obligations are necessary to reach clearly defined general interest objectives, are proportionate and are transparent.[674]

497. Must-carry obligations are prescribed in order to ensure diversity in the programming selection that is provided for the viewers when there is a scarcity of transmission tools compared to the number of channels. When the situation is reversed, that is, there is a content scarcity compared to the transmission capacities, the same purpose (diversity) may be achieved with must-offer obligations. The Hungarian law prescribes both of them under different conditions. In the era of digital transmission, when terrestrial frequencies are no longer provided to the individual media service providers by the State, must-carry rules would remain the only regulatory tool by which a State can influence how likely a programme gets to the audience. The law maintains this possibility only for public service and community linear media – mainly, but not exclusively, audiovisual. In absence of frequency licences, this can be used as a 'reward' for undertaking public service obligations.[675]

498. The new rules are more precise and somewhat more relaxed than the previous regulations. However, the competence of the Authority did increase in this respect, too. It has the right to give the must-carry status (i.e., the entitlement to be transmitted) to two linear public services and one linear community media service provider beyond those regulated by the law (*see* paragraphs 475–477). The transmitters do not qualify as 'clients' in the procedure, so they do not have the right to participate in the process or even appeal against the decision.[676]

499. The law lists a number of public interests that may justify this kind of market regulation. The place of the rules in the act (in chapter 'Pluralism') also signifies the intended purpose of these rules by the legislator. The listed interests are – preserving, protecting and developing Hungarian, national, ethnic and European

674. Directive 2002/22/EC of the European Parliament and of the Council of 7 Mar. 2002 on universal service and users' rights relating to electronic communications networks and services (Universal Service Directive) Art. 31. OJ L108/51, http://eur-lex.europa.eu/LexUriServ/LexUriServ.do?uri=OJ:L:2002:108:0051:0051:EN:PDF.

675. Gábor Polyák, *A médiarendszer kialakítása: a piacra lépés és a hozzáférés alkotmányjogi, közösségi jogi és összehasonlító jogi elemzése* 304–305 (HVG-ORAC 2008).

676. §75(3) Mttv., *see also*, Gábor Polyák, *A médiapiac szabályozása az új médiatörvényben*, 1 Médiakutató 24 (2011).

culture; fostering national and ethnic minority languages; satisfying the informational needs of citizens; helping them to participate in a democratic public sphere; and preserving the plurality of opinions.

500. Must-carry obligations apply to both radio and audiovisual distributors, especially cable television networks, satellite distribution networks, and terrestrial distribution networks (with the exception of analogue audiovisual transmitters), and also to transmission systems that use Internet Protocols if the nature and conditions of such service are equal to programme distribution, or if they substitute programme distribution through other methods.[677] However, the obligation may extend to any other service provider which distributes programmes in any other transmission system if the users or subscribers use this system as their primary means to receive radio and audiovisual media services. Such systems and networks are regularly (but at least in every third year) controlled and analysed by the Media Council (regular review is required by the Universal Service Directive). If the council finds that prescribing a must-carry obligation is justified in regard to the network or operating system, it shall prescribe a must-carry obligation to all service providers and operators that transmit through that system or network.[678]

501. Networks, which primarily transmit audiovisual media services, are not obliged to carry radio media services.[679] If a distributor/transmitter performs its services through more than one transmission system or distribution network, the obligation applies separately to each system or network.[680]

502. Programme distributors are obliged to transmit four linear audiovisual public media services and three linear radio services (i.e., all channels of the national public media services). No fee may be demanded from subscribers for making these channels available beyond the costs of access. Neither distributors nor the media service providers may demand a fee for this transmission.[681] An amendment added two more channels to this obligation in 2014. In case the distributor provides HD quality, it is obliged to carry the mentioned public service channels in HD quality and to make these available in the first places of the channel distribution.[682] Distributors are obliged to make these channels available in a basic package that contains only these channels.[683]

503. Programme distributors have an obligation to enter into a contract with up to three regional or local audiovisual media services or up to 10% of their total

677. §73(2–3) Mttv.
678. §73(4) Mttv.
679. §73(5) Mttv.
680. §73(6) Mttv.
681. §74(1) Mttv.
682. Amending Act CVII of 2014, effective since 1 Jul. 2015.
683. §74(2) Mttv.

capacity if they receive a reasonable offer.[684] In addition, another two local audio-visual media services must be distributed if the local media service providers' reception area is directed specifically to the inhabitants of that area and they make a reasonable offer. If a distributor's service covers separate areas, this obligation applies to each area separately.[685] However, satellite programme distributors form an exception – they are not obliged to carry local services.[686]

504. Certain programmes of the public broadcaster must be carried out free of charge on the terrestrial digital platform, specifically on the network with the widest coverage.[687] Also, in respect of the network with the widest coverage and of the mobile-received networks, the must-carry obligation applies to the multiplex operator toward a television provider that has been in business for at least four years, carrying at least two programmes focused on news and public affairs for the information of citizens, as well as toward nationwide community radio providers in business for at least three years. The beneficiaries of these obligations can be unambiguously identified as Hír TV and ATV. However, their business model was based on the fees received from cable and satellite distributors for their programme, which they nearly lost because of this legal change – if their channels had been accessible to the general public free of charge, their cable distributors would not have paid to them for the programme any longer. This was remedied by AH designing a paid programme package that featured no channels other than the two news television stations mentioned for several months.

505. The must-carry obligation also applies to no more than four nationwide general-content broadcasters.[688] Yet, despite the fact that the winning bidder made a commitment to contracting two new channels, neither is actually available on this platform. One of the channels never really took off, while the other decided that being carried on the terrestrial platform free of charge was not worth its while since the marginal increase in advertising revenues would not make up for the missed broadcasting fees. Even the two national commercial stations allowed themselves to be bogged down in lengthy legal disputes before they were willing to sign a contract for digital distribution.

506. Beyond the State public service channels, the Media Council may grant must-carry statuses to certain other channels (detailed below in paragraph 480). It is also the Media Council's competence to supervise whether the distributors fulfil their must-carry obligations.[689]

507. In addition, the Media Council may define at most two other linear public media services or at most one linear community media service, with which programme distributors would be obliged to enter into a contract. In the latter case, the

684. §75(1) Mttv.
685. §75(4) Mttv.
686. §75(2) Mttv.
687. §25 of Dtv. (Act LXXIV of 2007 on Digital Transition).
688. §39(2)c of Dtv.
689. §182. bj, x; §75(3) Mttv.

community media services must be different from those already entitled to be carried out (because of their local relevance). When passing this decision, the Media Council must consider the plurality of the media market and of information providing, the achievement of the public service goals (as defined in the act), and preservation and augmentation of culture. Distributors are not considered clients in this procedure, which means that they are not entitled to participate in the process or appeal against the decision.[690] This provision envisages that more public service channels will come into existence in future. The programme distributor's own information channels or media services that are provided by a company owned or influenced by the distributor cannot be considered when prescribing the above obligation.[691]

508. Dominant distributors are obliged to carry three more linear community audiovisual media services (at most) if they receive reasonable offers. If only one more linear community audiovisual media service must be carried out, but more suitable service providers apply, the distributor must execute an open, transparent procedure in which it is obliged to choose impartially and upon objective criteria between the contractual offers of the media service providers. An offer may be rejected for technological reasons only if the claim endangers the operational security or network unity. Economic reasons may be grounds for rejection only if the discrepancy between the fees offered and the costs (including from regular profit) makes the agreement impossible. The burden of the proof is on the distributor to prove that carrying the programme is unjustified either for economic or technological reasons.[692]

509. The Media Council publishes the starting of its procedure and the decision it passed. A court appeal has no delaying effect on the decision's application, and even the court does not have the right to suspend the application of the decision. The decision is immediately enforceable without regard to an appeal.[693] While in the case of must-carry obligations, the situation would not necessarily require an immediate application, as court procedures tend to drag on, it is in the interest of the entitled media service provider to enjoy immediate enforcement. The application of the decision is controlled and supervised by the Media Council.[694] If the distributor has violated the must-carry rules, the Media Council sets a twenty-day deadline first and then starts the sanctioning procedure.[695]

510. Programme distributors are obliged to send their contracts concluded within their must-carry obligations (and their modifications) to the Authority within thirty days and inform the Authority about the termination of the contract within

690. §75(3) Mttv.
691. §75(6) Mttv.
692. §75(7–11) Mttv.
693. §75(14) Mttv.
694. §75(15) Mttv.
695. §75(16–17) Mttv.

thirty days.[696] Both distributors and media service providers are obliged to reveal data relating to the must-carry obligation upon notice from the Authority.[697]

511. Under the previous regulation, in a case initiated by a media service provider, the authority (ORTT) found that the distributor (*CaraCom Kábel-TV és Internet Szolgáltató Kft.*) violated its must-carry obligation and obliged it to start negotiations with the applicant within fifteen days.[698]

§2. Other Access Obligations for Networks

I. Must-Offer

512. In case there is content scarcity at a certain platform, the purpose of ensuring diversity may be served by imposing a must-offer obligation to content providers so as to ensure the presence of certain programmes at the platform in question. In competition law, vertical integration is one of the conditions of the must-offer obligation, whereas having SIP on the market is the other. The Mttv. enforces both aspects – a must-offer obligation is prescribed to media service providers with SIP (*see* paragraph 508 below) and to content providers whose owner is a dominant distributor (*see* paragraph 481) and owns an influencing share. The obligation applies to all linear audiovisual services of such a service provider.[699] This might discourage launching their own channels by distributors, thereby exercising a chilling effect on the proliferation of television programmes.[700]

513. The offer may be rejected only if its fulfilment is impossible for technical or economic reasons and if the parties are unable to find a compromise. In case of doubt, the burden of the proof is on the obligated media service provider.[701] The law ensures strong protection to distributors at this point, although it might have been justified to ensure a right for content providers to abstain from including their service in programming packages with content with which they disagree.[702] But perhaps the market might regulate this problem automatically. The remaining contractual conditions shall be defined by the parties according to the principles of equality, technology neutrality, economy of scale, and at an affordable price level. The obligated media service provider may not unjustly differentiate between distributors' contractual offers and may not demand in the contract that another service or product be bought by the distributor.[703] The price may be amended only once a year. A principle of equality shall be deemed violated, especially if the obligated media service provider unjustly sets out certain technological conditions that a

696. §77(1) Mttv.
697. §77(2) Mttv.
698. HS/2133-1/201 decision.
699. §78(1) Mttv.
700. Gábor Polyák, *A médiapiac szabályozása az új médiatörvényben*, 1 Médiakutató 24–25 (2011).
701. §78(6–7) Mttv.
702. Gábor Polyák, *A médiapiac szabályozása az új médiatörvényben*, 1 Médiakutató 21–27 (2011).
703. §78(3) Mttv.

dominant number of the distributors is unable to fulfil or if the fee is defined so as to be acceptable only for a few programme distributors (including providing a discount for higher turnover).[704] In case the amount of the fee is disputed, the burden of the proof of proving the lawfulness of the fee's definition and of the observation of the principle of equality during the procedure is on the obligated media service provider.[705]

514. The obligated media service provider shall define the framework conditions that are deemed rational, justified, transparent and controllable and publish them on its website. The framework conditions shall contain especially the principles of how the fees are defined, how they are paid, the procedure leading to concluding the contract, the manner and conditions of using the service, its potential limits – whether economic, technological or other; the cases and conditions of amending and terminating the contract; cases of suspending the service; what constitutes breach of contract and what are its consequences. In case of amending the framework conditions, the new conditions must be published at least thirty days before stepping into effect. The Authority shall supervise whether the rules on the framework conditions are followed.[706] The contracts and their amendments shall be sent to the Authority within thirty days by the obligated media service provider. In case the contract terminates, the Authority shall be notified within thirty days as well.[707] All affected media service providers and distributors are obliged to provide data relating to the must-offer obligation to the Authority.[708]

515. In cases where the contract cannot be concluded within thirty days of making the offer, the distributor may initiate a dispute procedure with the Authority. The same possibility applies if the media service provider violated the contractual or legal rights or interests of the distributor.[709]

516. A distributor qualifies as dominant if the number of its subscribers is beyond 100,000 (regardless of the platform or network), or if its distribution service is accessible publicly, without a subscription fee, and it reaches more than one-third of the population of Hungary, and the yearly revenue of the distributor (or of a company that has an influential share in it, or in its owner) that arises from programme distribution on the territory of Hungary (or adjacent services, with exception of analogue broadcasting) exceeds HUF 1 billion. In case of doubt, the distributor must prove that it does not belong in this category.[710] Interestingly, the law fixes the conditions, leaving no room for the Authority to define a relevant market and to weigh what is considered the dominant position in that market.

704. §78(4–5) Mttv.
705. §80(2) Mttv.
706. §79(1–5) Mttv.
707. §81(1) Mttv.
708. §81(2) Mttv.
709. §80(1) Mttv.
710. §73(7) Mttv.

517. In a specific rule that is similar to the must-offer obligation, the law prohibits national commercial audiovisual linear service providers from demanding a fee from programme distributors for carrying their programmes until the digital transition is finished.[711] This means that they must rely on the shrinking advertising revenues. The frequent amendment of the final date of digital switch-off makes planning difficult for the two national commercial television channels (RTL Klub and TV2).[712]

II. Conditional Access

518. Most provisions regarding conditional access have been based on the Access Directive.[713] Operators of any kind of Conditional Access System (CAS) are obliged to ensure technical conditions for distributors or operators of transmission networks so as to control the transmission cost-effectively, in order to enable them to fully control the services and the number of subscribers.[714] In addition, if they provide conditional access services to digital television and radio services, they are obliged to provide fair, rational and equal technical services to each media service provider, services that enable the reception of the services of the latter by those subscribers who have the digital decoders. They are also obliged to keep separate financial accounts regarding their activity as conditional access providers.[715]

519. Programme distributors are obliged to operate CASs which enable parents to restrict their children's access to content not recommended for minors.[716]

711. §207(6) Mttv.
712. The final date of the digital switch-off was amended three times during 2011 (§38(1) Dtv.). The final date at 24 Jan. 2012 was – 31 Dec. 2014.
713. Now recaset by the Directive (EU) 2018/1972 of the European Parliament and of the Council of 11 Dec. 2018 establishing the European Electronic Communications Code (Recast) replacing the Access Directive: Directive 2002/19/EC of the European Parliament and of the Council of 7 Mar. 2002 on access to, and interconnection of, electronic communications networks and associated facilities, OJ L 108 (2002), 7.
714. §30(1) of Dtv.
715. §30(2) of Dtv.
716. §30(5) of Dtv.

Chapter 8. Standards and Interoperability

Ágnes Urbán

520. Hungary uses the Digital Video Broadcasting (DVB) standards for digital television. The DVB group was founded in September 1993 and standards were developed for satellite (DVB-S, 1993), cable (DVB-C, 1994), terrestrial (DVB-T, 1995) and mobile broadcasting (DVB-H, 2004). Originally, DVB was developed for Europe, but it became a worldwide standard.

521. There are no special, State-driven standards on the cable, satellite and IPTV market. DTT is different because its development is policy-driven, and although the DVB standard is accepted, there are some open questions. The standard excludes some key elements of digital television, like Application Programming Interface (API), CAS and the Electronic Programme Guide (EPG).

522. In 2008, the NHH issued tenders for licences to set up and operate digital terrestrial radio and television networks. AH was the winner of both tenders; the service was launched in December 2008. The service is built on the ETSI (European Telecommunications Standards Institute) standards. Law prescribes that all programme distributors and media service providers shall strive to apply open API,[717] and the contract between the authority and AH includes this obligation as a firm requirement. Programme distributors', media service providers' and manufacturers' access conditions to API have to be fair, rational and equal.[718] AH has to ensure the technical conditions for the cost-effective control of CAS in order to get exact data about services and suppliers.

523. The EPG service provider is obliged to ensure access to the interface to the required extent for the media service providers under fair, rational and equal conditions – as it is also prescribed by the Access Directive.[719] Law prescribes, however, that public service programmes shall have priority access in a given multiplex.[720] In case the EPG provider has a controlling relationship with a media service provider, these obligations apply only if in the same reception area no other independent EPG provider is available for users.[721] Obligation of MPEG-4 compression standard was also set in the contract between NHH and the authority; therefore, Hungary was one of the pioneers using this state-of-the-art technology in digital terrestrial broadcasting. High-definition quality or the 16:9 screen format was not a requirement.

---

717. §31(1) of Dtv.
718. §31(3) of Dtv.
719. Official Contract of NHH (2008). Accessible at: http://www.nmhh.hu/dokumentum.php?cid=16376, and Directive 2002/19/EC of the European Parliament and of the Council on access to, and interconnection of, electronic communications networks and associated facilities (Access Directive).
720. §33(2) of Dtv.
721. §34(1) of Dtv.

Part IV. Cross-Ownership Regulation

524. The 2010 Media Law has deregulated cross-ownership, that is, the possession of various types of media outlets such as printed press and broadcasters. The rules on ownership concentration of media service providers have been tailored to fit the digital market, with special regard to the terms and methods of regulation. However, the rules on analogue (radio) broadcasting companies remained largely the same.

525. The rules on analogue linear radio media services have remained the same as in the previous law. An analogue linear radio media service provider may not have more than one national, two regional and four local, or twelve local analogue linear radio services. A national analogue linear radio media service provider or a company which has an influencing share in it may not acquire an influencing share in any other media service provider or distributor (an exception is if the national linear radio media service provider provides only thematic services).[722] Licences of a media service provider and of companies under its influencing ownership shall be regarded as being on the one hand.

526. A regional or local linear media radio service provider or its owner may not acquire influencing ownership in another regional or local linear media radio service providing company, with the exception of the reception areas of the two radios overlapping by at most 20% or an unused programming time remains after the decision of the tender, and – while publishing a new tender – the unused programming time is contracted with the radio media service provider in question, provided that the acquired programming time differs 80% from its current programming time, and none of them exceeds four hours.[723]

527. An important new element of the law is that the Media Council acts as an expert authority (*szakhatóság*) in procedures at the Competition Authority if any of the merging parties have editorial liability and if their primary objective is to transmit media content through a telecommunication network or by a press product. According to law, a fusion may not be allowed if it violates the rules of the media law (Mttv.). As this rule refers to all other rules of the media law, including its principles, it leaves ample room for the Media Council to reject approvals. The procedure of the Media Council is unfolded below in paragraphs 536–540.

722. §71(1) Mttv.
723. §71(6)b Mttv.

528. Interestingly, while cross-ownership between media service providers and press product owners is not regulated by law, the Media Council may interfere in market processes (mergers and acquisitions) not only between these actors but also between press product owners, as happened in the *Axel Springer-Ringier* case in 2011.[724] The Media Council prohibited the merger of the print publishers Axel Springer and Ringier in 2011, proceeding in its role as an expert authority, delivering its opinion to the Competition Authority.[725] The Competition Authority may pass only a stricter decision than the Media Council's opinion. In 2014, both Ringier and Axel Springer sold part of their portfolio to an Austrian enterprise called Vienna Capital Partners and asked again for merger permission, which was approved this time.[726]

529. The merger of more than 450 printed press products into one holding (KESMA) was defined as one 'serving important national economic interests'.[727] (*See* more on KESMA in Part I. Overview of Media Markets and Main Actors, and §194) This category was created in 2013 by a simple amendment to the Competition Act: ' The Government is empowered to declare a concentration of undertakings to be of national strategic importance by decree in the public interest'[728] (The rule was activated in twenty-one cases since 2018, the KESMA case).[729] This means that the Competition Authority is not entitled to start an investigation in the case. In absence of an investigation by the Competition Authority, the Media Council is also not required to provide its expertise. The governmental decree that qualified the KESMA merger as of national importance was attacked at the Constitutional Court by one-quarter of the MPs. The Constitutional Court rejected the complaint[730] (*See* more under the Constitutional Court decisions in §194 to the AB decision).

530. Mttv.'s new rules on the prevention of media monopolies have created two different categories of influential media service providers with a special audience share. One is called *media service providers affected by rules on limiting media market concentration* (hereinafter – 'affected' media service providers), *see* more below in paragraphs 536–538; whereas the other category is called *SIP media service providers* (Jacot-Guillarmod media service providers with SIP, discussed in detail below in paragraphs 536–537).

724. *See* more in: Mihály Gálik & Artemon Vogl, *Az új médiakoncentráció-szabályozás első vizsgája: az Axel Springer és a Ringier kiadói csoport meghiúsult összeolvadása a magyar piacon*, 3 Médiakutató (2011).

725. The opinion of the Media Council was first published only after claimed under the FOI law and published by the civil media analyst group Mérték Médiaelemző Központ. https://mediatorveny.hu/dokumentum/89/nmhh_szakhatosagi_allasfoglalas.pdf.

726. A médiatanács hozzájárult az Axel Springer-Ringier fúzióhoz, 30 May 2014. http://www.napi.hu/magyar_vallalatok/a_mediatanacs_hozzajarult_az_axel_springer-ringier_fuziohoz.582036.html.

727. Government Decree 229/2018. (XII. 5.).

728. New §24/A and §97 of the Act on Unfair Market Behaviour and Competition Limitation. In effect since 22 Nov. 2013.

729. https://index.hu/gazdasag/2018/12/07/nemzetstrategiai_szempontbol_kiemelt_jelentosegu_osszefonodasok_2018_vegeig/.

730. 16/2020. (VII. 8.) Constitutional Court decision. http://public.mkab.hu/dev/dontesek.nsf/0/12bda2b452503d2dc12583a5006153a1/$FILE/16_2020%20AB%20határozat.pdf.

531. It is the Media Council's right to decide which provider qualifies either as an SIP provider or as an 'affected' provider. The rules on defining SIP providers and 'affected' providers are the same. The Media Council shall start its procedure against any provider or only against providers about which it suggests that they may belong in the category. The procedure may start with a request for data which must be fulfilled by the media service provider under the burden of a fine. When defining the audience share, the previous calendar year shall be taken as a basis,[731] but the measuring phase may be contracted out by the Media Council.[732] The audience share shall extend to all linear media services distributed by the media service provider, or by another media service provider under its influencing share, or by any of its owners, or by a media service provider under the influencing share of its owner in Hungary.[733] In its decision, the Media Council defines the exact content of some content obligations that are imposed on SIP media service providers.[734]

532. The Media Council may, instead of passing a decision upon request of the service provider, conclude an official contract with the media service provider about its qualification as an SIP media service provider and the exact scope of its content obligations. The law allows a different balancing method regarding the content obligations listed by law in §32 and §§38–39, but the provider may not be exempted from the fulfilment of those obligations.[735] However, the method and manner of fulfilling the obligations may be defined in the contract, which then cannot be changed unilaterally by the Media Council. Concluding a contract may be advantageous to the media service provider because it provides legal security as it remains effective until defined in it by the parties and may be amended only by the mutual agreement of the Media Council and of the SIP media service provider.[736] By contrast, a decision of the Media Council would remain effective only until next year's decision steps into effect. Obligations that arise from the qualification would also be effective from 1 January next year.[737] Decisions of the Media Council in respect of defining the SIP media service providers and of preventing media market concentration may be appealed against at the Capital Administrative and Labour Court (*Közigazgatási és Munkaügyi Bíróság*), but the appeal may be based only on violation of law. The court shall decide within sixty days and no appeal or renewal of the procedure is allowed. Supervising of the decision is possible if the request arrives within fifteen days of the court. The Supreme Court decides within sixty days. All courts shall give priority to the case (*soron kívül jár el)* and have reformatory rights, i.e., may change the decision of the Media Council.[738]

---

731. §70(11) Mttv.
732. §69(3) Mttv.
733. §70(4) Mttv.
734. §70(8) Mttv.
735. §70(10) Mttv.
736. András Koltay, András Lapsánszky & György Andrássy, *A médiaszabályozás kommentárja* 183 (CompLex 2011).
737. §70(11) Mttv.
738. §70(9–9a) Mttv.

533. ‘Affected’ media service providers are those linear audiovisual and radio media service providers that have a yearly average audience share of at least 35% or that have a yearly average audience share of at least 40% together on the linear audiovisual and radio market (this shall be calculated by adding the audience share reached separately on the radio and on the audiovisual market), and all of their owners, or all persons and enterprises that have an influencing share in their owner, belong in this legal category.[739] Both ‘affected’ and SIP media service providers are identified by the Media Council in an official procedure every year until 30 September.[740]

534. ‘Affected’ media service providers are subjected to two obligations. On the one hand, they are prohibited from starting another media service or acquiring ownership in any enterprise that provides media services – this obligation is effective by force of law automatically from the date they are identified as ‘affected’ media service providers by the council in its official resolution. On the other hand, they are obliged to increase plurality of the media market by amending their programming structure so that the ratios of Hungarian programmes and of programmes produced by independent programme producers are increased or in any other manner.[741] How this obligation shall be fulfilled, shall be negotiated with the Media Council – the ‘affected’ media service provider is obliged to submit its plan of measures that are meant to increase plurality for approval to the Media Council (unless an official contract is concluded by it and the Media Council, *see* in paragraph 507 below).[742] In case the media service provider cannot prove that the planned measures are suitable to increase media pluralism and decrease the information monopoly, the Media Council rejects its approval of the measures, motivating why they are not appropriate to decrease existing monopoly and increase plurality of the media market and plural information providing.[743] Then, the provider is obliged to resubmit a new plan not later than thirty days; otherwise, the Media Council may impose a procedural fine (up to HUF 25 million). In case the new plan is unsuitable for increasing media pluralism, the Media Council may impose a fine of up to HUF 200 million.[744]

535. In order to define those measures that are supposed to increase plurality of the media market, the media service provider may request the Media Council that, instead of passing a resolution, it concludes a contract with the service provider for one year. The request may be expressed within thirty days after the resolution about being identified as an ‘affected’ service provider and shall be finished within three

739. §68(1) Mttv.
740. §70(7), (11) Mttv.
741. §68(1) Mttv.
742. §68(4) Mttv. The claim for approval must be submitted within six months after the Media Council decided about the media service provider’s qualification as being significantly influential – in case of delay, the Media Council may impose a procedural fine (up to HUF 25 million, §156(2) Mttv.).
743. §68(7) Mttv.
744. §68(4–8) Mttv.

months. The Media Council is entitled to consider whether it accepts the undertakings offered by the media service provider or not.[745] In case the contract is not concluded within three months, the service provider is obliged to submit the application for approval of its plan for measurements within six months (the deadline must be kept under threat of a fine), and the approval procedure starts again.[746]

536. SIP media service providers are those linear audiovisual or radio media service providers that have at least a 15% yearly average audience share if at least one of their media services reaches a 3% yearly average audience share.[747] These media service providers are subject to special content obligations defined in §32 and §§38–39 (detailed below). In 2011, the Media Council decided that Magyar RTL (provider of RTL Klub), MTM-SBS (provider of TV2), Advenio (provider of linear radio service Class FM), FM1 (provider of Neo FM) qualified as SIP media service providers and defined their obligations in official resolutions.[748] The Media Council approved the acquisition of the IKO Group (IKO Media Holding and IKO Televisions) by M-RTL. IKO owned 31% of the shares of M-RTL.[749] SIP media service providers are subject to content obligations: they are obliged to publish a public announcement of the official catastrophe-prevention forces in case it imparts information about expectable events that endanger or harm human life or property or about the minimizing of the consequences of such events.[750] Linear audiovisual SIP media service providers are obliged to broadcast on all working days (reduced in 2019, *see* §443)at least twenty minutes news programmes between 6 and 9 pm but not more than 45 minutes. Linear radio SIP media service providers are obliged to broadcast on all working days at least ten and at most 45 minutes of uninterrupted independent news programmes between 6:30 and 8:30 am. News content taken from another media service provider or news of criminal themes that do not serve the purpose of providing democratic information may not take longer than 35% of the news programme on a yearly average. If the media service provider has more than one media service, this obligation must be performed in the service with the highest yearly average audience share. In all media services distributed digitally, the SIP media service providers must ensure that at least a quarter of the films and series are produced in a language other than Hungarian and published between 7 and 11 pm (including those ending after 11 pm) shall be accessible in the original language as well.[751]

---

745. §68(3) Mttv.
746. §68(4) Mttv.
747. §69(1) Mttv.
748. 1326/2011. (X. 5), 1327/2011. (X. 5), 1314/2011. (X. 5), 1315/2011. (X. 5) Media Council decisions. Accessible at www.mediatanacs.hu, http://www.mediatanacs.hu/uploads/28/50/13185074961327-2011_mt_kozig_hat_honlapra.pdf, http://www.mediatanacs.hu/uploads/28/50/13185074761315-2011_mt_kozig_hat_honlapra.pdf, http://www.mediatanacs.hu/uploads/28/50/13185074901326-2011_mt_kozig_hat_honlapra.pdf, http://www.mediatanacs.hu/uploads/28/50/13185074691314-2011_mt_kozig_hat_honlapra.pdf.
749. 1309/2011. (X. 5) Media Council decision, accessible at: http://www.mediatanacs.hu/hatarozatok.php?menu_id=38&h_id=15726.
750. §32(6) Mttv.
751. §38 Mttv.

537. In addition, linear audiovisual SIP media service providers are obliged to ensure that all public announcements, news programmes, political information programmes and films, as well as programmes specifically produced for people with hearing impairment, shall be accessible with Hungarian subtitles or with sign language interpretation from 2015. This shall be achieved gradually so that at least four hours of such programmes shall be provided in 2011, six hours in 2012, eight hours in 2013, and ten hours in 2014.[752] In 2019, rules on radio concentration were relaxed, allowing one owner to hold several licences in the same area. Licences are awarded for ten years instead of seven and can be extended for seven years instead of the previous five. The law also declares that the media service provider is not entitled to renew the licence, nor is the Media Council obliged to conclude a contract on the basis of such an initiative.[753]

752. §39 Mttv.
753. §48 Mttv. effective since 1 Aug. 2019.

Part V. Supervision: Media Regulator

538. Hungary has had a convergent Media and Telecommunication Authority since 2010. The Authority consists of its president, who passes decisions in telecommunication matters; the Media Council, which is responsible for supervising media content, both in the field of audiovisual and radio services, printed press and online journals; and the office which performs administrative tasks and passes decisions in cases of lesser importance in both sectors. Where both the office and the Media Council are entitled to perform an administrative action, the law – and this monograph – uses the word 'Authority'. The Mttv. considers the Media Council, the president of the Authority and the Office of the Authority all as separate bodies within the Authority with their independent competences.[754] In fact, decisions are taken by the president of the Authority in telecommunications matters, by the Media Council in media matters, and by the Office of the Authority in administrative matters. The Office of the Authority also acts as an administrative background organization for both the Media Council and the president of the Authority.[755]

754. §109(3) Mttv. In addition, the Administrative Spectrum Management Authority, which performs non-civil spectrum management administrative tasks of the government. (§109(8–9) Mttv.).
755. §123(4) Mttv.

Chapter 1. Organization

§1. The National Media and Telecommunication Authority

539. The National Media and Telecommunication Authority (NMHH) is a legally independent regulatory authority[756] which is subordinate only to the law. It carries out the government's policy in the field of spectrum management and telecommunication and has broad powers in the area of media supervision via the Media Council. Tasks may be prescribed by laws or by other legal rules issued upon empowerment of laws.[757]

540. The president of NMHH is appointed by the President of the Republic, upon the recommendation of the Prime Minister, for nine years and cannot be re-elected.[758] Requirements of personal conditions are: having an active right of election (to be electable in parliamentary elections), having a clean slate, not having been sentenced by prohibition to work in this activity, having a degree of higher education in the field of legal, economic or social sciences and having at least five years' experience relating to authority supervision of media services or press products, having a scientific title in any of those fields of study in the subject of media or telecommunication or having at least ten years' practice in an institute of higher education.[759] The Prime Minister shall consult civil organizations before making the recommendation in the following manner: it shall ask the Public Service Body, the National Telecommunication and Informatics Council and those self-regulatory, interest-representative and professional organizations of telecommunication service providers, media service providers, programme distributors and journalists, which have been operating nationally for at least five years, to make suggestions on the person for candidacy to the president of the Media Authority.[760] The organizations make their suggestions in writing and give reasoning, as well as present the professional curriculum of the recommended person.[761] The president is entitled to appoint two vice presidents for an unlimited time and may dismiss them at any time without reasoning.[762] The president may entitle the vice presidents with the competence to decide cases at second instance. Vice presidents may not be instructed in their task of deciding cases at second instance.[763] The president's mandate may terminate – by lapse of time, resignation, death or dismissal by the Prime Minister or – if he or she is not elected as president of the Media Council.[764] The last element was inserted by an amendment in May 2012 and practically raised the position of president of the Media Council to a higher rank than the president of the Authority (the two positions shall be fulfilled by the same person). After this amendment, the

756. Article 23. Basic Law.
757. §109(1–2) Mttv.
758. §111/A(1), (3) Mttv.
759. §111/A(2) Mttv.
760. §111/A(4) Mttv.
761. §111/A(5) Mttv.
762. §113(6) Mttv.
763. §112(1–2) Mttv.
764. §113(1)a–e Mttv.

president of the Media Council will also become the president of the Authority, while in the original version, the president of the Authority was also to become president of the Council. As the president of the Media Council is elected with two-thirds of the votes in Parliament, theoretically, this situation better agrees with democratic norms and may better serve the independence of the Authority. However, in the concrete situation, all presidents of both organizations were elected with the votes of only one party in the Parliament, Fidesz. The first president was herself, a previous senior official and MP of Fidesz. After her early death, the second president, Mónika Karas, was similarly elected with the votes of only the Fidesz in 2013 and then András Koltay in 2021. Under normal circumstances, the two-thirds majority would be regarded as a guarantee of independence of the president of the Authority. However, within the Hungarian Parliament, even in 2021, Fidesz possessed two-third of the votes and did not hesitate to use this power to define the new president of the Authority, even against the votes of oppositional parties. Political analysts name this move as the key factor in the pre-term resignation of Mónika Karas in 2021.[765] Her office would have terminated in 2022 after the parliamentary elections, and Fidesz feared losing its two-thirds majority (it did not).[766] Her early resignation allowed Fidesz to appoint the new, loyal president, András Koltay, for nine years in December 2021.[767]

541. It should be noted that no legal changes were applied to implement the AVMS Directive's Article 30[768] as the current procedure of election was regarded as sufficient. As noted in the previous paragraph, the appointing committee's qualified majority was even reduced to a simple majority. The requirements of Article are nevertheless not completely fulfilled (*see* §166.), in particular the de facto criteria of independence.[769]

542. The Prime Minister may dismiss the president only for four reasons – if incompatibility is not resolved within thirty days, if he or she was sentenced to

765. https://english.nmhh.hu/article/160287/Dr_Monika_Karas, *see also*: https://www.szabadeuropa.hu/a/karas-monika-nmhh-mediatanacs-lemond/31512069.html. The resigning president received a considerable compensation: appx. EUR 111.000 after taxes. https://hungarianpolitics.com/2021/11/15/head-of-hungarys-media-authorities-resigning-will-get-41-million-ft-in-severance-pay/.

766. https://www.euronews.com/2022/04/03/hungary-election-live-voting-closes-as-viktor-orban-seeks-fifth-term-in-office.

767. 37/2021. (XII. 14.) *OGY hat. https://www.parlament.hu/az-orszaggyules-altal-valasztott-kozjogi-tisztsegviselok-megbizatasi-ideje.*

768. Article 30 AVMS Directive on independence of the regulatory authorities of Member States.

769. Media Pluralism Monitor reported each year insufficience of NMHH's independence: 2016: 5–6, 2017: 7, 2018–19: 11, 2020: 11–12, 2021, 2022: 17. For de facto criteria, *see* Hans Bredow Institute (2011): *Indicators for Independence and Efficient Functioning of Audiovisual Media Services Regulatory Bodies for the Purpose of Enforcing the Rules in the AVMS Directive* (INDIREG). Brussels: European Commission. *See* further: Polyák Gábor (2022): *Monitoring the Independence of the Media Regulatory Body as an Effective Enforcement Mechanism for the Implementation of the AVMSD.* Journal of Digital Media & Policy, online first 4 August, https://doi.org/10.1386/jdmp_00106_1. NMHH's reaction to criticisms: NMHH (2023): *Médiaszabadság-jelentések értékelése*, https://nmhh.hu/dokumentum/241040/mediaszabadsag_jelentesek_ertekelese_NMHH.pdf.

imprisonment or prohibition from professional activity, if he or she was placed under guardianship, or if he or she did not perform his or her duties imputably for longer than six months.

543. The president of the Authority appoints the director of the office for an unlimited period of time and may dismiss him or her at any time in a justified decision.[770] The director may not be instructed when exercising his competence in passing decisions at the first instance. He or she must satisfy the same personal conditions as the president.[771] The president is entitled to appoint vice directors upon recommendation of the director.[772]

§2. The Media Council

544. The Media Council (*Médiatanács*) is a body within the Authority responsible for media matters under the supervision of the Parliament, having its own competence and legal personality. It is the legal successor of the Hungarian Radio and Television Body (*ORTT*). It shares the same office as the Authority.[773]

545. Its members are elected by the Parliament for nine years with a two-thirds majority. The four members shall be elected together on a list.[774] The members are recommended by an ad hoc committee in which each parliamentary political faction delegates one member whose vote shall be equal to the ratio of the faction that delegated him or her.[775] The time span for delegating members to the committee is defined by the parliamentary resolution about setting up the committee. If any of the parliamentary factions does not delegate its members to the committee within the set time, the committee starts the nominating process without that member.[776] The committee makes its recommendation with consensus, or, if it is unsuccessful until a date which is thirty days before the lapse of mandate of the existing Media Council members, then with a two-thirds majority.[777] If the recommendation cannot be made with a two-thirds majority within eight days, then a new delegating committee must be elected.[778] The members (and the president) may be re-elected unless their mandate ceases because of incompatibility, dismissal or exclusion.[779]

770. §§114(1), 115(1–2), (5), (7) Mttv.
771. §115(2) referring back to §111(4) Mttv.
772. §117 Mttv.
773. §123(1)(4) Mttv.
774. §124(1) Mttv.
775. §124(3–4) Mttv.
776. §124(5) Mttv.
777. §124(3), (6) Mttv. Or, if the mandate terminates for a reason other than the lapse of time, then within thirty days after getting knowledge about the termination.
778. §124(7) Mttv.
779. §125(5) Mttv.

546. The president of the Authority becomes automatically a president-appointee of the Media Council.[780] He or she is elected to become president of the Council by the Parliament on the same list as the other members of the Council.[781] Thus, it is not possible to express non-agreement against one or two members or the president separately, only to accept the whole list or reject it. If the president of the Authority loses her position because of resignation, death or dismissal by the Prime Minister, her position as president of the Media Council ceases immediately.[782] In this case, the voting is individual.

547. Detailed provisions of incompatibility apply to the members, president, vice president, director and vice directors of the Media Council, excluding bearing positions in public authorities and other official bodies and in companies related to the media or telecommunication field.[783]

548. The mandate of the members and of the president of the Media Council terminates when the new members' and president's mandate starts.[784] A possible deadlock situation was eliminated by the said amendments of May 2012. The time of the mandate of the council's president is bound to the time of the mandate of the Authority's president, with the exception of the case when the new president of the Authority is not elected to become president of the Media Council within thirty days from his or her appointment by the Prime Minister to be Authority's president.[785] In this case, not only does the previous Media Council president remain in her position until Parliament is able to elect a new Media Council president, but the Authority's president loses his or her position. In fact, these amendments changed the power relationship between the two positions: instead of binding the mandate of the council's president to the Authority's president, now the position of the Authority's president is bound to the council's president, that is, parliamentary approval by a two-thirds majority of the votes.

549. The mandate of Media Council members may terminate by lapse of time, resignation, establishing incompatibility, dismissal, exclusion and death.[786] Incompatibility may emerge for the reasons listed in §118 Mttv. or if they refuse or omit to make a transparency-declaration about their property, or disguise important data or facts or do not show proof of their clean slate.[787] Dismissal of a member or the president is possible if they have been placed under guardianship that excludes the

780. §125(1) Mttv.
781. §124(1) Mttv.
782. §125(3) Mttv.
783. §§118 and 127 Mttv.
784. Similarly: If the mandate of the president of the Authority terminates by lapse of time, his or her mandate terminates on the date when the newly elected president's mandate starts (§216(8) Mttv.). (The law uses the word 'elected', although the president of the Authority is appointed by the president.) In other cases, the termination should become effective on the actual date of the event, such as death, resignation or dismissal by the Prime Minister.
785. §125(7) Mttv., referring also to 216(8) Mttv., effective from 19 Jun. 2012.
786. §129(1) Mttv.
787. §129(2) Mttv.

person's disposal capacity.[788] Exclusion may take place if the member or the president imputably does not perform his or her duties for more than six months or if a final court decision is imposed on the member or the president imprisonment or prohibition from professional activity because of a crime.[789]

550. The Media Council's full meeting is entitled to decide on questions of incompatibility, dismissal, and exclusion with a unanimous decision (the affected person is excluded from voting).[790] If a new round of voting is still unsuccessful, the president of the Media Council may recommend that the Parliament pass the decision, which may do so by a two-thirds majority.[791] If the president is affected in the case, the member defined by the schedule of the council shall proceed to exercise the competence of the president.[792]

551. The Media Council sponsors its Media Research Institute, which is a separate organizational unit of NMHH. It helps the operation of the Media Council and also performs scientific activities, such as in the field of social sciences relating to media, publishing professional publications, and organizing conferences. Its activity is supervised by the Media Council. Its head and its members are public servants of the Authority.[793]

§3. The Media and Telecommunication Commissioner

552. A commissioner was established as part of the Authority, but the first version of its regulation was annulled by the Constitutional Court as a whole. The reasons were that the commissioner had the same – almost unlimited – rights of investigation as the Authority, had the right to investigate at each media outlet even if no violation of the law was suspected, and reported about its activity – with special regard to the cooperative attitude of the media outlet – to the Authority.

553. The amendment of May 2012 re-regulated the commissioner's institution according to the principles set by the Constitutional Court. In telecommunication matters, the rules remained largely the same, except that the commissioner may proceed only upon complaint in all cases. The commissioner may conduct a mediation procedure with the telecommunication service provider. The result of mediation is laid down in an agreement which is published and sent to the complainant and the organization representing consumers' interests. The agreement is supposed to grant rights to the subscribers, users and consumers, which may be referred to in individual cases and be controlled by the Authority. Cooperative attitude of the telecommunication service provider is respected later in other cases by the Authority.[794]

788. §129(5) Mttv.
789. §129(6) Mttv.
790. §§129(3) and 129(7) Mttv.
791. §129(7) Mttv.
792. §129(8) Mttv.
793. §138 Mttv.
794. §142 Mttv.

554. In media matters, the commissioner may conduct mediation only with organizations of the media content providers (whether professional, interest-representing or self-regulative) and only if the complaint affects a substantial part of viewers, listeners, and readers. In a later phase of the procedure, the complainant and the media content provider complained of are also invited. The result is summarized in a report which is sent to the complainant, the media content provider in question and the relevant professional organizations. In the report that is sent to the Media Council and the president of the Authority quarterly, the commissioner must not include individual media content providers.[795] The report must not be published (!).[796]

555. The commissioner is appointed by the president of the Authority. Complainants may be anyone whose interests were infringed, or the imminent danger of their infringement exists, or an organization representing 'consumers', 'subscribers', 'users', 'viewers', 'listeners', or 'readers' interests. Subject to complaint can be a behaviour related to providing media services or press products or telecommunication services, which albeit does not violate any rule on media or telecommunication and does not fall in the competence of the Media Council, the president of the Authority or the Office of Authority, but causes or may cause infringement of the just interests of users, viewers, listeners or readers.

795. §143 Mttv.
796. §142/A Mttv.

Chapter 2. Tasks

§1. Tasks of the Telecommunication and Media Authority (NMHH)

556. Any tasks may only be defined by law or other rules issued upon empowerment of law.[797] Its task in relation to the telecommunication sector is to foster the undisturbed, successful operation and development of the telecommunication market, the protection of telecommunication operators and users, and the development and maintenance of fair, effective competition in the telecommunication sector, further supervising that organizations and persons that perform telecommunication activity show lawful behaviour.[798] In the field of telecommunication, no competences may be taken away from the Authority.[799]

557. The president of the Authority is entitled to issue decrees; this right is granted in the Basic Law (*see* above in paragraphs 121 and 124).[800] The Act on Telecommunications defines the content of this right in detail, listing the subjects in which the president of the Authority may issue decrees from one to twenty-six.[801] These include – national frequency division; principles and detailed conditions of the entitlement to use, transfer or lease frequencies, including establishing the fees payable for frequencies. These fees serve as an income of the Authority.[802]

558. The Authority has several tasks relating to the telecommunication sector. It is entitled to establish the necessities of and give recommendations on legislation and amendments in relation to telecommunication; it assesses and continually analyses the operation of telecommunications and related informatics market; evaluates the situation of the telecommunications market continually and prepares comparative analyses about that; performs market inquiries; proceeds in relation to the fulfilment or the violation of obligations established individually for certain service providers; proceeds in case a rule of telecommunication has been violated, or in legal disputes related to contracting; performs telecommunication and postal official duties defined in other laws; exercises the State's ownership management rights in respect to radio frequencies and identifiers and performs civil management of them; and performs official duties defined in other laws.[803] The law on *electronic telecommunication* provides for its tasks in further detail, among others, about performing market analysis of electronic communications markets, in line with the EC Recommendation on relevant product and service markets within the electronic

797. §109(2) Mttv.
798. §109(5) Mttv.
799. §109(7) Mttv.
800. Article T(2) of the Basic Law.
801. §182(3) Act C of 2003 on Telecommunications.
802. §134(1) Mttv.
803. §110a–i Mttv.

communications sector susceptible to *ex ante* regulation.[804] Starting a sector inquiry in case a distortion in the telecommunication market is suspected is the right of the president of the Authority.[805]

§2. TASKS OF THE MEDIA COUNCIL

559. The law lists the tasks of the Media Council at two points: prescribing general and specific tasks. Below, first, we discuss general tasks, then the various specific tasks like market analysis and sector inquiry, fact-finding, extraterritorial jurisdiction, licensing and deciding about balanced information. Sanctioning powers will be discussed in a separate Chapter.

I. General Tasks

560. The Media Council (§132):

- controls and enforces press freedom within the frames of the Mttv. and the Smtv.;
- publishes and decides tenders for media services that use limited resources owned by the State;
- performs supervisory and controlling duties prescribed by law by way of recording the programme, or examining the programmes recorded by the media service provider, or upon an authority's initiative;
- operates a monitoring and programme-analysis service through its office;
- expresses its opinions about the draft laws on media and telecommunication;
- regularly controls the observation of the public contracts it concluded;
- develops position papers and recommendations on theoretical questions of the development of the Hungarian system of media services;
- initiates procedures in relation to consumer protection and the prohibition of unfair market practices;
- prepares a report to the European Commission on the fulfilment of programming quota obligations;
- if necessary, may initiate the amendment of the law (the Mttv.) at the responsible minister;
- assumes an initiative role in developing media literacy and media consciousness in Hungary, harmonizes other State participants' activity relating to media literacy, helps the government to prepare the regular report to the EU on this subject matter;
- performs other duties defined in this law or in another legal rule that may be issued according to this law.

---

804. §62 and in general §§10–13 Eht. (Act C of 2003 on Electronic Telecommunications).
805. §69 Eht.

561. In addition, the Media Council's specific official competences (in which it exercises State power) are as follows (§182):

(1) it performs the general supervision of the public contracts it concluded;
(2) supervises the application of the legal provisions below:
  (a) rules on the protection of children and youth;
  (b) rules on transmission of events that are of major importance for society;
  (c) rules on extraordinary situations that affect media services;
  (d) obligations on quotas;
  (e) rules on commercial advertisements;
  (f) rules on product placement;
  (g) rules on political advertisement, public announcement and social purpose advertisement (with the exception of the length of the advertisement which is one minute – this shall be supervised by the Office of the Authority);
  (h) rules on advertising and teleshopping;
  (i) must-carry rules and must-offer rules;
  (j) rules on the plurality of media services;
  (k) rules on performing duties of the public service media.
(3) supervises whether Articles 14 and 16–20 of the Smtv. are respected (content rules);
(4) exercises public power in case of violations of the law by media service providers settled in another State;
(5) upon request of the media service provider, it performs prior classification: decides in an official resolution in which category (in respect of the protection of minors) a certain programme should belong;[806]
(6) concludes a public contract with media service providers about exemption from programming quotas;
(7) defines (in its tenders) the lowest possible fee payable for media licence;
(8) carries out the tasks related to tenders of radio licences and of licences for fulfilling public duties;
(9) proceeds in respect of the renewal of analogue linear media service licences;
(10) proceeds in respect of the conclusion of public contracts;
(11) carries out the tasks related to the media service providers' joining into networks or their extension of their reception area;
(12) exercises the competences related to qualifying media services as community services and supervises their operation;
(13) identifies SIP media service providers (*see* paragraphs 502–509 and defines their obligations);
(14) proceeds in respect of enforcing the obligations of SIP media service providers (with the exception of the obligations regarding accessible content to people with hearing impairment – this shall be done by the Office of the Authority);

806. Examples to this type of decision are: 249/2012. (II. 7); 248/2012. (II. 7). Under the previous law, such prior classification was deemed as a form of censorship and rejected by the previous Authority.

(15) performs the public duties relating to controlling market ownership concentration;
(16) carries out sector inquiries;
(17) carries out market surveillance procedures;
(18) proceeds in legal disputes defined by the Mttv. (explained in more detail below in paragraphs 544–545);
(19) performs duties in respect of temporary media service contracts;
(20) gives expert opinion to other authorities in cases defined by the Mttv. and by the competition law;
(21) proceeds in balanced information cases related to public media service providers or SIP media service providers;
(22) defines the events of major importance for society in an official resolution;
(23) defines those public service and community media services that benefit from must-carry obligation;
(24) performs the official duties related to the procedure and decisions of self-regulatory bodies;
(25) exercises other competences as defined by law.

The Media Council performs further tasks in which it does not exercise State power (*nem-hatósági hatáskör*). These include developing recommendations and opinions; giving information and reports to the Parliament and the European Commission; managing MTVA, defining and publishing the detailed rules of managing MTVA, and approving its yearly plan, subsidizing policy, account, and general tendering conditions; cooperating with media authorities of other Member States; and performing tasks in relation to co-regulatory organizations, etc.[807]

562. The Office of the Authority also performs certain subsidiary tasks next to the Authority. These include, for example, keeping the registries (all media services must be registered in Hungary, including printed and online press), defining the media licence fee of those linear media service providers that need only registration to provide their services (rather than a frequency licence), supervises whether certain rules of the law are followed. It also proceeds in case the unbalanced nature of information is complained of, and the complained programme was not provided by a SIP media service provider (*see* paragraphs 536–537), nor by a public media service provider (in these cases, the Media Council shall proceed, discussed below in paragraph 592). It helps the Media Council by preparing, monitoring, and analysing cases in ways defined by the law.[808]

563. In general, the Authority is entitled to supervise the compliance with the rules of Mttv., Smtv., its own resolutions, as well as with the contracts on media services and other public contracts.[809] In case it finds that its resolution was not complied with, it may consider whether to start an enforcement procedure under the

807. §183 Mttv.
808. §184 Mttv.
809. §167(1) Mttv.

Administrative Procedures Act or an official procedure according to the Mttv. leading to the application of the legal consequences defined in the Mttv.[810]

564. Until 31 May each year, the Media Council submits a report of the previous year to the Parliament. The report is obliged to evaluate the situation of freedom of speech, opinion and the press, the balanced nature of information providing, changes in the ownership structure of media service providers and programme distributors, the standing of frequency management serving the satisfaction of the need for media services, and the changes of the economic and financial situation of media services.[811]

II. Market Analysis, Sector Inquiry

565. The Media Council performs market supervision (*piacfelügyelet*) on the media market.[812] It makes a market supervision plan every year up to 1 December, paying attention to that year's experiences. The plans shall be published on its website. However, the council may also perform market supervision activities other than those included in the plan.[813] They may be reviewed after the first semester and adjusted if necessary. The market supervision procedure shall finish within sixty days, with a possible extension of forty-five days.[814] The council makes a yearly report about the fulfilment of its market supervision plan, its results, outcomes and the recommendations for legal amendments on the basis of the market supervision decisions. The report shall be published on the Media Council's website.[815]

566. As a result of the procedure, the Media Council evaluates how the inspected services or activities comply with the law. In case of legal violations, it evaluates them one by one and also jointly, then imposes a legal consequence (*see* below in paragraphs 580–586). In absence of a violation of the law, it may define obligations and the conditions of their fulfilment and define the methods and directions of State interference in order to prevent violation of law or to promote voluntary compliance; the aspects of developing such a State strategy and media policy conclusions.[816]

567. The Media Council starts a sector inquiry (a different procedure from market supervision, *ágazati vizsgálat*) if market conditions show that the media market

810. §167(2) Mttv.
811. §133 Mttv.
812. The Mttv. defines as purpose of the market supervision: the interest of an undisturbed, successful, diverse operation of the media market, the protection of interest of programme distributors, media service providers, press product publishers, viewers, listeners, readers, subscribers and users; the preservation of national culture and the diversity of opinions; to promote a fair and effective market competition; getting information about market processes; and to evaluate, analyse and supervise the media policy and other aims.
813. §168(8) Mttv.
814. §168(1), (3) Mttv.
815. §168(7) Mttv.
816. §168(6) Mttv.

competition is getting distorted or getting limited.[817] This procedure shall not affect the competence of the Competition Authority to carry out a sector inquiry as defined in the law relevant to safeguarding competition and unfair market practices.[818] As a result of the sector inquiry, a fine of 0.5% of the previous year's net income of the violator, or, if there is no income or it is not revealed, between HUF 50,000 and HUF 50,000,000 may be imposed. In case information is not provided or not appropriately provided, the Media Council may impose a fine between HUF 50,000 and HUF 3,000,000 on the executive officer of the media service provider that violated the law. In case of repeated violation, the Media Council *must* impose this fine.[819] The Media Council informs the media service providers about starting the sector inquiry by publishing this on its bulletin board and on its website. It shall be regarded as delivered after fifteen days.[820]

568. In case the Media Council finds, as a result of its administrative monitoring procedure, that the competition in the media services market may get distorted or limited, and it holds that this cannot be remedied by applying the Media Council's powers, it may initiate a procedure of competition supervision at the Competition Authority. It is not clear whether the Competition Authority may consider whether to follow the initiative or not, but it shall not start a procedure if a sector inquiry is or has been in progress in the same subject and regarding the same period. In a case where a competition supervisory procedure is not justified or impossible because of a lack of competence, and neither the Media Council nor the Office of the Authority can cure the problem in their scope of competence, the Media Council shall inform the body entitled to issue legal instruments.[821]

569. The Media Council is entitled to give an expert opinion to the Competition Authority in concentration cases when at least two of the merging organizations are media content providers (this term includes printed and online press as well).[822] The Competition Authority may not decide without such an opinion, but it may depart from the opinion by prohibiting a merger or takeover that was approved by the Media Council, or it may apply further obligations as conditions of the merger or takeover.[823] The Media Council must not deny the approval of the concentration if the number of remaining independent opinion sources on the relevant media content market is enough to ensure the possibility of getting diverse information.[824] Observers have said that in the *Ringier-Springer* case, where the Media Council denied approval, diversity could have been better preserved by allowing the merger because the market situation threatened the termination of at least one national daily paper.[825]

817. §169(1) Mttv.
818. §169(2) Mttv.
819. §169(4) Mttv.
820. §169(3) Mttv.
821. §170(3) Mttv.
822. §171(1) Mttv.
823. §171(4)a–b Mttv.
824. §171(2) Mttv.
825. *See* more in: Mihály Gálik & Artemon Vogl, *Az új médiakoncentráció-szabályozás első vizsgája:*

III. Fact-Finding

570. The Authority is entitled to access, examine, copy or extract any document or tool containing information (even secrets protected by law) that relates to media services, publishing press products or programme distribution.[826] The Mttv. mentions 'Authority' here because both the Media Council and the Office of the Authority may exercise these rights. Practically, this means that this procedure may be applied in telecommunication cases as well as media matters. The wording also implies that no Media Council resolution is needed for fact-finding actions, only an administrative decision of the Authority, signed by its president. The Authority is entitled to oblige the parties or other participants of the process, their employees and mandated persons, and persons in any other relationship with them, to pass on the necessary information either in writing or verbally, in a format that is suitable for comparison, defined by the Authority.[827] In cases specifically justified, the Authority may oblige other persons or organizations to provide data or tools of verification. A decision of this effect may be appealed against at the Capital Administrative and Labour Court, which shall decide within eight days. The court appeal has a delaying effect, but the resolution is final.[828]

571. The Authority may also oblige the parties to make a declaration under threat of a fine.[829] Witnesses may be interrogated about business secrets of the parties even if they did not get an exemption from keeping the secret.[830] However, – after the latest amendment – documents created in connection with the communication between the client and his or her attorney may not be examined, confiscated, or used as proof, provided that this nature of the document is shown on the document itself.[831] The information and documents acquired this way may be used in another procedure if specifically justified and if it is necessary for the appropriate or efficient enforcement of the law or to ease the burden of the parties.[832] Reasons or a method for justification are not provided in the law, however. The Authority may impose a procedural fine on any participant of the procedure: parties or other persons who are obliged to cooperate in order to clarify the situation. A fine may be imposed if a person shows a behaviour which may result in a delay of the procedure or frustrate the revelation of the true facts or which is intended at such a result.[833] The highest amount of this fine is HUF 25 million (but only HUF 1 million for a natural person).[834] In addition, for hindering the procedure, or for not providing information or not appropriately providing it, a fine of HUF 3 million may

az Axel Springer és a Ringier kiadói csoport meghiúsult összeolvadása a magyar piacon 3 Médiakutató (2011).

826. §155(2) Mttv.
827. §155(3) Mttv.
828. §155(4) Mttv.
829. §155(3) Mttv.
830. §155(8) Mttv.
831. §155(5)a Mttv. effective from 3 Jul. 2012.
832. §155(9) Mttv.
833. §156(1) Mttv.
834. §156(2) Mttv.

be imposed – and in case of repeated violation of these rules, it *must* be imposed – on the CEO of the organization that violated the law.[835] When imposing the fine, the Authority shall consider the net income of the previous year and whether the violation was repeated.[836]

572. Until recently, the Authority was entitled to demand every data and information, even secrets protected by law, from any enterprise that was subject to the Mttv. It was possible to oblige them by official resolution to regular or continuous data submission, even by way of a monitoring system installed at the premises of the enterprise, by telecommunication methods. If the obligation was not fulfilled or not appropriately fulfilled, the Authority was entitled to impose a fine of up to HUF 50 million. This whole section, however, was annulled by the Constitutional Court on 19 December 2011.[837] This was one of the two sections that were annulled with immediate effect. The court's argumentation held that this was an unnecessary restriction of press freedom, especially because this type of data collection did not have a constitutionally justified legitimate reason. The necessary data can be collected during the procedures when they are needed, said the Constitutional Court. The court retained several other sections that provided for the collection of the necessary data, among them §155(1–8) the Mttv.[838]

IV. Legal Disputes

573. The Media Council is entitled to decide in legal disputes between media content providers or distributors, for example, in cases of contracting obligation, if a contract cannot be concluded because of a lack of agreement between the parties.[839] If a media content provider or distributor is of the opinion that another media content provider or distributor has violated its right or lawful interest, incorporated in any rule on media administration or in a contract concluded on the basis of such rules, it may ask the Media Council to decide. The procedure may be initiated within six months of the injury.[840] The Media Council shall send the application to the other party and ask it to submit its declaration and proofs within a deadline not longer than ten days.[841] The Media Council may oblige the other party to submit necessary data or make a declaration.[842] A meeting may be held at the discretion of

835. §156(3) Mttv. and §38(4–5) Eht.
836. §156(4) Mttv.
837. 1746/10 ABh annulling among others §175 of the Mttv.
838. Further sections allowing collection of data are: §22(8) Mttv. (The media service provider is obliged to provide data monthly to the Media Council so as to enable the controlling of following the rules on programming quotas.); §195(4) Mttv. (The Media Council may demand data from the self-regulatory organization about the companies that belong under their umbrella).
839. §§172(1), 174(1) Mttv.
840. §172(1) Mttv. (or later if the applicant got knowledge about the injury only later, or was hindered in filing the application, but not later than one year after the injury).
841. §172(7) Mttv.
842. §173(5) Mttv.

the Media Council. The meeting is not public.[843] The Media Council may apply for an interim injunction if necessary to prevent the threat of severe injury of interests because of the violation of the law if the injury cannot be prevented otherwise and if the injunction is proportionate with the goal to be achieved.[844] The other party may appeal against the injunction to the Capital Administrative and Labour Court, but the appeal does not have a delaying effect. The court shall decide within fifteen days in a non-contentious (written) procedure, and its decision is final (no appeal against the court decision is possible).[845]

574. The law does not provide for what the relationship of this procedure to a normal court procedure is; that is, if any of the parties initiates a court procedure in the same subject matter, does that prevail over the Media Council's procedure? The author is of the opinion that – while the Authority's expertise may be useful at several points – nobody should be deprived of access to the regular courts. Each person, even legal persons (if both of the parties are media content providers or distributors), are entitled to be able to have their legal disputes settled by independent regular courts. This right is also granted by the Basic Law.[846]

V. Extraterritorial Jurisdiction

575. The law entitles the Media Council to enforce certain parts of the law in respect of media content providers established in another Member State of the EU. It follows Articles 3 and 4 of the AVMS Directive. In 2010, the European Commission asked the Hungarian government to make certain changes in this part of the law, among others, to bring it in line with the AVMS Directive.[847] A few differences have remained despite the efforts of the Hungarian government to fulfil the request. For example, the Directive provides that domestic rules on foreign broadcasts may be applied only provisionally, but the Mttv. contains no reference to the temporary nature of these rules.[848] Another difference from the AVMS Directive is that no prior approval of the European Commission is required by the Mttv. for imposing a fine on a foreign media service provider, obliging it to publish a statement, or suspend its service in case the service provider had settled abroad with the intention to circumvent Hungarian regulations. The Mttv. provides that the draft resolution shall be sent to the commission, but – unlike the Directive – it does not require waiting for the commission's approval. Whereas the AVMS Directive provides that '[a]

843. §173(1) Mttv. Before amendment of May 2012, the meeting was to be held upon request of any of the parties.
844. §173(6) Mttv.
845. §173(9) Mttv.
846. Article XXVIII(1) Basic Law.
847. http://europa.eu/rapid/pressReleasesAction.do?reference=SPEECH/11/6&format=HTML&aged=0&language=EN&guiLanguage=en.
848. Article 3(2) AVMS Directive and Preamble (36).

Member State may take measures … only if the following conditions are met: (…) (b) the commission has decided that the measures are compatible with Union law … '.[849]

576. Other provisions – in line with the AVMS Directive – entitle the Media Council to oblige a linear audiovisual media service provider to publish a statement defined by the council or to suspend its service for a period ranging from fifteen minutes up to one week.[850] These provisions apply if the media service obviously and severely violated the rules on the protection of minors and the prohibition to incite hatred against any nation, community, minority, majority, church or religious group, and the violation occurred at least two times during the previous twelve months; further, if both the service provider and the European Commission were informed in writing about the violations and the planned measurements of the Media Council. Further requirements are that no agreement came to settlement with the Member State where the service provider is established within fifteen days after notification and the violation still exists or is repeated. The resolution shall be sent to the European Commission at the same time as it is communicated, which may decide within two months if the Media Council should retract its resolution.[851]

577. Transposing Article 3(4) AVMS Directive (almost literally following the Directive), the law also entitles the Media Council to apply consequences against on-demand audiovisual services if their services are accessible in the territory of Hungary. A service distributed also in Hungary may be suspended by the Media Council, or a service provider may be obliged to publish a statement defined by the Media Council in respect of its service distributed in Hungary. The conditions for applying these consequences are that such measure is necessary for the protection of public order, prevention, detection and investigation of crimes, violation of the prohibition to incite hatred, or for the protection of minors, public health, public security, national security, consumers or investors; that the media service injures or severely endangers one of these interests, and is proportionate to the goal that is to be achieved.[852] Before this resolution is issued, the Media Council is obliged to ask the EU Member State in which the media service provider is established to take the necessary measures. If these are not done or not appropriately done, the Media Council sends the draft resolution to the Member State and the European Commission.[853] In exceptionally urgent cases, for the protection of the viewers' interests, the Media Council may pass an interim resolution which is immediately enforceable. This shall be sent to the European Commission and the relevant Member State at the same time as it is communicated to the media service provider.[854]

849. Article 4(4)b AVMS Directive and §179(5) Mttv.
850. After negotiations with the European Commission, the law was amended so that a fine can only be applied against linear service providers (audiovisual and radio) if they settled abroad with the intention to circumvent Hungarian laws.
851. §176 Mttv.
852. §177(1) Mttv.
853. §177(2) Mttv.
854. §177(3) Mttv.

578. In Hungary, the Media Council may supervise certain content requirements against radio, printed and online press (although after several amendments, printed and online press is subject to somewhat fewer rules). If the content of such providers is directed at Hungary or is accessible in Hungary, the Media Council may oblige the content provider to publish a statement if it seems necessary to protect the public order or to prevent, detect or investigate a crime, in case the rules on the prohibition to incite hatred, the protection of minors, public health, public security, national security and the protection of consumers or investors were violated, or severely endangered, and if such measurement is proportionate to the interest to be protected.[855] No other consequences may be applied, however, such as suspension of service or a fine (after the amendments required by the European Commission). The Media Council shall ask the competent Member State to take measures before starting such a procedure, and only if the Member State did not fulfil the Media Council's request within a reasonable time or did not fulfil it appropriately may the Media Council start its own procedure.[856] In an exceptionally urgent case, the Media Council may issue an interim order which is immediately enforceable. The Media Council sends such an order to the relevant State and asks for the State's action at the same time.[857]

579. Further, in line with Article 4(3)b of the AVMS Directive, the law entitles the Media Council to apply the Mttv. and the content rules of Smtv. on linear audiovisual media services also in cases where they direct their services wholly or mostly towards the territory of Hungary if they established themselves outside Hungary in order to circumvent the stricter rules of the Mttv. and Smtv. When establishing the latter condition, the council shall examine where the main sources of advertising and subscription are, what is the main language of the media services, in which Member State the main scene of its reportages is, and which Member State's audience its programmes target.[858] The Media Council is obliged to ask the EU Member State under whose jurisdiction the media service provider falls to take the necessary measures.[859] If the competent Member State does not take appropriate measures within two months, the Media Council may apply a fine or oblige the service provider to publish a statement defined by the Media Council or suspend the service.[860] The Media Council sends the draft resolution to the European Commission before it communicates. In case the European Commission requires the Media Council to retract its decision, it is obliged to follow the instructions.[861] Interestingly, the AVMS Directive requires at this point that the European Commission's positive reply is necessary for taking the measure, which condition is not required under Mttv. (as mentioned above in paragraph 546).[862]

855. §178(1) Mttv.
856. §178(2) Mttv.
857. §178(3) Mttv.
858. §179(2) Mttv.
859. §179(3) Mttv.
860. §179(4) Mttv.
861. §179(5) Mttv.
862. Article 4(4)b AVMS Directive.

580. The same set of rules apply to radio services, printed press, and online journals if their content is directed wholly or mostly towards the territory of Hungary and if they had settled outside Hungary in order to circumvent the stricter rules of the Mttv. and Smtv. The only difference is that the European Commission does not receive the draft resolutions.[863]

VI. Licensing

581. The Media Council is not only entitled to prepare, publish and decide tenders for licences, but it also may give a licence for three years without a tender (*see* paragraph 547).[864] Rules and the content of the tender are defined by the Media Council, while procedural details are defined by Ket. (Act on Administrative Procedures) and Mttv. Chapter III. The law lists only basic rules and principles; for example, that decision shall be based on the criteria published in the tender.[865]

582. The council is also entitled to amend the published tender while paying respect to the principles of objectivity, transparency and equal treatment.[866] It may also retract a tender until fifteen days before the submission deadline.[867] The law lists obligatory contents of a tender, their formal requirements and reasons for invalidity because of their content.[868]

583. The council is entitled to terminate the tender without decision in several cases:

§61 (1) Mttv.

- if no tender offers are received;
- because of a newly emerged circumstance the tender becomes unnecessary (*okafogyott*);
- according to the Media Council's discretion, media policy aspects or principles and goals included in the law or in the tender call cannot be achieved;
- none of the applicants fulfil the goals and principles of the law, or declaring any of them as winner, would endanger rational, responsible, proper management of the frequencies.

584. The decision may be appealed against within fifteen days upon reasons of the law's violation. The provision that after thirty days, the decision could not be appealed, even if it was not communicated to the person entitled to ask for remedy,

863. §180(1–4) Mttv.
864. §48(3) Mttv.
865. §60(4) Mttv.
866. §53(1–4) Mttv.
867. §53(5) Mttv.
868. §§56–57, 59 Mttv.

was annulled in 2012.[869] The appeal needs to be submitted to the Media Council which shall forward it to the court within fifteen days. The Capital Administrative and Labour Court shall decide within sixty days, and no appeal or renewal of the procedure is allowed. However, review of the decision may be requested within fifteen days, but the request must arrive at the court within this deadline. The Supreme Court shall decide within sixty days. All courts shall give priority to the case (*soron kívül járnak el*).[870] The tender documents count as legal secrets, and the Media Council may not disclose any information included in the offers until the contract is concluded.[871]

585. For a maximum of three years, the Media Council may issue a licence for media service without tender for the reason of fulfilling public duties. The media service provider who asks first shall receive such a licence if it fits the conditions to fulfil the public duty, which may be – (a) media services in case of or related to an officially promulgated emergency situation or a natural disaster affecting a substantial area of the country, or industrial disaster; (b) serving a community's special educational, cultural, informational needs or needs related to a specific event affecting that community.[872]

586. Upon request, the Media Council may give a right to provide temporary media services for a maximum of thirty days in order to utilize unused local frequencies.[873]

587. Contracts concluded with the predecessor of the Media Council (ORTT) that granted frequency licences had to be renewed according to Mttv. The Mttv. originally contained guarantees for media service providers, ensuring, among others, that the new conditions may not be worse than the previous conditions and making sure that the situation becomes legally settled even if the media service provider would not take the necessary steps. The Media Council was obliged to finish the procedure within ninety days; if the procedure was not started in time by the media service provider, to start it itself; if the contract is not concluded, to define the conditions in a resolution – where the conditions may not be worse for the media service provider than those in the previous contract.[874] These rules were annulled in the amendment of May 2012, arguing that they will not be necessary in the future.

588. Tendering is meaningful only in the radio market because of the complete digitalization of the television market. However, the radio market saw significant changes after 2010, the decisions in their entirety, and some individually, raising even international attention and criticism. In 2011, the frequency used by Klubradio, a talk-and-news radio, was offered in an invitation to tender under the condition that

869. §62(5) Mttv.
870. §62(6) Mttv. (amended in 2012).
871. §62(7) Mttv.
872. §48(4) Mttv.
873. §65(1) Mttv.
874. Previous §207(1–5), effective until 2 Jul. 2012.

applicants offer mainly music and only a little talk. As no other frequency was offered for talk content, it became clear that Klubradio could not continue its operation. However, it still applies to the frequency and loss.[875] The winning company (which had a murky background) soon offered its new licence for sale. Before this could have happened, the Capital Court annulled the tender decision upon appeal of the Klubradio, excluded the winner from the competition because of a formal mistake (lack of signature on the tender documents) and ordered to carry out a new tender.[876] The Media Council, in the new procedure, excluded all applicants from the procedure, with the reasoning that signatures were missing from the (empty) backsides of pages in the tender documents.[877] This reasoning was successfully contested in court, and Klubradio's tender application was found to be legally valid.[878] In 2014, according to the decision of the High Court of the Capital, the Media Council was obliged to provide an official, local, community licence to the radio station. During the legal battles, Klubradio broadcast its programme through temporary licences of local frequencies that were renewed on a case-by-case basis. In 2016, *Kúria* (the highest court) awarded a compensation of HUF 108 million (EUR 580,000) to the radio.[879] In 2021, Klubrádió's licence was not renewed and the frequency was awarded to a government-friendly media group.[880] In 2022, the Commission referred Hungary to the Court of Justice for breaching EU telecoms rules with disproportionate and discriminatory actions that prevented Klubradio from continuing its activity in the radio broadcasting sector.[881]

589. The Media Council's tender decisions altogether gave more room for radios close to the governing Fidesz party and of religious content (*see also* paragraph 38 above). This happened on the basis of providing more local content, but then the Media Council approved their unification into a national network which eliminated all local content of these radios.[882]

875. 1983/2011. (XII. 20) Media Council decision.
876. Judit Muhari, *A bíróság másodszor is a Klubrádió javára ítélt,* http://www.nepszava.hu/articles/article.php?id=530945, Népszava, 16 Mar. 2012; Új győztest kell hirdetni a 95, 3-as frekvenciára. http://index.hu/kultur/media/2012/03/14/klubr_radio/, Index, 14 Mar. 2012.
877. Mérték Médiaelemzö Mühely: Médiatájkép Egy Hosszú; Vihar Után. Médiapolitika 2010 után. 2021. https://mertek.eu/wp-content/uploads/2021/12/MertekFuzetek24.pdf. A Klubrádiónak az üres hátlapokat is alá kellett volna írnia, http://nol.hu/belfold/mszp__a_mediatanacsnak_mennie_kell__0706, NOL, 6 Jul. 2012.
878. Fővárosi Ítélőtábla, K.2.27.474/2012/5.
879. Jogerős: 108 millió forintos kártérítés jár a Klubrádiónak, June 2016, available at: https://media.mandiner.hu/cikk/20160607_jogeros_108_millio_forintos_karterites_jar_a_klubradionak.
880. Beswick Emma, *Klubrádió: Frequency of Hungarian Independent Radio to be Taken over by Group Close to Orbán* (2021), https://www.euronews.com/2021/04/11/klubradio-frequency-of-hungarian-independent-radio-to-be-taken-over-by-group-close-to-orba.
881. EC Press Release (2022) Media freedom: the Commission refers Hungary to the Court of Justice of the European Union for failure to comply with EU electronic communications rules, https://ec.europa.eu/commission/presscorner/detail/en/IP_22_2688.
882. A médiatanács frekvencia pályáztatási gyakorlata, in Mérték Médiaelemző Műhely, https://mertek.eu/2012/02/22/a-mediatanacs-frekvencia-palyaztatasi-gyakorlata/, March 2012.

VII. Deciding about Balanced Information

590. The Media Council is entitled to decide a case where someone complains that a media service provider did not provide balanced information. The obligation to provide balanced information is prescribed by Smtv. (§13) and Mttv. (§12(2)):

> §13 Smtv.
> Linear media services that perform informative activity are obliged to impart balanced, objective, topical, factual and diverse information in their news and information programmes about events that are meaningful for the citizens of Hungary and the members of the Hungarian nation, and about discussed questions, as well as about local, national and European events that may attract public interest.
> §12 (2) Mttv.
> Balancedness of information providing shall be ensured – depending on the nature of the programmes – within the individual programmes, or within the serial of the regularly published programmes.

591. The rule in the Mttv. prescribes an interpretation of internal pluralism substantially stricter than usually known in the media legal theory literature (mentioned above in paragraphs 191 and 394).[883] The consequences, however, have been moderated after the European Commission exercised pressure on the Hungarian government in February 2011 (*see* paragraph 392 above). After this amendment, printed press and online journals are no longer subject to this obligation, and the only consequence to be applied against media service providers is obliging them to publish a statement. Although still a State interference in freedom of expression, this means a lesser burden on service providers compared to a fine or suspension of service. The disadvantage of the regulation is that it conserves the old system which was problematic in itself.[884] While the scope of the law is rather narrow, and so are procedural deadlines, complaints arrive in all topics and times. As a result, a majority of complaints get rejected by the Authority (previously, a specific body, the Complaints Commission, discussed these cases). The Complaint Commission's practice was far from being standardized and was unpredictable.[885]

592. According to the regulation, if any viewer or listener is of the opinion that a media service provider violated the rules above, he or she may initiate a procedure. If the media service provider has SIP (*see* paragraphs 536–537) or is a public service media provider, then the Media Council has the competence to proceed; in other cases, the Office of the Authority proceeds. Before initiating the procedure at the Media Council, the applicant shall contact the media service provider directly in writing within seventy-two hours after the objected programme and demand that the

883. As this concept has originated in the German jurisprudence, *see*, BVerfGE 57, 295.
884. Judit Bayer, *Kiegyensúlyozottság és kampány a médiában* 93–108 (Péter Bajomi-Lázár, Róbert Kotroczó & Miklós Sükösd ed., L'Harmattan 2007); Judit Bayer, *A Panaszbizottság ügyei*, 3 Médiakutató (2001).
885. *See* more on this in: Judit Bayer, *A panaszbizottság ügyei*, 3 Médiakutató (2001).

provider publish a statement that would make the information balanced.[886] The media service provider shall accept or reject the objection within forty-eight hours and inform the complainant immediately about its decision. The deadlines are important because the complainant may initiate the procedure at the Authority within forty-eight hours after communication of the service provider's decision. In case there was no decision, or it was not communicated, the complainant has ten days after the programme to start the procedure at the Authority. Also, if the media service provider does not implement its own decision, the complainant may initiate the procedure – in this case, within forty-eight hours after the deadline for publishing the statement has lapsed. The Authority shall decide within fifteen days or may postpone its deadline once, for a maximum of eight days.[887] The media service provider is obliged to present a copy of the objected programme upon notice of the Authority, without delay.[888] In case the Authority finds that the media service provider indeed violated the obligation to provide balanced information, it may oblige the media service provider to publish a statement defined by the Authority in the date, time and manner as defined by the Authority, without any comments – or allow the possibility to the complainant to present his or her opinion. No other consequences may be applied.[889] The decision of the Authority may be appealed against, and the review of the second instance decision may be requested (by the party in the procedure or by another participant with respect to provisions in the decision specifically affecting him or her) from the Capital Administrative and Labour Court which shall decide within sixty days, in a non-contentious procedure. No appeal or renewal against the decision of the court is allowed, but review may be requested within fifteen days (the request shall arrive at the court within this deadline). The Supreme Court shall proceed within forty-five days. All courts shall give priority to the case (*soron kívül jár el*). Also, the first instance decision of the Media Council may be appealed against; the same procedural rules apply as described above.[890]

593. Even today, an overwhelming majority of complaints get rejected because of delay or other procedural mistakes (among others, Decisions: 920/2011. (VII. 6.); 558/2011. (IV. 28.); 559/2011. (IV. 28.); 1870/2011. (XII. 14.); 317/2012. (II. 15.); 379/2012. (II. 22.); 377/2012. (II. 22.); 376/2012. (II. 22.); 376/2012. (II. 22.); 114/2012. (I. 18.); 118/2012. (I. 18.); 119/2012. (I. 18.); 120/2012. (I. 18.); 87/2012. (I. 11.); 92/2012. (I. 11.)).

594. In November 2011, a reporter on public service television cut a report about Daniel Cohn-Bendit's press conference so that it made him seem as if not having replied to a sensitive personal question and as having escaped from public scrutiny before the end of the conference. The falsified coverage spurred several dozen complaints, but all were belated and had to be rejected for that reason.[891]

886. §181(2) Mttv.
887. §181(3) Mttv.
888. §181(4) Mttv.
889. §181(5) Mttv.
890. §181(7–8) Mttv.
891. For example, decisions from 1870/2011. (XII. 14) to 1878/011. (XII. 14), and also from 29/2012. (I. 11) throughout to 86/2012. (I. 11).

595. Decisions rejected in merit (rather than procedural reasons) are, for example, 1879/2011 (XII. 14); 1880/2011. (XII. 14); 924/2011. (VII. 6); 921/2011. (VII. 6); 925/2011. (VII. 6); 320/2012. (II. 15); 374/2012. (II. 22); 252/2012. (II. 7); 251/2012. (II. 7); 109/2012. (I. 18).

596. Some cases even reached the courts – On 23 October 2006, when riots occurred on the streets of Budapest, a media service provider presented the results of an opinion poll, and, according to the Complaints Commission, more opinions should have been presented, juxtaposed to each other. However, in court, it was not proven whether another opinion poll existed, and it was not the task of the court but that of the commission to decide this. The Capital Court ordered a new procedure before the Complaints Commission (4.Kf.27.722/2010/6).

597. Objections may be submitted only by a person directly affected (EBH2006.1479). A social organization which is specialized and empowered to disclose and step up against legal violations may also submit an objection (KGD2004.23).

598. ORTT found that a programme titled 'The price of truth' (*Az igazság ára*) that violated several laws on human dignity and informational self-determination. Participants of the show had to respond to unexpected questions relating to their private lives while being attached to a lie detector. The Court of First Instance found that the participants had the right and the possibility to set their own limits and gave their agreement to the show. Upon appeal, the Supreme Court found that the show's concept and intended effect was to achieve the participants' disclosure of their private secrets against their own will publicly, causing the injury of both their right to informational self-determination and dignity. In case the lie detector showed that someone lied, either the right to reputation or the right to privacy was infringed. An informed consent to disclosing the secrets was bound to be missing, as this gave the necessary excitement to the show. The original decision was upheld (EBH2010.2197).

Chapter 3. Sanctioning Powers

599. Dramatic increase in the level of fines was one of the peculiarities of the Hungarian media law reform. The fines are considered high even in an international comparison.[892] The fines are, especially if imposed repeatedly, capable of disabling the further operation of media outlets on the Hungarian market. Commenters fear that it would cause a chilling effect on the general media scene.[893]

600. Beyond the high fines, the Authority may suspend the services of not only linear media service providers but also on-demand service providers and online journals. This decision may be enforced through ISPs whom the Media Council may oblige to not transmit the content in question. It may order ISPs and programme distributors to suspend a service if its provider did not pay a fine or did not publish a statement according to the Authority's decision.[894] The same applies to online journals as well: they may be fined or obliged to publish a statement (not be suspended), but if they do not follow this decision, the Authority orders their ISP to suspend their service.[895]

601. Even after the Constitutional Court decision and the following amendment in May 2012, the Media Council still may supervise sections 14 and 16–20 of Smtv. also in relation to press products, and may also impose sanctions in this regard.[896] Violating the rules on registration may also be sanctioned with HUF 1 million.[897] If this fine is not paid, the Authority may order an ISP to suspend the journal's service (*see* paragraphs 240 and 600).

602. Co-regulation agreements concluded with representatives of the associations of printed press, online journals, on-demand service providers and advertisers provide some protection to these industry actors from being sanctioned for violation of the content rules of Smtv. (§§14–20). However, the co-regulation system does not prevent the Media Council's procedure and sanctioning.

603. The Media Council and the Office of the Authority may apply many different kinds of sanctions against any person who violates any rule on media administration.[898] While 'rules on media administration' primarily mean the Mttv. and

---

892. Hungarian Media Laws in Europe, https://cmds.ceu.edu/projects/hungarian-media-laws-europe.
893. Attila Mong, *A szabadság gyeplői – öncenzúra a magyar sajtóban*, http://mertek.postr.hu/a-szabadsag-gyeploi-oncenzura-a-magyar-sajtoban/ (25 Apr. 2012); Hungarian Media Law: International Mission Condemns Chilling Effect and Calls for Change, http://www.cij.hu/en/hungarian-media-law-international-mission-condemns-chilling-effect-and-calls-for-change-2/, CIJ (16 Nov. 2011).
894. §189(2–3) Mttv.
895. §189(4) Mttv.
896. To sum up, the content restrictions of Smtv. that remained valid also for press products are: §14(2), §16, §17, §19(3)(4a), §20. These embrace the topics of: prohibition to show people in humiliating, exposed situation, respect the constitutional order, prohibition to incite hatred or exclude any minority or any majority, restrict access for the protection of minors, prohibition to show a minor in a way which may be harmful for him or her, and basic rules on advertising.
897. §45(8) Mttv.
898. §185(1) Mttv.

Smtv., they also include rules other than laws, like the decrees issued by the president of the Authority[899] and decisions of the Authority. The Media Council and the Office of the Media Authority (hereinafter called together as the Authority[900]) shall pay attention to the principles of proportionality, equal treatment and gradation when they apply the consequences, considering the weight and the repetition of the violation of the law.[901]

604. If the violation is of a minor nature, and no repetition can be observed, the Authority may just summon the content provider to stop the violation and refrain from doing it in the future. It may also oblige the content provider to act lawfully in the future and define its conditions. It may set a deadline of no longer than thirty days.[902]

605. In case the violation is repeated, the Authority may fine the executive officer of the enterprise up to HUF 2 million, depending on the weight, nature and individual characteristics of the case.[903]

606. When applying consequences, attention is to be paid to the weight of the infringement, its repetitiveness, continuity, time span, the material gain achieved through the violation and the injury to interests caused by it, the number of persons who suffered an injury or are endangered by it, damages caused by it and its effect exercised on the market, the violations of personal rights, as well as other aspects evaluable in the individual case.[904] The consequences may also be applied jointly.[905]

607. Below first, the applicable consequences will be listed in short, and then they are unfolded in more detail with some explanation, where necessary.

608. The Authority may:

(1) exclude media service providers from tenders of the MTVA for a defined period;[906]
(2) impose a fine;[907]
(3) oblige the content provider to publish a statement or the decision on the opening page of its website, in its press product, or in a programme defined by the Authority, in the manner and for the time as defined by the Authority;[908]

899. *See* in more detail above in para. 126. Article T(2) of Basic Law and §182(3) of the Eht.
900. ORTT ceased in 2010 and the Media Authority – incorporating the Media Council – took its place.
901. §185(2) Mttv.
902. §186(1) Mttv.
903. §187(1) Mttv.
904. §187(2) Mttv.
905. §187(5) Mttv.
906. §187(3)a Mttv.
907. §187(3)b Mttv.
908. §187(3)c Mttv.

(4) suspend the exercise of media services licence;[909]
(5) erase a media service provider from the register or terminate the public contract with immediate effect if a repeated grave violation was committed.[910]

609. Fines are diversified depending on the type of the medium:[911]

- SIP media service providers and 'affected' media service providers (*see* definition above in paragraphs 503–509) up to HUF 200 million.
- Other media service providers: HUF 50 million.
- National daily papers: HUF 25 million.
- National weekly papers and journals: HUF 10 million.
- Other daily papers, weekly papers and journals: HUF 5 million.
- Online journals: HUF 25 million.
- Programme distributors: HUF 5 million.
- ISPs: HUF 3 million.

610. The Media Council may order the publication of a statement or a resolution on the opening page of the website, in a press product or in a defined programme, in a defined manner, and for a defined time. This sanction is similar to the rectification but is a legal consequence of an administrative nature rather than civil. Its main goal is the public representation of the Authority's opinion; thus, more of a general preventive effect is foreseen than retaliation or specific prevention.

611. The Media Council may suspend the right to provide media services (*jogosultság*) for a defined period.[912] It also applies to those service providers which provide their services on the basis of registration only, like digital linear or on-demand service providers. The period of suspension differs according to the weight of the legal violation. In case of 'normal violation', the suspension may extend from fifteen minutes to twenty-four hours; in case of grave violation, from one hour to forty-eight hours; in case of repeated and grave violation, from three hours to one week.[913]

612. Suspension cannot be applied against press products and online journals as a legal consequence for a legal infringement, but in case an online journal does not follow the final resolution of the Media Council, the Media Council may order that their service be suspended by the ISP.[914]

909. §187(3)d Mttv. The formulation refers to a licence, while no licence, only registration, is needed in all cases but the analogue linear radio services.
910. §187(3)e Mttv.
911. §187(3)(ba–bh) Mttv.
912. §187(3)d Mttv. The word *jogosultság* has a wider meaning than the word 'licence' (*engedély*).
913. §187(3)d Mttv.
914. §189(3–4) Mttv.

613. Finally, the Media Council may erase a media service from the registry or terminate the public contract with immediate effect. This may be applied only against audiovisual and radio services and no press products.[915]

614. The law also defines what shall be deemed as repetitive violation: if the same violating behaviour has been committed (on the same legal bases and violating the same section of the law) in the same subject matter at least twice within 365 days, not counting minor violations of the law.[916]

615. A further very powerful right of discretion in the hands of the Media Council is to decide whether to start a procedure or not. For example, in the *Cohn-Bendit* case (mentioned above in paragraphs 565 and 318), the Media Council decided not to start a procedure on the basis of violating human dignity.[917] It also denied starting a procedure in relation to a documentary film on public service television that – in the view of civil groups, experts and human rights NGOs – represented the Roma minority in a seriously one-sided, prejudicial manner.[918]

616. The Media Council has several decisions in which it decided not to start a procedure against a media service provider without giving the reasons.[919] Some of these decisions specify which section of the law was violated in which period and declare that only no administrative procedure will be started. The appearance of such decisions alone may be regarded as a warning against the relevant media service provider, exercising a chilling effect without giving reasons or a possibility to dispute. Uncertainty about the Media Council's practice is a powerful tool for chilling effect. As of now, there are no signs that the Media Council would use its discretionary power in an impartial manner.[920]

617. In general, the Media Council has been relatively modest in applying its sanctioning competences in the first year of its existence. It passed relatively few

915. §187(3)e Mttv.
916. §187(4) Mttv.
917. 1870/2011. (XII. 14) §14 of Smtv. prescribes that media service providers should in all their content, and during its preparation, respect human dignity.
918. *See* the Media Council's blog entry: Nem volt törvénysértő a Pesty Fekete Doboz, http://mediatanacs.blog.hu/2012/05/30/nem_volt_torvenyserto_a_pesty_fekete_doboz (30 May 2012); and the story in the news: Th. B., Tiltakoztak Pesty romafilmje ellen, http://index.hu/kultur/media/2012/03/20/tiltakozasi_hullam_indult_pesty_romakrol_szolo_dokumentumfilmje_miatt/ (20 Mar. 2012). The video report in question can be viewed at: A cigány-magyar együttélés, http://videotar.mtv.hu/Videok/2012/03/09/17/Pesty_Fekete_Doboz_2012_marcius_7__A.aspx, Pesty Fekete Doboz (7 Mar. 2012).
919. 122/2012. (I. 18); 175/2012. (I. 25); 322/2012. (II. 15); 382/2012. (II. 22) Media Council decisions.
920. A médiatanács frekvencia pályáztatási gyakorlata, in Mérték Médiaelemző Műhely, https://mertek.eu/2012/02/22/a-mediatanacs-frekvencia-palyaztatasi-gyakorlata, March 2012. *See also* Klubradio decision [1983/2011. (XII. 20)] and sanctioning decisions of the two national commercial channels, discussed in paras 556–557. On the Klubradio case, *see*, Gábor Polyák, *Dupla vagy semmi – ítéletek a Klubrádió ügyeiben*, in Mérték Médiaelemző Műhely, http://mertek.postr.hu/cimke/Klubrádió (19 Mar. 2012).

sanctioning decisions. In advertising cases, it typically issued a warning[921] or a very low fine (HUF 28,000).[922]

618. However, one national television channel, RTL Klub, was fined to several hundreds of millions in 2011. The penalty levied for the wrong classification of a reality show broadcast during November–December 2010 was approximately HUF 144 million,[923] and another HUF 88 million penalty was imposed on the same legal basis a week later (for violations committed in January 2011).[924] Penalties were defined in the media service contract between the Media Council and M-RTL which was still in effect until a new public contract was concluded under the new regulation in 2011. However, the other national commercial television channel, TV2, was not supervised in this period, only after the old contracts lost their effect, and was sanctioned significantly (approximately one-fiftieth) less for similar violations of the law, for its very similar reality show. The fine (rather than penalty) was only HUF 1 million for similar reality shows broadcast in September-October 2011[925] and HUF 4 million a month later.[926] Altogether, until the end of March 2012, TV2 was fined HUF 18 million for about 150 episodes of the programme series.[927] RTL Klub received a penalty of about HUF 300 million for the same. The official explanation was that the two reality shows were of different nature, and RTL Klub's lasted for longer.

619. In relation to other programmes on the same channel as TV2, the Media Council imposed a fine of HUF 2.5 million against TV2 for violating the categorization rule in the protection of children[928] and 5 million for violating human dignity.[929]

620. The Media Council established that Viasat Broadcasting UK violated the rules on protecting children but did not apply any consequences. Viasat is settled in the UK, and the council should have started diplomatic negotiations with the home country in order to apply any consequences.[930]

621. The Media Council issued only a warning in cases of violation of the rules for the protection of minors against Chello Central Europe cable television channel (172/2012. (I. 25)) and against the Hungarian Television M1 (173/2012 (I. 25)).

921. For example, 1761/2011. (XII. 1); 419/2012. (II. 29); 421/2012. (II. 29); 422/2012. (II. 29); 219/2012. (II. 1) 220/2012. (II. 1), 221 … 222 … 168/2012. (I. 25); 170/2012. (I. 25); 174/2012. (I. 25); 111/2012. (I. 18) Media Council decisions.
922. 420/2012. (II. 29); or HUF 50,000 in the case 111/2012. (I. 18). Media Council decisions
923. 624/2011. (V. 11) Media Council decision.
924. 668/2011. (V. 18) Media Council decision.
925. 110/2012. (I. 18) Media Council decision.
926. 321/2012. (II. 15) Media Council decision.
927. 581/2012. (III. 28) Media Council decision.
928. 415/2012. (II. 29) Media Council decision.
929. 417/2012. (II. 29) Media Council decision.
930. 413/2012. (II. 29) Media Council decision. *See* §§176, 179 Mttv.

622. The Media Council's official decisions are not to be appealed to the council itself, but the Capital Administrative and Labour Court may review and change the decisions if one of the parties or other participants of the procedure requests so within thirty days after their communication.[931] The court decides in an administrative procedure whether the Media Council violated the law and may change the decision.[932] Although the Commentary of Mttv. argues that the court has full competence to control the lawfulness of the Media Council's decision,[933] the author finds Pp. more instructive; this law says that:

> § 339/B of Pp.
> An administrative decision passed in a competence of discretion shall be regarded as lawful, if the administrative body revealed the facts to the extent necessary, followed the procedural rules, the aspects of discretion can be established, and causality of considering the tools of evidence can be seen in the justification of the decision.[934]
>
> According to this, courts cannot overrule the causal relationship, or the weighing of facts, or the balancing of arguments in the Media Council's reasoning, if the court is satisfied to see that such were given by the Media Council. There is an intense debate about this between the Media Council and the Center for Media and Communication Studies in Budapest.[935]

623. The application for judicial review does not have a delaying effect on the decision's enforcement, but the applicant may ask the court to suspend its enforcement.[936] The Capital Court's first instance decision is the final decision in several cases: reviewing decisions on tenders and awarding licences,[937] probing enforcement decisions of the Authority,[938] reviewing interim injunctions by the Authority,[939] obliging other persons than those participating in a procedure to yield data, information and tools of verification.[940] Certain minor decisions (*végzés*) of the Media Council, which may be reviewed separately from the whole decision, should

931. §§163(1), 165(3), (6) Mttv.
932. §§163(1–2), 164(3) Mttv.
933. '*sőt kiterjed a közigazgatási döntésben foglalt mérlegelési jog, mérlegelési szempontok felülvizsgálatának ok-, illetve jogszerűségére is.*' András Koltay, András Lapsánszky & György Andrássy, *A médiaszabályozás kommentárja* 318 (CompLex 2011).
934. Pp. Ch. XX. 'Court Review of Administrative Decisions' §339/B. Original text: '*Mérlegelési jogkörben hozott közigazgatási határozat akkor tekintendő jogszerűnek, ha a közigazgatási szerv a tényállást kellő mértékben feltárta, az eljárási szabályokat betartotta, a mérlegelés szempontjai megállapíthatóak, és a határozat indokolásából a bizonyítékok mérlegelésének okszerűsége kitűnik.*'
935. CMCS, Hungarian Media Laws in Europe, http://medialaws.ceu.hu/ and *see* the reply of the Authority: A Közé p-eur ópai Egyetem kalandjai a magyar médiaszabályozással, http://mediatanacs.blog.hu/2012/01/10/a_kozep_europai_egyetem_kalandjai_a_magyar_mediaszabalyozassal (10 Jan. 2012).
936. §163(3) Mttv.
937. §62(6) Mttv.
938. §§161(2) and 189(8) Mttv.
939. §173(9) Mttv.
940. §155(4) Mttv.

be appealed within fifteen days.[941] If the Office of the Authority decides at first instance, its decisions may be appealed against the Media Council at second instance, unless the Mttv. or the Act on Administrative Procedures excludes this.[942]

624. The Media Council may not be subjected to a supervisory procedure as it has no supervisory organ in State administration.[943]

941. §163(5) Mttv.
942. §165(1) Mttv.
943. §163(6) Mttv. *See also*: András Koltay, András Lapsánszky & György Andrássy, *A médiaszabályozás kommentárja* 125 (CompLex 2011).

Selected Bibliography

§1. Books

Bajomi-Lázár, Péter. *A magyarországi médiaháború*. Budapest: Új Mandátum, 2001.

Bajomi-Lázár, Péter. *Média és politika*. Budapest: PrintXBudavár, 2010.

Bajomi-Lázár, Péter. *Mai magyar média: főiskolai tankönyv*. Budapest: Zsigmond Király Főiskola, 2005.

Bajomi-Lázár, Péter. *Média és társadalom*. Budapest: PrintXBudavár, Médiakutató Alapítvány, 2008.

Bajomi-Lázár, Péter, Kotroczó Róbert & Sükösd Miklós. *Kiegyensúlyozottság és kampány a médiában*. Budapest: L'Harmattan, 2007.

Bárándy, Gergely. *A gyűlöletbeszéd Magyarországon*. Budapest: Scolar, 2010.

Bayer, József & Bajomi-Lázár Péter (eds). *Globalizáció, média, politika: a politikai kommunikáció változása a globalizáció korában*. Budapest: Magyar Tudományos Akadémia Politikai Tudományok Intézete, 2005.

Bayer, Judit. *A háló szabadsága: az internet tartalmának szabályozási problémái a véleménynyilvánítás szabadsága tükrében*. Budapest: Új Mandátum – Zsigmond Király Főiskola, 2005.

Bayer, Judit, et al. *A közszolgálati média és az európai versenyjog: közszolgálatiság a változó világban*. Budapest: L'Harmattan: Magyar Tudományos Akadémia Jogtudományi Intézete Infokummunikációs Jogi Centrum, 2010.

Gálik, Mihály & Polyák Gábor. *Médiaszabályozás*. Budapest: KJK-Kerszöv, 2005.

Gálik, Mihály & Vogl Artemon. *A média koncentrációjának mérése*. Budapest: AKTI, 2009.

Halmai, Gábor. *A kifejezés szabadsága az Alkotmánybíróság joggyakorlatában*. Budapest: COLPI, 1996.

Halmai, Gábor. *A véleményszabadság határai*. Budapest: Atlantisz, 1994.

Halmai, Gábor. *Alkotmánybírósági esetjog*. Budapest: CompLex, 2007.

Halmai, Gábor. *Kommunikációs jogok*. Budapest: Új Mandátum, 2002.

Halmai, Gábor. *Sajtószabadság és személyiségi jogok. Alapjogi bíráskodás I.* Budapest: INDOK, 1998.

Incze, Kinga. *Magyarországi médiapiaci körkép*. Budapest: AKT 2010.

Jany, János, Ilosvai Gábor & Bölcskei János. *Médiajogi kézikönyv I.* Budapest: Osiris, 2000.

Jóri, András. *Adatvédelem és információszabadság a gyakorlatban*. Budapest: CompLex, 2010.

Koltay, András, Lapsánszky András & Andrássy György. *A médiaszabályozás kommentárja*. Budapest: CompLex, 2011.

Lazarsfeld, Paul F., et al. *Média, nyilvánosság, közvélemény: szöveggyűjtemény*. Budapest: Gondolat, 2007.

Lenkovics, Barnabás & Székely László. *A személyi jog vázlata*. Budapest: Eötvös József Könyvkiadó, 2002.

Majtényi, László. *Az információs szabadságok: adatvédelem és a közérdekű adatok nyilvánossága*. Budapest: CompLex, 2006.

Majtényi, László (ed.). *Az odaátra nyíló ajtó*. Budapest: Adatvédelmi Biztos Irodája, 2001.

Majtényi, László, et al. (eds). *Az elektronikus információszabadság*. Budapest: Eötvös Károly Intézet, 2005.

Molnár, Péter. *Gondolatbátorság: szólásszabadság és közbeszélgetés az Egyesült Államokban és Magyarországon*. Budapest: Új Mandátum, 2002.

Pázmándy, Kinga. *Modern reklámjog*. Budapest: HVG-ORAC, 2007.

Petrik, Ferenc. *A személyiség jogi védelme*. Budapest: HVG-ORAC, 2001.

Pikó, András, Wisinger István & Zöldi László. *Általános médiaismeret*. Budapest; Pécs: Dialóg Campus, 2007.

Polyák, Gábor. *A műsorterjesztőket terhelő továbbítási kötelezettségek*. Budapest: AKTI 2008.

Polyák, Gábor. *Az audiovizuális médiaszolgáltatások meghatározása és szabályozási terhei*. Budapest: AKTI, 2007.

Polyák, Gábor. *Médiapolitikai szöveggyűjtemény*. Budapest: Gondolat, AKTI 2010.

Polyák, Gábor. *Versenyjogi és médiajogi eszközök a médiakoncentráció korlátozásában*. Budapest: AKTI, 2008.

Polyák, Gábor. *A médiarendszer kialakítása: a piacra lépés és a hozzáférés alkotmányjogi, közösségi jogi és összehasonlító jogi elemzése*. Budapest: HVG-ORAC, 2008.

Sajó, András. *A szólásszabadság kézikönyve*. Budapest: KJK-KERSZÖV, 2005.

Sarkady, Ildikó. *Médiajogi írások*. Budapest: Új Mandátum, 2005.

Sipos, Balázs. *Média és demokrácia Magyarországon: a politikai média jelenkortörténete*. Budapest: Napvilág, 2010.

Székely, László. *Magyar sajtó – és médiajog*. Budapest, Pécs: Dialóg Campus, 2007.

Tóth, Tihamér (ed.). *A reklámjog nagy kézikönyve*. Budapest: CompLex 2009.

Udvary, Sándor. *Alkotmányos médiajog?*. Budapest: Károli Gáspár Református Egyetem Állam – és Jogtudományi Kar, 2008.

Zlinszky, János. *A közszolgálati média és az emberi méltóság alapértéke*. Budapest: Alkalmazott Kommunikációtudományi Intézet, 2008.

I. English

Bayer, József, Jensen Jody & Orsolya Frank. *From Transition to Globalization: New Challenges for Politics, the Media and Society*. Budapest: Magyar Tudományos Akadémia Politikai Tudományok Intézete, 2007.

Castendyk, Oliver, Dommering Egbert & Scheuer Alexander. *European Media Law*. Alphen aan den Rijn: Kluwer Law International, 2008.

Dési János, et al. (eds). *Antisemitic Discourse in Hungary 2000–2003*. Budapest: B'nai B'rith Budapest Lodge, 2004.
Goldberg, David, Prosser Tony & Verhulst Stefaan. *EC Media Law and Policy*. London, New York: Longman, 1998.
Majtényi, László (ed.). *The Door Onto the Other Side*. Budapest: Adatvédelmi Biztos Irodája, 2001. (Also shown in Hungarian, double language book).

§2. Chapters and Articles

Bayer, Judit. 'Médiajog'. In *Magyar médiatörténet: a késő Kádár-kortól az ezredfordulóig,* edited by Péter Bajomi-Lázár. Budapest: Akadémiai Kiadó, 2005.
Bayer, Judit. 'Gondolatok a szólásszabadságról az ORTT Panaszbizottsága kapcsán'. *ELTE Annales* (December 1998).
Bayer, Judit. 'A kiegyensúlyozottság vizsgálata. A Panaszbizottság jogi szabályozása'. In *Kiegyensúlyozottság és kampány a médiában*, edited by Péter Bajomi-Lázár, Róbert Kotroczó, Miklós Sükösd. Budapest: L'Harmattan 2007, 93–108.
Bayer, Judit. 'A Panaszbizottság ügyei'. *Médiakutató*, 2001/3, 52–62.
Donges, P. 'Autonomie sichern, Offenheit erhöhen – Sicherung des Public Service'. In P. Donges & M. Puppis (eds). *Die Zunkunft des öffentlichen Rundfunks – Internationale Beitraege aus Wissenschaft und Praxis.* Köln: Halem Publications, 2003, 59–61.
Gosztonyi, Gergely. 'A közösségi médiaszolgáltatók a hatályos magyar jogi szabályozásban'. *Médiakutató,* 2011/4.
Halmai, Gábor. 'A véleménynyilvánítás szabadsága'. In *Emberi Jogok,* edited by Gábor Halmai & Tóth Gábor Attila. Budapest: Osiris, 2003, 423–478.
Horányi, Özséb. 'A panasz jogintézménye az elektronikus médiában'. In *Rendszerváltás és kommunikáció*, edited by Erika Sárközy. Budapest: Osiris, 1999.
Majtényi, László. 'Az információs jogok'. In *Emberi Jogok*, edited by Gábor Halmai & Tóth Gábor Attila. Budapest: Osiris, 2003, 577–628.
Polyák, Gábor. 'A médiapiac szabályozása az új médiatörvényben'. *Médiakutató,* 2011/1, 21–27.
Polyák, Gábor. 'A közszolgálati médiaszabályozás alkotmányjogi pozíciói'. *Jura,* 2007/2, 133–143.

Selected Bibliography

Index

The numbers here refer to paragraph numbers.

Index

www.ingramcontent.com/pod-product-compliance
Lightning Source LLC
LaVergne TN
LVHW011127300926
849160LV00008B/541
9789403515786